AMONG THE TRUTHERS

AMONG THE TRUTHERS

A JOURNEY THROUGH
AMERICA'S GROWING
CONSPIRACIST UNDERGROUND

JONATHAN KAY

HARPER

An Imprint of HarperCollins*Publishers*

www.harpercollins.com

HarperCollins books may be purchased for educational, business, or sales promotional use. For information, please write: Special Markets Department, HarperCollins Publishers, 10 East 53rd Street, New York, NY 10022.

FIRST EDITION

Designed by William Ruoto

Library of Congress Cataloging-in-Publication Data

Kay, Jonathan
   Among the truthers : a journey through America's growing conspiracist underground/ Jonathan Kay.—1st ed.
      p.   cm.
   Summary: "America is awash with conspiracy theories, and the shared view of reality we once took for granted has been permanently shattered. Jonathan Kay uses the 9/11 Truth movement as a springboard to examine this fragmented national mindset."
—Provided by publisher
   ISBN 978-0-06-200481-9 (hardback)
   1. Conspiracy theories—United States. 2. Political culture—United States. 3. United States—Politics and government—2009-
I. Title.
HV6275.K39   2011
001.90973—dc22

                                                      2011006813

11 12 13 14 15   ID/RRD   10 9 8 7 6 5 4 3 2 1

| CONTENTS |

Acknowledgments. ix

Preface xi

Introduction: Stumbling on the Truthers 1

Don't Call Them "Nutbars" 4

Some Caveats 19

Part 1 | The Truth Movement and Its Ancestors

1   American Conspiracism: A Brief History. 25

Programmed for Conspiracy. 25

Populism and Paranoia: How Politics Shaped American
Conspiracism 33

The Men in Black: How Technology Shaped American
Conspiracism 51

The Emergence of "Flowchart Conspiracism". 57

2   Warrant for Genocide, Blueprint for Paranoia 65

A Dark Fairy Tale. 67

Singularity 71

Boundless Evil 76

Incumbency 81

Greed 83

Cui Bono? 87

Hypercompetence 89

Covering Their Tracks 93

3   False Flags and Lava Lamps: The Birth of a Conspiracy Movement 99

Ken Jenkins: Videographer, Flower Child, Truther 99

Operation Northwoods and Its Legacy 106

Project for the New American Century: A Modern Northwoods . . . 116

4   "Show Me the Birth Certificate": Conspiracism in the Age of Obama . . 121

Joseph Farah: Birther Extraordinaire 121

Drinking Tea in Nashville 124

Enter the False Prophet 135

Glenn Beck and the New Populism 138

Part II | Meet the Truthers

5   Why They Believe: A Psychological Field Guide to Conspiracists 149

The Midlife Crisis Case 151

The Failed Historian 159

The Damaged Survivor 170

The Cosmic Voyager 179

The Clinical Conspiracist 183

The Crank 187

The Evangelical Doomsayer 196

The Firebrand 199

6   The Church of Conspiracism 205

Enter Satan 205

The Devil's Legacy 211
Lives of the Prophets. 215
The Cultic Milieu. 218

Part III | Accessories to Trutherdom

7   Democratizing Paranoia: How the Web Revolutionized Conspiracism . .227
The Legacy of Flight 800 227
Muckraking 2.0 230
Through the Internet's Looking Glass 238
The Revolution Will Be Televised 250
History Belongs to the YouTube Victors. 258

8   Tin-Foil Mortarboards: Conspiracism's Ivy League Enablers 261
Jacques Derrida's Hall of Mirrors 261
Among the Antiracists 273
Lessons from the *Yale Law Journal* 279

9   The *Protocols* Revisited: The New Face of Anti-Semitic Conspiracism. .285
Showdown in the Bowery 285
Conspiracism's Hateful Sidekick. 289
A New Home on the Left 294
The 9/11 Effect. 300
Jews Drift Right 305

10   Confronting Conspiracism. 309
A Pound of Cure. 309
An Ounce of Prevention 316

Index. 329

| ACKNOWLEDGMENTS |

This book is dedicated to my father, Ronald, whom I followed into the study of science and engineering; and my mother, Barbara, who passed on to me her love of books. He gave me the tools to understand how the world works. She gave me the tools to put that understanding into words.

This book would not exist without the support I received from my employer, Canada's *National Post* newspaper—and, in particular, publisher Doug Kelly and editor Steve Meurice. I also received important assistance from Mark Dubowitz and his team at the Foundation for Defense of Democracies, which provided me with logistical support during my trips to Washington, D.C. Over the last two years, I have been very proud to call myself a fellow at the FDD.

Additional thanks go to Michael Levine, for his tireless efforts to promote the project before I'd written a single word; my researcher, Timothy Mak; my editors at HarperCollins—Jennifer Lambert and Alex Schultz in Toronto, and Adam Bellow in New York. I would also like to express appreciation to my friend Michael Ross, who trusted me to help edit his 2007 book, *The Volunteer*. It was thanks to that collaboration that I first realized how satisfying and enjoyable the act of creating a book could be.

Finally, I am grateful to my wife, Jennifer, who set me free to travel across North America, interviewing the people discussed in this book. Jennifer also endured many evenings of my droning on about the various flavors of Trutherdom. Never once did she say, "If you don't mind, I'll wait for the book."

ERRATA

| PREFACE |

At 9:40 on the morning of November 1, 1755, Portugal was rocked by the most deadly earthquake in the recorded history of Europe. In Lisbon alone, more than thirty thousand people perished. Many victims were entombed in their churches, which collapsed around them as they celebrated All Saints.

The scene that emerged when the earth stopped shaking was one of Last Days. A tsunami swallowed the city's harbor, killing many of the survivors who'd assembled on the shore. A fire at the Royal Hospital roasted hundreds of patients alive. Gallows sprouted up on the city's hilltops, from which were hanged the desperate looters trying to survive amidst the ruins.

In purely quantitative terms, death on this scale was not uncommon in eighteenth-century Europe, which often was ravaged by wars and plagues. But the sudden, spectacular nature of the Great Lisbon Earthquake filled Europeans with a special kind of terror. Indeed, the impact of this horrific event on European thought and culture has sometimes been compared to that of the Holocaust. Most significant, perhaps, was the space that opened up for radical challenges to the authority of the Church, as Enlightenment philosophers asked how the benevolent God of the Christian Bible could permit such a catastrophe.

One of those men was François-Marie Arouet, better known by his pen name, Voltaire. In his 1756 "Poem on the Lisbon Disaster," he pronounced his despair—"Oh unhappy mortals! Oh wretched earth! Oh dreadful gathering of so many dead!"—but also his anger, aimed at contemporaries who depicted the event as just another mysterious subplot in God's master plan:

Come, ye philosophers, who cry, "All's well,"
And contemplate this ruin of a world.
Behold these shreds and cinders of your race,
This child and mother heaped in common wreck,
These scattered limbs beneath the marble shafts —
A hundred thousand whom the earth devours,
Who, torn and bloody, palpitating yet,
Entombed beneath their hospitable roofs,
In racking torment end their stricken lives.
To those expiring murmurs of distress,
To that appalling spectacle of woe,
Will ye reply: "You do but illustrate
The Iron laws that chain the will of God"?
Say ye, o'er that yet quivering mass of flesh:
"God is avenged: the wage of sin is death"?
What crime, what sin, had those young hearts conceived
That lie, bleeding and torn, on mother's breast?
Did fallen Lisbon deeper drink of vice
Than London, Paris, or sunlit Madrid?

Three years later, in *Candide*, Voltaire satirized this superstitious attitude through the character of Pangloss, a philosopher who greets every unspeakable tragedy—including the Great Lisbon Earthquake itself—with fatuous syllogisms aimed at proving ours to be "the best of all possible worlds." Throughout their shared adventures, Candide holds Pangloss in awe. Only in the book's final pages, as the two men find themselves tending a subsistence farm in an obscure corner of the Ottoman Empire, does a skeptical Candide glimpse the truth that life can be cruel and random, and that the best course is simply to muddle through, using our wits as well as practically possible.

Or as Candide put it in the book's last line, in response to one of Pangloss' particularly ambitious flourishes: "Excellently observed. But let us cultivate our garden."

In the two and a half centuries since Voltaire helped usher in the Enlightenment, Western societies gradually, fitfully have come to embrace rationalism and skepticism. We have separated church and state, enshrined science, questioned God, elevated materialism over piety, swept aside the divine right of kings, and otherwise followed the skeptics' claim that our world is shaped by human agency, in all its cruel imperfection, not some grand blueprint imposed from on high. America itself, founded by rational deists, has long been considered the crown jewel of the Enlightenment.

Yet there are risks inherent in the rationalist project, as the philosophers themselves sometimes acknowledged. A little learning is a dangerous thing, wrote Alexander Pope—a reminder to those who embraced the ideal of universal enlightenment that human reason remains an imperfect tool and that skepticism can be a two-edged sword. Even now, the intellectual edifice we've built on these foundations occasionally teeters, shaken by the tectonic social forces set in motion by depression, war, and terrorism. "Let us cultivate our garden" may be persuasive advice in normal times. But when skyscrapers crumble, when great powers are laid low, we demand a grander narrative than mere chaos, and grander villains than mere criminals and lunatics. In France after the French Revolution, on America's Great Plains following the depressions of the late nineteenth century, in Germany after World War I, and across the Western world in the shadow of Cold War hysteria, JFK's death, the Vietnam War, Watergate, and the rise of the 1960s counterculture—these have been the moments when shrieking prophets and conspiracy theorists found their followers. Americans now are living through another such moment, one that began with the collapse of the Twin Towers, and has continued through the aftershocks emanating from Afghanistan, Iraq, the 2008 financial crisis, and the crippling recession that followed it.

On the op-ed pages of the *New York Times* and on the airwaves of NPR, America's respectable intellectuals reassure one another that we are merely passing through a transient phase—a rekindling of populist agitation that comes and goes with the political tides. It's just a matter of waiting it out. But the evidence suggests that America's state of intellectual agitation in the aftermath of 9/11 isn't a temporary phenomenon. Like the Lisbon Earthquake, it has had far-reaching social, political, and psychological consequences that have yet to be fully absorbed or understood.

The reason for this goes in part to the nature of terrorism itself, which—after eliciting a brief spasm of patriotism and national solidarity—inevitably shrinks a society's common political center. Since 9/11, America has been implicitly divided between those who believe the country had provoked its enemies, and those who don't; between those who believe America needs to retreat from the world stage, and those who want to project freedom and democracy more aggressively than ever; and, in the purely domestic arena, between those who embrace the romantic project of returning America to its original "pure" libertarian social contract, and those who see its future in the image of the modern, multilaterally encumbered European welfare state. Like an earthquake, 9/11 produced a great fissure through the heart of America's political center—with two increasingly polarized ideological camps sniping at one another on radio, cable TV, and blogs from either side of the divide.

It is not just politics that separate these two camps, but the very manner by which they answer fundamental questions about the world. Is the earth getting hotter, or is global warming a hoax engineered to bring America into a UN-controlled One World Government? Is America led by a brilliant visionary—or a fifth columnist intent on bringing America down in the name of some sinister Afrocentric, Islamist, or communist agenda? Is socialized medicine necessary to make America a humane society, or is it a Malthusian plot to put Granny before a death panel? Which is to say: The basic building blocks of our political reality.

Many books have been written about the geopolitical fallout from 9/11. This book is about its seismic effects on the country's collective intellect—9/11's *cognitive* consequences.

In the past, such rifts have been healed by America's intellectual and political establishment, which has thrown bridges across the political spectrum at several critical historical junctures. A century ago, the extremes of populism gave way to progressivism, and then the New Deal. The Depression ended in FDR's war economy, and then the prosperous, relatively apolitical Pleasantvilles of the 1950s and 1960s. Even as late as the 1990s, American scholar Francis Fukuyama was predicting that ideological conflict itself was becoming a thing of the past, thanks to the universal embrace of core Western values. Ten years after 9/11, not even America (much less the world) seems anywhere near Fukuyama's "end of history," in large part because the institutions that we once counted on to discourage radicalism and guide our society toward common ground—organized religion, a vibrant academy, an influential mainstream media, and a respected central government—no longer command the public trust.

Voltaire is venerated for rebelling against the suffocating religiosity of Pangloss, which required a total, fatalistic submission to the whims of God. But the Christian intellectual monopoly that the Enlightenment overturned at least provided society with a shared frame of reference. Moreover, it also provided a cosmic explanation for evil—the main preoccupation of the secular conspiracy theorists who have proliferated in our own age. Voltaire himself understood all this, which is why he detested atheism even as he challenged the power of the Church. "The man who believes in God will recover from his excitement," Voltaire wrote. "He can be violent but for a moment, while the atheist is a monster all his life."

In the postmodern marketplace of ideas, there is little check on popular "excitement." Gaian environmentalism, healing crystals, and dilettante variations of Asian spirituality are claimed to be coequal in status to established Western faiths; and a wave of aggressive atheists—from Christopher Hitchens to Richard Dawkins—treat religion as a species of mental illness. Certainly, America remains home to legions of deeply observant Christians. But increasingly, they regard themselves as besieged combatants in an endless culture war against everyone else, with no shared moral language with which to negotiate an armistice. As for the dwindling tribe of equally embattled rationalists who take comfort in atheist tracts, it must be pointed out that attacks upon religion are not the same as the enlightened defense of reason originally offered by such figures as Bacon and Descartes.

Far from healing this growing cognitive rift, the secular academy has fetishized it: Many of the most revered liberal arts scholars of the postwar era have cast doubt on the very idea that language can act as a bridge between people holding different viewpoints. Thanks to the rise of identity politics, it is imagined that words—and even facts—have no meaning independent of the emotional effect they produce on their audience: Everyone feels entitled to their own private reality. And so the idea of rationally negotiating a consensus truth about the way our world works came to be seen as not only impossible, but undesirable—a trap created by society's privileged caste to justify their position. "There is one thing a professor can be absolutely certain of: Almost every student entering his university believes, or says he believes, that truth is relative," wrote Allan Bloom in his 1987 book *The Closing of the American Mind*. "The study of history and culture teaches that all the world was mad in the past; men always thought they were right, and that led to wars, persecutions, slavery, xenophobia, and chauvinism. The point is not to correct the mistakes and really be right; rather, it is not to think you are right at all."

Yet even Bloom would have been astonished by the intellectual balkanization created by the World Wide Web. For the first time in history, ordinary people now can spread their opinions, no matter how hateful or eccentric, without them first gaining the approval of editors, publishers, broadcasters, or paying consumers. At the Web's birth in the mid-1990s, it was imagined that these new information technologies would usher in an Enlightenment dreamworld of mutual understanding and rationalism. Instead, the opposite has happened: Rather than bring different groups into common discussion, they instead propelled radicals into their own paranoid echo chambers. They have also provided a stage for the most megalomaniacal of these radicals to act out their conspiratorial scripts—such as WikiLeaks founder Julian Assange, whose publication of hundreds of thousands of classified documents apparently was motivated by his desire to undermine Washington's ongoing "authoritarian conspiracy" against "a more just society."

Perhaps most worrying of all is the general disrepute into which authority figures of all stripes have fallen—especially our government and elected officials. The proportion of Americans who say that they "basically trust their government" has dropped from a high of 73 percent in 1958, when pollsters first asked the question, to just 22 percent in 2010. And there is a direct line from this statistic to the men and women profiled in this book. "I am old enough to remember having to sign up for selective service during the Vietnam War and also vividly remember the denied 'conspiracy theory' that Johnson and the military staged/lied about Tonkin Gulf," a Boston, Massachusetts–based conspiracy theorist named Mark McKertich told me. "Forty years later, we now know it was a theory based in fact. A lot of us have no patience to wait forty years for the truth about 9/11 to be revealed."

Indeed, a series of blows to official credibility, including the unsatisfying Warren Commission Report on the JFK assassination, the secret bombing of Cambodia and the military cover-up of My Lai, a program of foreign coups and assassinations by the CIA, and other questionable activities officially denied and only brought to light after the fact have all but destroyed Americans' faith in the pronouncements of their government.

The media fares no better: Many Americans now regard journalists with the same jaded skepticism that they apply to pop-up Internet ads and infomercials. In part, this is because the major news organizations—formerly represented by the reassuring face of Walter Cronkite, the most trusted man in America—are now dominated by Ivy League elitists and California Google jockeys. In part, it is because cost pressures have dumbed down broadcast media to a format so compressed that the crawl text on some headline news services doesn't even allow space for verbs. And in part it is because Americans now are simply more sophisticated consumers of news, for the obvious reason that they have more sources than ever to compare.

But the larger problem for the media is that, since the 1960s, they have been undermined by a dual critique that comes (ironically) from both the left and right. Conservatives increasingly see the media as a liberal-elitist establishment that is complicit in a whole range of partisan sins—including the uncritically reverential treatment accorded Barack Obama during the 2008 presidential campaign. (As Bernard Goldberg put it in his 2009 book, *A Slobbering Love Affair:* "I could not remember a time when so many supposedly objective reporters had acted so blatantly as full-fledged activists for one side—and without even a hint of embarrassment.") Many liberals, meanwhile, see the media through the lens of a left-wing critique whose central text is Noam Chomsky's *Manufacturing Consent,* a staple of liberal-arts reading lists that presents corporate-owned news media as lackeys to society's wealthy stakeholders. Even if the two angry poles of the political spectrum agree on nothing else, their attitude toward the media has fused together in a common posture of aggressive skepticism. Moreover, the media's failure to take this two-pronged assault seriously enough to respond to its major assertions—and more important, perhaps, its refusal to acknowledge the grain of truth in these critiques—has further compromised its authority as an arbiter of what is "true" or "real" in American life.

In sum, the media have ceased to be the source of an accepted common vision of events and have come to be seen instead as interested partisans manipulating public perceptions for hidden commercial or ideological ends. Even if a majority of Americans do not actually share these suspicions, the generalized mistrust of the "official version" of events has made many of them less critical of formerly outlandish explanations, which are now entertained as equally plausible "alternative narratives."

The result of all this is nothing less than a countercultural rift in the fabric of consensual American reality, a gaping cognitive hole into which has leaped a wide range of political paranoiacs previously consigned to the lunatic fringe—Larouchites, UFO nuts, libertarian survivalists, Holocaust deniers, and a thousand other groups besides. Even conspiracy theories that were discredited generations ago suddenly have sprung back to life, as if animated by electroshock. Explaining his decision to run a 1999 cover story questioning "who in fact was the bard, the usual suspect from Stratford, or Edward de Vere, 17th Earl of Oxford?" *Harper's* then-editor Lewis H. Lapham—the very caricature of a coastal, salon-dwelling sophisticate, which is to say, someone who should know better—recalled that his interest in the controversy was first piqued in 1972, "not a year conducive to belief in the masterpieces of the official doctrine." Such talk is eerily reminiscent of Orwell's reflections on the nature of totalitarian propaganda.

Conspiracy theories, the subject of this book, are both a leading cause and a symptom of this intellectual and civic crisis. When a critical mass of educated people in a society lose their grip on the real world—when they claim that George W. Bush is a follower of Nazi ideology, that Barack Obama is a Muslim secretly plotting to impose Sharia law on America, that the United States government is controlled by Israel, or that FEMA is preparing to imprison political dissidents in preparation for a totalitarian New World Order—it is a signal that the ordinary rules of rational intellectual inquiry are now treated as optional. It is not unusual for intellectuals and politicians to reject their opponents' arguments. But it is the mark of an intellectually pathologized society that intellectuals and politicians will reject their opponents' *realities*.

As I argue in Chapter 5—my field guide to the different breeds of conspiracy theorist—people come to their paranoias for all sorts of complicated reasons. Some of the figures profiled within this book are Marxists. Others are anti-Semites, or radical libertarians, or religious fantasists. Some defy ideological categorization. But they are all bound together by one increasingly common trait: They have spun out of rationality's ever-weakening gravitational pull, and into mutually impenetrable Manichean fantasy universes of their own construction. Much of this book is devoted to the task of exploring those fantasy universes and delving into the minds of those who create them—an inquiry that is a critical first step in defending the rationalist tradition.

It is important to concede that some conspiracies are very real. Watergate was no myth. Neither was Iran-Contra, or the Teapot Dome scandal. There is always a tiny grain of truth at the core of popular conspiracy theories, even in the case of concocted ones. Or at least some vexing question. *How did Adolf Hitler exterminate European Jewry without the Allies finding out about it earlier? How was Lee Harvey Oswald able to shoot JFK twice within such a short period of time? Why does the U.S. flag appear to flutter in the moon-landing footage?* In most cases, experts can provide persuasive answers. But sometimes, the truth is that we simply don't know. The world is a complicated place, and some aspects of even the most heavily scrutinized historical events always will remain fissures in society's intellectual foundations. In normal times, those fissures remain small and inconsequential—fodder for campus crackpots and late night AM call-in shows, perhaps, but nothing more. But in a society whose public intellectual foundations have been compromised over decades, those cracks will spread until the entire edifice is threatened.

That is what has happened to the United States, a place where millions of American "Birthers" accuse their president of being a foreign-born illegal alien. Other right-wing conspiracists, including no less a political celebrity than the Republicans' 2008 vice-presidential candidate, accused Barack Obama of creating "death panels" that would send the old and crippled to early graves. In bookstores and movie theaters, Dan Brown became a cultural force of nature by peddling discredited fantasies about Christian conspiracies, freemasonry, and secret societies.

Most infamously, there is the 9/11 "Truth movement," whose members have concluded that the September 11 attacks were actually part of an "inside job" hatched by ultra-hawkish elements within the U.S. government in order to secure a pretext for war abroad and draconian repression at home. In the Truther vision of America, our elected government is nothing but a smokescreen for Deep State actors—arms dealers, oil companies, neoconservative ideologues, Strangelovian Pentagon warmongers—who pull our elected politicians' puppet strings, and control our society at all levels through bribery, murder, and extortion.

Despite this otherworldly premise, the 9/11 Truth movement has become a mass phenomenon in the last ten years, spawning best-selling books, conferences, a pseudo-academic journal, and dozens of heavily surfed websites. A 2006 Scripps Howard poll of over one thousand U.S. citizens found that 36 percent of Americans believe it was either "somewhat likely" or "very likely" that "federal officials either participated in the attacks on the World Trade Center and the Pentagon, or took no action to stop them." About one-sixth of the respondents also agreed it was at least "somewhat likely" that "the collapse of the twin towers in New York was aided by explosives secretly planted in the two buildings."

For some Truthers, including many of those I've interviewed for this book, the idea that elements within the Bush administration used self-inflicted mass murder as a launching pad for geopolitical adventurism has become a full-time, all-consuming obsession. They include white-collar professionals like Richard Gage, a mild-mannered California architect who spent twenty years designing office buildings and strip malls before giving up everything—his wife, his home, his job—so he could travel the world preaching the gospel that the Twin Towers were felled by controlled demolition; and Steven Jones, a famous Brigham Young University physicist renowned for his work with cold fusion back in the 1980s, who then went on to lead a group called Scholars for 9/11 Truth and Justice. Actor Daniel Sunjata is a Truther (and even was permitted to deliver an in-character Truther monologue during a 2009 episode of the FX Network television drama *Rescue Me*). So is former pro wrestler and Minnesota governor Jesse Ventura, who went on to host a TV series dedicated to conspiracy theories; Charlie Sheen, who in September 2009 published a lengthy Truther-themed pseudo-interview with Barack Obama; Van Jones, the presidential advisor who was forced to quit his post after it was disclosed that he'd signed a petition seeking a new investigation into 9/11; Jared Loughner, the gunman who shot Congresswoman Gabrielle Giffords; as well as Fidel Castro and Hugo Chavez. In November 2010, as I was preparing final edits for this book, FOX News Channel analyst (and former New Jersey Superior Court judge) Andrew Napolitano told his audience: "Twenty years from now, people will look at 9-11 the way we look at the assassination of JFK today. It couldn't possibly have been done the way the government told us."

Iranian president Mahmoud Ahmadinejad is a Truther, too, naturally. In September 2010, he told the United Nations General Assembly that the 9/11 attacks were staged by elements within the U.S. government in order "to reverse the declining American economy and . . . save the Zionist regime." Just a few days later, he visited Yale University, where he lectured a graduate seminar on "U.S.-Iranian Diplomacy." Hillary Mann Leverett, the senior research fellow who organized the event, claimed Ahmadinejad's smooth performance at Yale demonstrated that he is "not a crazy, irrational leader." On the modern American campus, accepting the truth of 9/11 (not to mention the Holocaust—which Ahmadinejad also doubts) apparently is no longer a prerequisite for "rational" thinkers.

Despite all this, the 9/11 Truth movement mostly has been ignored by the mainstream media. In some scattered instances, Truthers have appeared on television (usually, on community access), and a few popular left-wing columnists (such as Robert Fisk of Britain's *Independent*) have expressed skepticism of the conventionally accepted account of the 9/11 attacks. But in general, mainstream authors and publishing houses have shunned Truthers. To provide them with any sort of media platform, the theory goes, is to "dignify" their position as respectable—the "other side" in a debate we should not even be having.

But having spent the last three years interviewing Truthers, reading their literature, attending their events, and surfing their discussion forums, I've come to a different conclusion. The Truther phenomenon—like the broader intellectual trend it epitomizes—is simply too important to ignore. Truther theories may be nonsense, but the disturbing habits of mind underlying them—a nihilistic distrust in government, total alienation from conventional politics, a need to reduce the world's complexity to good-versus-evil fables, the melding of secular politics with apocalyptic End-Is-Nigh religiosity, and a rejection of the basic tools of logic and rational discourse—have become threats all across our intellectual landscape. Moreover, journalists' refusal to engage intellectually with conspiracy theorists only serves to justify their claim—made on both sides of the political spectrum—that the mainstream media is nothing more than a trade shop for establishment propagandists.

You can't defeat the Enlightenment's enemies unless you understand them. And that is the project I ask my readers to embark on as they read this book. Those of us who continue to adhere to the rationalist tradition must commit to its defense, as though the year were 1755 and not 2011. For if the Great Lisbon Earthquake can be said to have inaugurated the Age of Reason, 9/11 and its consequences may yet prove to mark its end.

AMONG THE TRUTHERS

What is madness? To have erroneous perceptions and to reason correctly from them.

—*Voltaire*

I remember when
I remember, I remember when I lost my mind
There was something so pleasant about that place
Even your emotions have an echo in so much space
And when you're out there, without care
Yeah, I was out of touch
But it wasn't because I didn't know enough
I just knew too much

—*Gnarls Barkley, "Crazy"*

David Rockefeller owns several homes. So it is hard to say whether he was at his East Sixty-fifth Street double-wide Manhattan townhouse during the afternoon of September 10, 2009. But if he was, he would have seen a remarkable spectacle on the curbside below: A hundred young protestors wearing black T-shirts emblazoned with the words, "INVESTIGATE 9/11." Their leader, a Brooklyn College student and full-time rabble-rouser named Luke Rudkowski was screaming at the man's home: *"You will never have a New World Order!"*

Many Americans probably are unaware that the ninety-six-year-old Rockefeller is still alive (as of this writing)—much less that he is leading the fight to create a one-world government.

But for Truthers, the Rockefeller family is an enduring obsession. David Rockefeller chaired the organization that initiated the creation of the World Trade Center in 1960, with backing from his late brother, Nelson, then-governor of New York. Since the Rockefeller family helped create the Twin Towers, the Truther theory goes, they must have given the green light for their destruction.

After lecturing the nonagenarian for a while, the group walked over to the Council on Foreign Relations building on East Sixty-eighth, whereupon they broke into alternating chants of "Down with the CFR!," and then, apropos of nothing, "No vaccines! No vaccines!" At one point, the ringleaders screamed out to the CFR president, "Come out Richard Haass!" (He never complied.) Banners were unfurled, and passing motorists were invited to honk in support. Many of the protestors carried stacks of black-and-white leaflets titled "Ten Reasons For Starting A New 9/11 Investigation," and enthusiastically handed them out to passersby.

Most people in the crowd were teenagers and twentysomethings. But there were a few older, eccentric types—including one memorable specimen in glasses and purple track pants. Several were holding "Ron Paul for President" and "End the Fed" signs, in tribute to the various enduring conspiracy theories about the Federal Reserve. (According to radio host Alex Jones, who is profiled later in this chapter, JFK was murdered because he tried to dismantle the Fed.) One neatly trimmed man in his thirties, who told me he was a professional graphic designer, had produced a slick-looking placard with the images of Adolf Hitler, Josef Stalin, and Barack Obama side by side, emblazoned with the words "It Begins With Hope & Change."

Screaming the loudest was a short, tattooed, dreadlocked fellow named Craig Fitzgerald—a man described to me as a "32nd-degree Scottish Rite Mason." Fitzgerald occasionally took breaks from slogan-chanting so that he could lecture fellow protestors about the Illuminati. "Hegel was *possibly* a member—it's hard to be sure," he told one. "But [Johann Gottlieb] Fichte—there's no question. He was in the group. You have to do your research. A lot of the patterns and sequences we're seeing now descend from Bavaria."

Then it was up Fifth Avenue and on to Michael Bloomberg's house on Seventy-ninth Street. Unfortunately, no one seemed quite sure where the place was. And so for a while we ended up milling about around the Ukrainian Institute of America, a beautiful French Gothic–style mansion on the south side of Seventy-ninth, passing out more leaflets to pedestrians. (Inside the Institute, confused Slavs looked out from behind curtains, wondering what exactly their countrymen had done to bring down the Twin Towers.)

Later on, the whole group would reconvene at a Flatiron-district bar called Slate for speeches, as well as a recitation of poetry dedicated to 9/11 first responders, written by a middle-aged fellow named Jerry Mazza:

> How do you do this to them,
> Lady of Liberty,
> take theirs away, their freedom
> to work and be again.
> these giant people whose inner
> steel melted finally from thermate
> and poisons in the air,
> the steel blown up in a cloud
> that stole the sky and the streets.

As I sat there observing this surreal scene, nursing my beer, and scribbling down as many of Mazza's earnest lyrics as I could, my mind gradually began to drift. I wondered, not for the first time: "How exactly did I end up here?"

Don't Call Them "Nutbars"

My introduction to the 9/11 Truth movement came through an unlikely avenue: the staid world of Canadian politics.

In the run-up to Canada's 2008 federal election, the center-left Liberal party (Canada's version of the U.S. Democrats, or Labour in the UK) was low on money and staff. Fundraising efforts had been subpar. As a result, many candidates got their party's blessing before receiving a thorough background check.

One of the grass-roots party members who slipped under the radar was Lesley Hughes, an earnest middle-aged mother and community activist running under the Liberal banner in the midwestern city of Winnipeg. Like most Liberals, Hughes was decidedly left of center on foreign policy issues. But as one local blogger discovered with a Google search, her views went beyond her party's standard cant: A 2002 column she'd written for an obscure publication argued that sources known to her "suggest[ed] CIA foreknowledge and complicity of highly placed officials in the U.S. government around the attacks on the World Trade Center."

She also wrote that "Israeli businesses, which had offices in the Towers, vacated the premises a week before the attacks, breaking their lease to do it," suggested that the war in Afghanistan was part of a U.S. plot to seize natural gas and drugs, and cited reports to the effect that Osama bin Laden had been treated at an American hospital in Dubai.

Following the revelations, Hughes was turfed from her party. In the process, she became a sort of lightning rod and martyr for North America's Truther movement—something I discovered when I wrote a brief blog entry on my newspaper's website casually criticizing Hughes' "nutbar" opinions. Within hours, my inbox was stuffed with comments from irate Truthers, slamming me for my naïveté.

Wrote one typical U.S.-based correspondent:

Let's set aside name-calling, and dare to follow facts and evidence. I would prefer the scenario that Muslim extremists were responsible for attacks on my country. That would be easier on me. However, as an American, I have allowed the 'military industrial complex' as President Eisenhower warned of, to align agendas with the neo-cons . . . Any actual clear-minded research leaves one with the revelation that such an event could not possibly have been orchestrated, directed, and carried out exclusively by Al-CIAduh . . . Do your own research, and the conclusion cannot be avoided: The events of, and since, 9/11/2001 were and are the actions of a global coup d'état. Having the courage to follow the evidence wherever it leads is not easy. It requires facing an ugly situation and sharing the responsibility for correcting it. I salute Lesley Hughes for answering the call to duty.

Like most journalists with a public email address, I find a lot of conspiracy-mongering in my inbox every day—mostly from isolated paranoiacs raging against landlords, ex-spouses, and municipal politicians. Sometimes, they send me thick sheaves of legal documents, proving how this or that governmental agency had conspired for decades against them; or hand-typed screeds all in caps about such and such a minority group. From the micrographia scrawled around the margins of these documents, and often on the envelope itself, you can tell before reading a word that you are dealing with a damaged mind.

Moreover, this was 2008, a time when large swathes of the West were in the grip of what Charles Krauthammer described as Bush Derangement Syndrome—"the acute onset of paranoia in otherwise normal people in reaction to the policies, the presidency—nay—the very existence of George W. Bush." As an editorial board member at a pro-American Canadian newspaper (one that had endorsed the invasion of Iraq, no less), I had grown inured to the many readers who accused me of being an apologist for a war criminal.

But the Truthers who contacted me were different. They were neither street corner paranoiacs nor standard-issue political partisans. Most were outwardly "normal," articulate people who kept up with the news and held down office jobs—but who also happened to have become obsessively fixated on very particular, and very radical theories about the people running the U.S. government. My initial batch of correspondents included: a mechanical engineer working at a nuclear reactor, a Finnish IT expert, a doctor, an explosives specialist, the president of a financial corporation, and several university professors. One woman I corresponded with, Elizabeth Woodworth, was formerly the head librarian at the British Columbia Ministry of Health Library and had since devoted herself to becoming a "voluntary assistant" to David Ray Griffin, a superstar Truther who placed forty-first on the New Statesman's 2009 list of the world's most influential people (more on him later in the book).

These people, I learned, aren't the loners of X-Files stereotype. Just the opposite: Like other dot-com-era conspiracists, Truthers have collaborated on the Internet to produce a dense mythology with a professional, even scholarly, gloss. And they know how to stay on message: Scrolling down through my incoming correspondence, I was struck by how faithfully Truthers hewed to the movement's main talking points:

- 9/11 was a secret plot led by Dick Cheney, Donald Rumsfeld, and Paul Wolfowitz as an excuse to launch imperial wars of conquest and seize the world's dwindling oil and natural gas supplies;
- Osama bin Laden is a patsy of the U.S. government, and al-Qaeda is a wholly controlled subsidiary of the CIA;
- Ill-trained al-Qaeda pilots could never have executed the maneuvers required to fly commercial jetliners into the World Trade Center and Pentagon;
- NORAD was intentionally made to "stand down" on

9/11 so that the hijacked planes could reach their destina-
tions;

- Preplanted bombs brought down the World Trade Center buildings after they'd been hit by aircraft;
- Liquid metal observed flowing from the World Trade Center was molten steel—the result of an exotic high-temperature, government-manufactured pyrotechnic explosive called thermite;
- The puffs of air and dust emitted from the lower floors of the Twin Towers as they fell, plus the neat free-fall collapse of the buildings into their own ground-level footprint, demonstrate the use of a planned demolition sequence;
- World Trade Center leaseholder Larry Silverstein publicly admitted that one of the WTC buildings had been "pulled down" by internal demolition;
- Stock-trading data show that multimillion-dollar bets were made on airline companies in advance of Sept. 11, 2001, suggesting investor foreknowledge of the 9/11 attacks.

I'd long assumed that abnormal theories came from abnormal minds. But these people couldn't be dismissed as freaks. Outwardly, in fact, they looked and sounded a lot like me. And when I look back at the genesis of this book, I think that was the crucial fact that drew me to them, and made me curious about what made them tick. Like many of the Truthers who emailed me, I, too, have a weakness for narrow, geeky pursuits—tabletop war games, chess problems, sports statistics, Internet flame wars. During a previous phase of my life, when I was pursuing my master's degree in metallurgical engineering, I would often spend sixteen hours a day in front of a computer, writing a mathematical simulation that perhaps two dozen other people in the world would find useful.

In other words, I know what it is like to become enmeshed

in all-consuming intellectual exercises that the people around you simply cannot understand—and perhaps even disdain. But for me, it was always a hobby or an academic pursuit—never a worldview or a political philosophy. This is the line these people had crossed. And I wanted to find out why.

A t first, I didn't take Lubo Zizakovic seriously.

In his lengthy email to me, the man claimed to be all sorts of things—a successful investment banker, a software entrepreneur, an award-winning business scholar who'd once shared a podium with George Bush Sr., a walk-on member of the University of Maryland basketball team, and, most memorably, a former defensive end with the New York Giants. When I reluctantly took Zizakovic up on his offer to meet for lunch at a sushi restaurant near my office, I expected to meet a confused man inhabiting a world of fantasy.

As soon as I walked into the restaurant, I knew otherwise. Lubo Zizakovic is six foot eight, trim as my wife's yoga instructor, with hands as large as small desk fans. No surprise that such a specimen would be able to make a career on the gridiron.

Despite his intimidating appearance, Zizakovic is no goon. During our meal of raw fish, he put me at ease, describing his experiences in professional football, the state of the global economy, his volunteer work for the Special Olympics, and the joys of raising a family on his large rural estate. The accomplishments he described to me are real, as is his career as an investment banker. And by all appearances, he's good at what he does.

But every once in a while, as he became animated about one point or another, I would see flashes of the 280-pound defensive end who drove opposing quarterbacks into the turf during the 1990s. Underneath his genteel, well-dressed investment banker exterior, Lubo Zizakovic harbors a lot of anger—anger that's been his constant companion since the defining historical event of our time.

"I was at [an investment banking] training session at Bricket

Wood just outside London [on 9/11]," he told me. "When a trainer came in to inform us of the first plane hitting [World Trade Center] 1, we all immediately reacted as if this were a curve ball being thrown at us as part of the training session. It was that outrageous.

"Once I realized that the attacks were for real, my first reaction was, 'My God! How could a group pull this off with such efficiency? Three out of four direct hits? Four of four hijacked planes? Where was NORAD? Where were the air defense systems?' I did my undergraduate work at the University of Maryland, so I spent a lot of time in the D.C. area, and I drove past the Pentagon often. I couldn't imagine how someone could pull this off."

In the days following 9/11, the Bush administration blamed al-Qaeda for the attacks, and even identified the nineteen hijackers who'd been on the four doomed airliners. But for Zizakovic—a man of Serbian ancestry whose distrust of the U.S. government became a fixation when NATO took sides against Slobodan Milosevic during the Balkan wars of the 1990s—the official explanation didn't hold up. In fact, it only heightened his suspicions.

"The U.S. government apparently had it all figured out immediately," he told me. "That was the first time I smelled a rat. [And] when the United States turned the entire world's sympathy to extreme hatred in such a short time, I knew something was wrong. When they attacked Iraq under false pretenses and found no WMD, I knew in my heart that a bunch of guys living in caves in Afghanistan didn't do 9/11.

"The clincher was listening to Bush say that Bin Laden might never be found. The U.S. military, with all of its modern satellite equipment and military might can find a needle in a haystack— but not a guy isolated in a single region? Common sense pointed to a cover-up early on, and I just had to spend some time finding concrete evidence . . . I [now] know beyond a shadow of a doubt that 9/11 was a criminal act executed by elements of the U.S. government—let's call it the shadow government—against its own citizens."

Michael Keefer epitomizes what most of us imagine when we hear someone described as "an academic." Tall, thin, bearded, gray-haired, and mild-mannered, Keefer shares a large century-old brick house in Toronto's West End with his wife, an acclaimed novelist. Bookshelves line the rooms, each crammed with classic texts accumulated over a four-decade career as a professor of English literature.

Bookish as he is, Keefer hails from a long line of fighters. His father—an elder in the Presbyterian Church—landed at Normandy. His grandfather was nearly killed at Gallipoli, and went on to serve in the Burma Corps during the Second World War. Keefer himself took a degree at Canada's Royal Military College in the late 1960s. As we talk in his living room, he directs my gaze to a portrait of an especially fierce-looking Keefer over the mantelpiece. "That's my double-great grandfather," he says. "His father and uncle and grandmother were booted out of New Jersey after the American Revolution. The family eventually moved to the Niagara Peninsula."

After graduation from RMC, Keefer became an officer in Canada's naval reserve, and then earned a doctorate at Sussex University in England. His thesis, researched during five years spent poring over Renaissance texts in Latin and German, was about the ideological origins of the Faustus myth. In time, he became an authority on both William Shakespeare and Christopher Marlowe, and published an exhaustive article on the philosophy of René Descartes.

And yes, he is a Truther.

Something about Keefer's personality had always lent itself to activism: Early in his career at Guelph University, he engaged in an unsuccessful four-year campaign to save a local heritage bridge from demolition. His awakening to more global causes began in the 1990s, when he organized fellow faculty members at Guelph in opposition to Canada's participation in the first Gulf War and the sanctions regime that followed. "It seems clear to me that what [the allies] had done in 1991 [were] war crimes," he told me. "Two UN guys resigned in protest over sanctions in Iraq—both denounced them as criminal. I was collecting information about stuff like that."

"Starting in about 2002," he tells me, "I'd begun noticing that computer security people were raising red flags over U.S. voting systems. On election night in 2004, I was carefully collecting exit-polling information from CNN. The next morning, I noticed that all of the key exit poll numbers had been changed overnight from what they'd been at midnight. They'd been changed to correspond to the final vote tally. I proved that the numbers had been fiddled, and published [my analysis] on the Internet. The piece had four-teen thousand hits within a week. My article basically argued that the 2004 election was stolen."

As he continued to research the 2004 election, Keefer found more dots to connect—including what he describes as evidence that the crucial Ohio results were sent to the office of Michael Connell, a Karl Rove confidante, before being certified by Ohio's Secretary of State. "Connell died in a plane crash in December [2008]," Keefer notes dryly. "It quite possibly was linked to the election shenanigans."

Based on these investigations, Keefer became more convinced that nothing announced by the U.S. government was as it seemed—including the "official" account of the September 11, 2001, attacks.

In the years following 9/11, Keefer—who'd formerly stuck to the world of academic journals and faculty meetings—began to surf the web, forging contacts with other left-wing authors and theorists. He became particularly influenced by the work of Michel Chossudovsky, a radical critic of the United States and globaliza-tion.

Keefer's theory of 9/11? "I concluded that a highly placed group within the U.S. government wanted to energize the U.S.

public into support for a radical program of redrawing the map in the Middle East and Central Asia. And I think they felt the only way they could get support for this geopolitical program was through some kind of mighty shock to the U.S. psyche. These people—whoever they were—both organized the absence of the American air defenses and the destruction of the Word Trade Center towers."

As our lengthy interview unfolded, Keefer began to detail his theory—as if supplying footnotes in one of his carefully researched academic papers on Renaissance-era philosophy: the timing of NORAD military training, suspicious plumes of smoke emanating from the North Tower, the behavioral oddities of 9/11 hijacker Mohammed Atta ("purported hijacker" is how Keefer describes him). All of this he recites calmly, methodically, authoritatively—as if what he was saying were not even controversial, let alone radical.

Then, suddenly, the conversation turned, and we found ourselves once more discussing Faustus, Descartes, and the frustrations of university politics. Within a few minutes, I'd half-forgotten that the brilliant scholar on the other side of my coffee cup imagined the U.S. government to be guilty of mass-murdering three thousand innocent people on a sunny morning in 2001.

When we parted ways, it was with a friendly handshake and a smile: Like most Truthers I'd met, he didn't begrudge the fact that I rejected his views. He was pleased that I'd taken the time to listen to him, and hoped that I'd eventually come around to the capital-T Truth.

Keefer and Zizakovic are just two of many conspiracy theorists I've met. I've chosen to include them in the first chapter because they exemplify the penetration of conspiracism into the well-educated middle class. Zizakovic is a respected and successful banker responsible for multimillion-dollar investment decisions. Keefer is an eminent author and university professor who is entrusted with the education of hundreds of young minds. Neither fit the stereotype of the antisocial conspiracy theorist scribbling out his obscure theses in a dingy student apartment.

They are alike in another way, too: For Keefer and Zizakovic, as for most Truthers, 9/11 is just the tip of the iceberg—a symptom of a far larger metaconspiracy organized by the world's secret elites.

In interview after interview, a conversation about 9/11 would inevitably come back to the same group of apparently disconnected individuals and corporations—Henry Kissinger, the Carlyle Group, David Rockefeller, the Rothschilds, George Soros (who seems to be considered, by Glenn Beck and others, a sort of honorary Rothschild in modern conspiracist lore), Unocal, Halliburton, the Bilderberg Group, the U.S. Federal Reserve, the Council on Foreign Relations, the International Monetary Fund, Dick Cheney, the CIA, the Mossad, Pakistan's ISI, Adnan Khashoggi, E. Howard Hunt, Zbigniew Brzezinski—along with theories linking them in complex and tantalizing ways. In the mind of the committed conspiracist, such theories multiply until they encompass literally every aspect of human life, from the water we drink (filled with fluoride, a "deadly neurotoxin" developed by the Nazis to "pacify concentration camp prisoners"), to the air we breathe (polluted by government-engineered "chemtrails" emitted by jet engines as they pass overhead), to the blood pumping through our veins (poisoned by government-mandated vaccines).

Keefer, for instance, suspects that 9/11 is but one chapter in a continuing saga of "false flag" operations hatched by elements within, or allied to, the United States government—including the bombing of the Bologna train station in 1980. He also believes there is evidence that "the occupation of Afghanistan is linked to U.S. government participation in the global drug trade"—an echo of 1980s-era charges that the CIA was trafficking cocaine in Central America as part of its campaign against Nicaragua's Sandinista regime.

When you talk to a conspiracy theorist, you can never be sure where your conversation will end up. One of the very first Truthers

I met—a charming, New York–based former newspaper columnist named Dallas Hansen, who'd lost his job as a result of his controversial views about the World Trade Center attacks—connected September 11 to a range of particularly jaw-dropping theories, spanning the assassination of JFK to the likely target of the next false-flag terrorist attack.

"My great-grandfather owned a bus line in Holland and hid Jews in his country home," he tells me. "My grandfather was a teenager who participated in ambushes of Nazi supply trucks . . . I'm not the first person to compare 9/11 to the Reichstag Fire, nor to notice a sort of fascism-lite has emerged. The news abounds with tales of police-state tyranny, from [people] being Tasered to death . . . to police forcibly withdrawing blood from 'drunk driving suspects.' "

Most memorably, he speculated that George W. Bush would retire to Paraguay so that he could enjoy the protection and fraternity of former Nazis. "Why in the world would he do that?" I asked. He responded that the fortunes of the Bush family have long been intertwined with those of the Nazis—and then described financial links between George Bush's ancestors and Hitler's regime.

(To my shock, I later found that Hansen's story had a germ of truth: A 2004 article in Britain's *Guardian* newspaper reported that "George Bush's grandfather, the late U.S. senator Prescott Bush, was a director and shareholder of companies that profited from their involvement with the financial backers of Nazi Germany." It was a classic example of an isolated historical factoid being used to justify an outlandish conspiracy theory—a pattern I would see repeated many times.)

As explained in more detail in Chapter 2, several common threads run through these theories, and they spooled over one another repeatedly during the course of my interviews. These include the belief that the path of history is controlled in secret by a small group of influential, fantastically wealthy people; that this power structure is murderous and morally corrupt; and that the political world we inhabit is fundamentally illusory, like the constructed reality in the 1999 film *The Matrix*.

"The world is ruled by an elite who make world events occur for their own benefit," declared Zizakovic when I asked him to describe how 9/11 figured in the sweep of modern history. "Read *The True Story of the Bilderberg Group* by Daniel Estulin [an influential conspiracist book summarized in the next chaper]. In 1954, the ruling elite started coordinating their efforts. They are a global shadow government with influence and control of just about every major government in the world . . . Their objective, which can be argued might already be achieved, is a one government world with one currency where the masses have no real wealth and all of the resources are in [the elite's] hands."

When a conspiracy theorist held forth in this way, I would usually just put down my pen and listen as we dove together down the rabbit hole. There's nothing else to be done: These metanarratives are so elaborate and ambitious that they essentially describe alternate moral universes—unrecognizable realms in which a Western government smashing airplanes into its own cities makes perfect sense.

Truthers' arcane, detailed theories about internal demolition, NORAD complicity, and CIA–al-Qaeda complicity aren't just paranoid fairy tales—they are foundational narratives in the construction of this alternate reality, told and retold at Truther gatherings in the same ritualized manner that psalms or Torah portions are read out at religious services. Like other radicalized political movements of our time, the Truth movement transcends activism: For many adherents, it has become the dominant spiritual force in their lives, a pattern described in detail in Chapter 6.

Certainly, the 9/11 Truth phenomenon cannot be explained as a merely political phenomenon. While I once supposed Truthers to be simply radical specimens of the anti-American, Bush-hating Left, many of the Truthers I've met actually turned out to be self-described conservatives who see 9/11 as part of a plot to strip Americans of their liberty, and transfer Washington's sovereign powers to the United Nations. With the liberal Barack Obama in power, this imagined day of reckoning only grows nearer.

F or Alex Jones, it all started with David Koresh and the Waco siege.

Jones grew up in the Dallas suburbs, just two hours' drive from the Branch Davidian ranch at Mount Carmel. In 1993, when Jones was barely out of high school, a seven-week Bureau of Alcohol, Tobacco, and Firearms (ATF) siege ended in the incineration of seventy-six cult members. He remembers being transfixed by the congressional hearings into the fiasco, which were broadcast by C-SPAN. The episode turned Jones into a full-time crusader against the United States government.

Koresh and his followers, Jones believed, were harmless innocents who'd been murdered by Attorney General Janet Reno and cynical ATF agents looking to boost their agency's profile. "I remember watching the TV screen and seeing that famous footage of the ATF loading their video cameras before going in," Jones told me. "They were going to lose their funding. This was [a] PR stunt. They were about to be abolished. That's why they did it."

Two years later, Timothy McVeigh bombed the Alfred P. Murrah building in Oklahoma City, an act intended to incite a popular revolt against the U.S. government. But Jones concluded the bombing actually was a part of a conspiracy, hatched by the feds themselves, to quash the nascent states'-rights movement. By this time, his opinion mattered: The twenty-one-year-old Jones already had his own cable-access television program. A year later, he began airing on radio. By the time George W. Bush was in his second term he arguably had become the most popular and influential conspiracist in America. His syndicated *Alex Jones Show* appears on dozens of AM, FM, and shortwave stations across the United States—a platform that gives him unparalleled influence within the Truther movement.

Jones believes that the 9/11 plot was an inside job, likely executed by using remote control technology to override the pilots of the commandeered aircraft. Under this theory, the nineteen hijackers were stooges who believed they were participating in a legitimate military exercise—though many of Jones' followers believe the men are still alive, and have developed a rich literature detailing their sightings.

When you ask Jones about all of this, one of the first things he'll tell you is that he "predicted" 9/11. What actually happened was this: On July 25, 2001, Jones warned viewers of his *Infowars* TV show that the U.S. government was planning a terrorist attack against its own citizens—flashing the White House's phone number so that people could call in and beg the president not to go through with the dastardly plot. In the broadcast, which now circulates widely on the Internet, Jones does not identify the World Trade Center as a future target, but he does declare—in typically Jonesian language—that "the United States is a shining jewel the globalists want to bring down and they will use terrorism as the pretext to get it done," and that Osama bin Laden is "the bogeyman [the government] need[s] in this Orwellian system."

Talking to Jones is exhausting. He spits out every sentence as if he were calling the police to report a crime in progress—footnoting each eyebrow-raising claim with scattered (but oddly precise) references to Internet news sources. As *Radar* magazine writer Jebediah Reed put it, he speaks "in a gravelly baritone fit for the public address announcer at a monster truck rally—a voice so gruff it almost sounds like he's faking it."

He throws around acronyms like "PNAC" (Project for the New American Century, a Truther obsession described in more detail later in this book), and talks casually of NATO's role in engineering "the 888 attacks" (his term for the brief 2008 war between Russia and Georgia). Jones has lived and breathed these sorts of conspiracy theories for years. It's not clear that this New World Order prophet could turn his obsession off—though he claims he'd like to . . . if only the world would let him. "Once you discover reality, what is being admitted, all the crimes, and you go around to the zombie-like media and tell people to read all this stuff, and they just giggle and say none of this exists, that government is good, it's upsetting, and so you try to wake people up," he tells me, slowing down the pace of his manic verbiage only slightly as he adopts the weary tone of a political martyr. "People laughed at us, and now it's all coming true. Even though I'm sick of doing this, I do it anyway. Somebody's got to do this."

One would have thought that the Republicans' across-the-board losses in the 2008 elections would have provided Jones with peace of mind: Surely, one of the first things that Barack Obama and incoming administration officials would do is unearth the murderous 9/11 lies of their ousted opponents.

But Jones—like other Truthers—scoffs at the illusion that Obama will ever willingly permit Americans to get at the truth ("smoking Demo-crack" many activists call it). When it comes to who calls the real shots in Washington, he tells me, there is no difference between Republicans and Democrats: "They answer to the same people. The president is nothing more than a pitch man—a Madison Avenue front." Like all committed conspiracy theorists, he is able to incorporate any new piece of information or historical development into a preexisting framework.

All governments, Jones believes, use terrorism and staged acts of warfare to hoodwink their citizens and gain support for their agendas—from the sinking of the *Maine*, to the Reichstag fire (Jones' favorite historical reference), to Pearl Harbor ("*The Honolulu Advertiser* newspaper was telling readers the attack was coming seven days before it happened"). In the case of Obama, Jones sees dark hints of things to come in the mused-about carbon tax, the proceeds from which, he believes, will one day be paid to a global overlord. The same goes for Washington's bank bailout: In a full-length film he's produced—*The Obama Deception*—Jones alleges "international bankers purposefully engineered the worldwide financial meltdown to bankrupt the nations of the planet and bring in World Government.

"Bottom line, the future as I see it is this: 70 percent *Brave New World*, 30 percent *Nineteen-Eighty-Four*," he tells me. "There'll be lots of video games, drugs, Soma, Prozac, parties—but if you get out of line, the SWAT team's coming."

Some Caveats

This is a book about American conspiracism's history and mythology (Chapters 1 through 4), psychological and religious roots (Chapters 5 and 6), propagation through modern media, academic and activist networks (Chapters 7, 8, and 9), and, more generally, the manner in which it erodes our society's collective grasp on reality. In Chapter 10, I offer suggestions for countering the spread of conspiracy theories—including a brief description of a hypothetical academic course that would give college students the tools needed to identify and debunk conspiracist ideologies.

Before proceeding further, let me offer five caveats about the way the material is presented.

First, this book focuses primarily on conspiracism in the United States and the Internet-based conspiracist culture that has grown out of it, with some coverage of prominent Canadian theorists who have taken an active role in promoting American conspiracist narratives. (True to its moderate stereotype, my native Canada has virtually no indigenous conspiracist culture of its own, except in regard to phobias of U.S. hegemony. And so its paranoiacs tend to co-opt American obsessions with JFK, 9/11, the USS *Liberty*, and the like.)

The 9/11 Truth movement is widespread beyond North America's shores—particularly in the Muslim countries of the Middle East and South Asia. But in these parts of the world, such theories are wrapped up in complicated ways with anti-Americanism, colonialism, and the long history of the West's interaction with what was once called the Third World—issues that lie beyond the scope of this book.

Second, this book is not intended as a rebuttal to conspiracists. Nor will I provide a complete recitation of their elaborate proofs. Those seeking a point-by-point rebuttal to the claims of the 9/11 Truth movement already have several fine resources at their disposal. In particular, I recommend the 2006 book *Debunking 9/11 Myths*: *Why Conspiracy Theories Can't Stand up to the Facts*, authored by the editors of *Popular Mechanics* magazine; Mark Roberts' *Links for 9/11 Research*; the websites 911 Myths, Debunking 911, and the blog *Screw Loose Change*. Readers who wish to devote more time to the issue might also consider reading the *Final Report of the 9–11 Commission*, released in 2004; Lawrence Wright's Pulitzer Prize–winning 2006 account of the history of 9/11, *The Looming Tower*; and, for those who share my interest in technical material, the National Institute of Standards and Technology's exhaustive *Final Reports of the Federal Building and Fire Investigation of the World Trade Center Disaster* (a twenty-million-dollar effort that took three years to produce, and drew on the efforts of three hundred staff and external experts). I also recommend a brief, but highly illuminating 2006 paper by explosives and demolitions expert Brent Blanchard entitled *A Critical Analysis of the Collapse of WTC Towers 1,2&7 From a Conventional Explosives and Demolitions Industry Viewpoint*. It can be found on the website of the *Journal of Debunking 9/11*, which contains a number of other interesting articles aimed at helping laypeople refute Truther claims.

Third, a note about terminology: Throughout this book, I employ the terms "conspiracy theory" (and, interchangeably, "conspiracism") to describe 9/11 Truth and similar movements. The phrase is defined by *Merriam-Webster's* as "a theory that explains an event or set of circumstances as the result of a secret plot." But that formulation is broad enough to encompass *actual* historical conspiracies, such as the plot to frame Alfred Dreyfus in the 1890s, the

1972 plot by members of the Committee to Re-elect the President to spy on the Democratic National Committee headquarters, and the actual al-Qaeda plot that led to 9/11. So instead, I adopt the narrower definition set out by Oxford University conspiracy theory scholar Steve Clarke and Brian Keeley of Pitzer College (formerly of Washington University): A theory that traces important events to a secretive, nefarious cabal, *and whose proponents consistently respond to contrary facts not by modifying their theory, but instead by insisting on the existence of ever-wider circles of high-level conspirators controlling most or all parts of society.*

Fourth, a caveat about the different types of conspiracy theories discussed in this book: As political scientist Michael Barkun has noted, conspiracy theories usually can be classified as either "event" or "systemic." In the former case, the conspiracist is merely seeking to explain a discrete event—such as, say, the moon landing, or a hypothetical Elizabethan plot to pass off Francis Bacon's plays as William Shakespeare's. In the case of systemic conspiracy theories, on the other hand, the theory purports to explain the operation of whole societies, and often the entire planet. This book deals primarily (though not exclusively) with systemic conspiracy theories, such as 9/11 Truth, since they are far more damaging to the marketplace of ideas. That said, I do not take pains in the text to assign conspiracy theories to one category or the other.

Fifth, a note about the people who are the subject of the case study at the heart of this book.

Many Americans view 9/11 Truthers as inherently contemptible. *Washington Post* columnist Charles Krauthammer, for instance, has declared that Truthers "derangedly desecrate" the victims of 9/11. While I understand why people hold that view, most Truthers I've met actually tend to be outwardly respectful of the innocent victims who perished in the World Trade Center and Pentagon attacks. In fact, many of the most prominent boosters of the Truther movement—including some of the so-called Jersey Girls—have themselves been 9/11 widows or first responders (a psychological phenomenon I describe in the "damaged survivor" subsection of Chapter 5). At Truther events I've attended in the New York City area, organizers have raised thousands of dollars for police and firefighters who became sick or injured on 9/11, and sometimes (though not always) there is plenty of genuine American patriotism on display.

Moreover, let it be said that not all conspiracy theories are equally malign.

Some of the conspiracist movements I discuss in this book—such as the Ku Klux Klan, *The Protocols of the Elders of Zion*, and Holocaust revisionism—are explicitly racist or anti-Semitic. By including these historical references, I am *not* suggesting that Truthers harbor any equivalent hatred. Most Truthers actually cast themselves as *enemies* of bigotry whose mission is to expose the truth about a racist, white, imperialist war machine originally set into motion by the Christian crusader George W. Bush.

It also bears mentioning that the Truth movement is entirely non-violent. Their meetings and literature typically are suffused with exhortations to tolerance and respect. When they demonstrate publicly, they get permits, and usually follow police instructions carefully. (I know this from eyewitness observations: I've marched with them several times, and have never seen anyone arrested.) Unlike hate-fueled conspiracist movements that fired adherents up by calling for pogroms against Jews or blacks (or even full-blown insurgency against the government), Truthers appeal to due process and the American Constitution. Their professed goal is to put America's leadership on trial according to the existing laws of the land.

The threat currently posed by modern conspiracists is not physical, but cultural. Like other groups that have effectively opted out of America's ideological mainstream, they threaten to turn the country into a sort of intellectual Yugoslavia—a patchwork of agitated cults screaming at one another in mutually unintelligible tongues. It's a trend that every thinking person has a duty to fight.

| **PART I** |

The Truth Movement and Its Ancestors

CHAPTER ONE

American Conspiracism: A Brief History

I worked for them . . . I took a position with a group of multinationals we call "The Company." They call every shot this country takes. What laws to pass. What judges to appoint. What wars to fight. The thing is—if you want to rise in the ranks like I did, you had to commit to leaving everything you knew behind. Because then you start to get access to the real information . . . information that people would do a lot of things to get their hands on—like harm your family.

—Prison Break, *Season 1, Episode 19, "The Key"*

I know I'm hardly the first one to decide I have had all I can stand. It has always been a myth that people have stopped dying for their freedom in this country, and it isn't limited to the blacks, and poor immigrants. I know there have been countless before me and there are sure to be as many after. But I also know that by not adding my body to the count, I insure nothing will change. I choose to not keep looking over my shoulder at "big brother" while he strips my carcass, I choose not to ignore what is going on all around me, I choose not to pretend that business as usual won't continue; I have just had enough.

—*Suicide manifesto left by Joseph Stack, who crashed a single-engine plane into an Austin, Texas, building housing IRS offices on February 18, 2010*

Programmed for Conspiracy

In the late 1990s, University of Michigan developmental psychologist Margaret Evans became interested in the question of why many Americans doubted the notion of biological evolution. So she began interviewing children of different ages and religious backgrounds about where they thought animals originated.

The responses she got, analyzed in a 2000 academic journal article, revealed an interesting pattern. The youngest subjects, aged four to seven, gave a range of answers—most along the lines of "from someplace else" or "out of the ground." But among eight-to-ten year olds, the responses were different: "Whatever their family background, most children in this age range endorse the idea that the first kinds of animals were 'made by someone,' and often that someone is God." Only in later years, as children developed the ability for complex, abstract thought, were they able to process the idea of evolutionary change.

Obviously, this reflects the fact that evolution is a complicated scientific concept. But Evans and other researchers believe there is more to it than that: From a young age, human brains seem programmed to see design and intention behind the world around them.

When asked about lions, children tell social science researchers that they exist so we can see them in the zoo. When asked why some rocks are pointy, children will respond: "so that animals won't sit on them." No less a thinker than Aristotle theorized that rocks fell downward so that they could take their natural place in the world. Only in the centuries since the Enlightenment has this outlook been systematically challenged. And even now, it continues to have its defenders—the campaign for "Intelligent Design" as an alternative to random genetic mutation and natural selection being the most prominent example.

Michael Shermer, the editor of *Skeptic* magazine, and executive director of the Skeptics Society, calls this mode of thinking "agenticity"—"the tendency to believe that the world is controlled by intentional agents, usually invisible, from the top down . . . souls, spirits, ghosts, gods, demons, angels, aliens, intelligent designers, and government conspiracies are all believed to haunt our world and control our lives . . . It even informs our [modern] belief in government."

How does this thinking evolve? The same way our bodies did.

"Picture yourself in the Neolithic environment of our evolutionary adaptation, and you're a hominid walking along and you hear a rustle in the grass," says Shermer. "Is it a dangerous predator or just the wind? Well, if you believed it was a predator, but it was just the wind, you've made a [false positive] error. But no problem—no big deal. On the other hand, if you believe the rustle in the grass was just the wind, and it's actually a dangerous predator, you're lunch. And so there's a high cost to making a [false negative] error. [Thus,] our default position is just to assume that all patterns are real. This is the evolution of 'patternicity' or superstition. There's been a natural selection in our cognitive processes of assuming that all patterns are real important phenomena. And we're the descendants of the most successful patternicity primates."

At the societal level, the "agenticity" and "patternicity" Shermer describes have shaped the foundational myths that humans develop to infuse meaning into life: We take comfort from the idea that the randomness of human life, with all the attendant sorrows and catastrophes, is actually part of some master plan created by a (usually) unseen higher power. In the Western literary tradition, the prototype was Odysseus, a long-suffering pawn in a feud between the protective Athena and the malicious Poseidon. Aeneas was buffeted by similar divine intrigues on his way to founding Rome. Indeed, the whole arc of Greco-Roman mythology, and even the Bible stories that replaced it, is premised on the idea that human events are guided by mysterious supernatural agents—conspiracy theories in robes and sandals.

In many cases, this conspiracist reflex has blended with tribalism, the human instinct that causes us to rally around our own kin groups, and demonize outsiders—especially during times of conflict or crisis. The most venerable example is the blood libel against Jews that periodically gained a following in medieval European societies (and still pops up in Muslim countries), according to which Jews were accused of killing gentile children and using their blood for the production of their Passover matzos. Such anti-Semitic conspiracy theories have been around in recognizable form since at least the time of the Crusades, when bellicosity toward Muslims morphed into a more general form of religious xenophobia.

The Crusades also led to a second and distinct form of conspiracism—one directed toward the Knights Templar and similarly secretive groups of monk-warriors. While these holy legions originally were organized to fight in the Middle East, they eventually set up banks and commercial networks, and exerted a sometimes malign influence on domestic affairs. As Daniel Pipes wrote in his 1997 book *Conspiracy: How The Paranoid Style Flourishes And Where It Comes From*, the Knights Templar "had a conspiratorial air about them . . . At the initiation ceremony, a candidate was told that 'of our order you only see the surface which is the outside,' implying that something very secret took place behind closed doors. At the end of the initiation, each knight kissed the adept on the mouth, an act with obvious homosexual overtones . . . Together, the spectacular rise, great power, and grisly end of the Templars [at the hands of King Philip IV of France] turned them into a permanent feature of European conspiracy theories."

By modern standards, these theories were simple narratives—folk tales for peasants—that purported to describe finite, localized plots against this or that monarch or town. But this began to change in the eighteenth century, as capitalism, industrialization, and urbanization transformed Europe. The French Revolution, in particular, demonstrated that a relatively small group of ideologically motivated radicals, armed with a universalist creed, could propel a state, and possibly even a whole continent, into mass upheaval. "If French fears from 1725 of a 'famine plot' to starve the country symbolize conspiracy theories before the French Revolution—a limited scheme aimed at monetary gain—fears after 1789 are captured by a supposed . . . plot to eliminate the monarchy, the church, and private property," wrote Pipes. "Just as the conspirators grew far more alarming, so did their goals—and the theories about them."

It is no coincidence that conspiracism took its modern form at the same time Edmund Burke was writing *Reflections on the Revolution in France*, which many historians identify as the original manifesto of conservative thought. Like the conspiracist creeds of the era, Burke's influential ideology was rooted in a nostalgia—or at least a respect—for the old order, and a (justified) fear that the revolutionary, abstract doctrines animating Europe would lead to tyranny and chaos.

The Freemasons and Jews figured prominently in conspiracy theories about the French Revolution that emerged in the early nineteenth century. But there was a new villain, as well—the Order of the Illuminati, a secret society founded on the precepts of humanitarian rationalism by an eccentric Bavarian law professor in 1776. Unlike the benign Masons, the Illuminati operated as a genuine cult, imposing secret rites on members, and forbidding interaction with outside society. Though the group would fizzle within a decade, and had only a few thousand members at its height, it remains an enduring fixation among conspiracists—including novelist Dan Brown, who put a lurid pseudo-Illuminati plot to destroy Vatican City at the center of his 2000 book, *Angels & Demons*.

Even before the French Revolution, the Marquis de Luchet warned Europe that the Illuminati aimed to "govern the world." Later on, in 1797, Scottish conspiracist John Robison wrote that the Illuminati had been formed "for the express purpose of rooting out all the religious establishments, and overturning all the existing governments of Europe." A year later, Augustin Barruel gave the Illuminati a starring role in his four-volume work *Memoirs Illustrating the History of Jacobinism*—in which he argued that the French Revolution resulted from a "triple conspiracy" of Freemasons, Illuminati, and anti-Christians who aimed at achieving the "overthrow of the altar, the ruin of the throne, and the dissolution of all civil society." His list of conspirators included many of the greatest minds of the Enlightenment, including Voltaire, whom Barruel imagines to be the French Revolution's true architect.

Foreshadowing the New World Order paranoia of the John Birch Society and other twentieth-century conspiracist groups, Barruel warned of a godless world republic that would be built on the ashes of the Vatican and the world's royal palaces. Within a few years, these dark rhapsodies were co-opted wholesale by anti-Semites (who simply replaced "Illuminati" with "Jews" in their propaganda), and would become the dominant theme of the anti-Semitic literature of the nineteenth and twentieth centuries—including *The Protocols of the Elders of Zion*, whose enormous influence on modern conspiracism will be discussed in detail in Chapter 2.

During the twentieth century, conspiracism became the animating creed at both extremes of Europe's political spectrum.

On the Far Right, fascists idealized the notion of a single-party state, infused with a single collective cultural identity, and launched murderous propaganda campaigns against any group that stood accused of thwarting this monolithic agenda. Adolf Hitler took this view to its defining extreme, basing his entire political philosophy on a delusional fear that Jews were conspiring to destroy not only the Aryan nation, but all of humanity. "Should the Jew, with the aid of his Marxist creed, triumph over the people of this world, his Crown will be the funeral wreath of mankind, and this planet will once again follow its orbit through ether, without any human life on its surface, as it did millions of years ago," he wrote in *Mein Kampf.* "And so I believe today that my conduct is in accordance with the will of the Almighty Creator. In standing guard against the Jew I am defending the handiwork of the Lord."

But conspiracism put down strong roots on the Far Left, too—fed both by Soviet propaganda about the United States, and the inherent nature of radical left-wing ideology, which presents capitalists as scheming parasites seeking to rob the proletariat of the value of their labor. Or as Marx himself put it in *Das Kapital*: "Within the capitalist system, all methods for raising the social productivity of labour are put into effect at the cost of the individual worker; all means for the development of production undergo a dialectical inversion so that they become means of domination and exploitation of the producers; they distort the worker into a fragment of a man." (This aspect of Marxism helps explain why former Marxist radicals so easily leap to other militant creeds, such as fascism, Islamism, or—as with WorldNetDaily editor Joseph Farah, profiled later in this book—ultrapopulist conservatism. Notwithstanding the numbing jargon about Hegelian dialectics and such, the real lure of Marxism for these ideologues is its fundamentally conspiracist vision of society.)

In the United States, where neither Marxism nor fascism ever became truly mass movements, conspiracism followed a different and more complicated pattern—one rooted in three intertwined influences.

First was America's religious tradition of apocalyptic millenarianism—a subject discussed in more detail in Chapter 4, in the specific context of Christian conservative conspiracy theories involving Barack Obama. It is a tradition that dates back to New England's witch hunts and the "Beast-watching" early Puritans, who linked the seven-headed beast of Revelation 13 with the Catholic Church and, later on, the British Empire. Many American conspiracists hitched their appeal to this Revelation-inspired vision of End Times, assigning the various roles of False Prophet, Antichrist, and Satan to popery, the Elders of Zion, the USSR, Nazi Germany, secular humanism, a "New World Order," or neoconservatism. The United Nations, which the rest of the civilized world tends to regard as a largely benign (if incompetent) organization, is an especially popular target: In the best-selling *Left Behind* series of novels, which portray earth in the agonies of the Rapture, the Antichrist figure takes the form of UN Secretary General "Nicolae Carpathia" (so-named, social critic Charles Pierce has quipped, "because the authors didn't think of calling him 'Evil J. Transylvania'"). According to this vision, the political battle for America is in fact a battle for the cosmos itself—with the conspiracists assigning to themselves the role of enlightened Prophets.

The second major influence on American conspiracism is the country's unique political culture. From early on in the nation's history (before it even became a nation, in fact), Americans viewed the United States as a land of economic and political freedom—a place where sturdy, independent yeomen could make their way in the world without much help from government or entanglement with their neighbors. This muscular, independent attitude extended into the realm of philosophy: Born amid the Enlightenment, with its emphasis on individual reason unfettered by authority, America produced a lively culture of homegrown inventors and scientists. As time would tell, it was also more hospitable than the nations of Europe to intellectual outsiders—oddballs, dissidents, heretics, fussy autodidacts, and skeptics—the sort of men who we would now call "cranks."

But this worldview sowed the seeds of its own destruction. Unfettered American capitalism in the nineteenth century permitted a concentration of economic power in a small handful of banks and conglomerates, whose abuses summoned into being a populist backlash, which in turn spurred the creation of an intrusive regulatory state. Meanwhile, on the international stage, America became liberty's defender of last resort in the face of the Soviet threat—a campaign that ultimately was successful, but only through the empowerment of what Dwight Eisenhower called the "military-industrial complex." The combined result was a country where the ideals of liberty conflicted with a reality in which power became concentrated in the hands of large, faceless corporate and governmental organizations whose very existence seemed a malign affront to the open character of America's early years.

The third major influence on the development of American conspiracism was technology. In the early and mid-twentieth century, in particular, Americans were confronted with a range of powerful new machines—from mass communications, to invasive medical imaging, to space travel, to nuclear energy—that were controlled by a new class of menacing technocrats. Thanks to America's massive wealth in the postwar years, the pace of progress was much faster than in other developed nations. While the new technologies improved the material lives of most Americans, they also increased their dependence on the government and large corporations, thereby increasing the scope for mass paranoia.

It is out of this three-part mix—religious apocalypticism, political populism, and rapid technological advancement—that America's unique brand of conspiracism emerged. I call the resulting pastiche "flowchart conspiracism"—because its trademark feature is the imagining of a complex organizational chart linking all of America's power centers, from media companies to drug makers to the CIA, to one central, all-controlling secular Antichrist.

Populism and Paranoia: How Politics Shaped American Conspiracism

From the Populist movement of the late nineteenth century, to the KKK, to the backlash against FDR's New Deal, to McCarthyism, the militia movement, Ross Perot, the films of Michael Moore, and the red-state rhetoric of Sarah Palin, Glenn Beck, and Lou Dobbs, American conspiracism has reflected a consistent political theme: Some cabal of coastal political elites, Ivy league intellectuals, "bankers" (sometimes, but not always, a code word for Jews), and corporate oligopolists are conspiring to sell out the nation's ordinary, hardscrabble working people. As I was reminded by a sixteen-year-old Minnesotan Truther whom I heard fulminating in New York City against "a tyrannical government and their oppressive regime of bankers, front men, and puppets" and "thieves who take our hard-earned money and ship it off to foreigners," much of the modern conspiracist mindset, and even its terminology, remains frozen in place from the Jacksonian movement of the early nineteenth century.

If conspiracism may be seen as a collective ailment, then the United States was infected at birth: British colonial rule under King George III truly was designed to keep Americans in a state of perpetual subservience, and to steal the fruits of their industry. Over time, resentment of this fact grew into a deep suspicion of government power more generally. "Society in every state is a blessing," Thomas Paine wrote in *Common Sense.* "But government even in its best state is but a necessary evil; in its worst state an intolerable one . . . Government, like dress, is the badge of lost innocence; the palaces of kings are built on the ruins of the bowers of paradise."

The violent boom-and-bust cycles of America's young, rapidly industrializing, hypercapitalist economy provided conspiracists with plenty of growth opportunities—but with an important New World twist. The authors of the *Protocols* and the conspiracist tracts that followed in the wake of the French Revolution were reactionaries who urged a return to a preindustrial, precapitalist Christian utopia ruled by benign, hereditary kings. In the United States, it was the opposite: American conspiracy theorists cast themselves as *defenders* of the revolution, on guard to protect their noble values from a backsliding into monarchist tyranny.

"A great part of both the strength and weakness of our national existence lies in the fact that Americans do not abide very quietly the evils of life," wrote historian Richard Hofstadter in 1955. "We are forever restlessly pitting ourselves against them . . . whether it be the force represented by the 'gold bugs,' the Catholic Church, big business, corrupt politicians, the liquor interests and the saloons, or the Communist Party, and that this evil is something that must be not merely limited, checked and controlled but rather extirpated root and branch at the earliest possible moment."

In his Pulitzer Prize–winning classic, *The Age of Reform*, and again in his famous essay, "The Paranoid Style in American Politics," Hofstadter traced the roots of the McCarthyite conspiracism he witnessed in his own era to eighteenth-century Jeffersonians and Federalists, who accused one another of seeking to reestablish a monarchy or subvert America's Christian character. The latter theme would endure throughout the nineteenth century—particularly in regard to Catholics, whose imagined role as Vatican-directed fifth columnists fueled the creation of the Order of the Star Spangled Banner (the Know-Nothings), as well as several short-lived anti-immigrant political parties. The Ku Klux Klan, though remembered by historians primarily for its violent campaigns against blacks, also trafficked in anti-Catholic propaganda—including the theory that Washington, D.C.'s Catholic churches were secret military bases from which papist hordes would emerge to install the pope as America's president. Even as late as the mid-twentieth century, it was not uncommon to hear claims that—in one Protestant propagandist's words—"Jesuits are prowling about all parts of the United States in every possible disguise, expressly to . . . disseminate Popery."

Conspiracy theories based on secret societies also gained adherents in nineteenth-century America. Following the mysterious 1826 disappearance of a disgruntled Freemason from Batavia, New York, anti-Masonry activists spawned a single-issue political party that managed to capture two state governorships before withering. Thanks to the stateside penetration of two influential (and poisonously anti-Semitic) English paranoiacs, Nesta Webster and Edith Starr Miller, anti-Illuminati conspiracism, too, enjoyed episodic popularity. Some Federalists even accused the Democratic-Republicans of being in the Illuminati's grip—quite an amazing claim given that not a single Illuminati leader is known to have ever traversed the Atlantic.

The most profound manifestation of conspiracism in nineteenth-century America came through the Populist movement that reached its zenith following the collapse of food, commodity, and land prices in the 1890s. As farmers' profits dwindled, many country dwellers (not entirely without basis) blamed their troubles on industrialization, immigration, financial speculation, corporate conglomerates, and the rise of urban machine politics. Their vision of America was famously captured by the sketch of an octopus with tentacles encircling all of the nation's workers and industries—an image that would go on to become an enduring staple of anti-Semitic paranoia (albeit with zoological variations: while many editions of the *Protocols* retained the octopine image, the Jew appeared in a British edition as a snake, and in a French edition as a spider).

Such notions eventually led to the broad notion that America's rural yeomen were locked in an existential war with bankers, railroad owners, mining magnates, and other conniving urban sophisticates. As one manifesto circulated by the Populist Party put it: "There are but two sides in the conflict that is being waged in this country today. On the one side are the allied hosts of monopolies, the money power, great trusts and railroad corporations, who seek the enactment of laws to benefit them and impoverish the people. On the other side are the farmers, laborers, merchants, and all others who produce wealth and bear the burdens of taxation. The one represents the wealthy and powerful classes who want the control of the Government to plunder the people. The other represents the people, contending for equality before the law, and the rights of man. Between these two there is no middle ground."

A similarly dark vision of society's divide came in *Caesar's Column*, a best-selling 1890 novel by Ignatius Donnelly, a lifelong crank and conspiracy theorist who later would go on to draft the preamble to the Populist Party platform. Foreshadowing more influential classics of the sci-fi genre, such as Yevgeny Zamyatin's *We* (discussed in more detail later in this chapter), *Brave New World*, and *Nineteen Eighty-Four*, Donnelly's lurid work portrays a dystopic America in the grip of a tyrannical syndicate known simply as the Oligarchy.

The work is stunning to read in the post-9/11 era: Though 120 years old, it closely tracks the modern-day Truther obsession with secret plots and weapons, apocalyptic state terrorism, mass civilian slaughter, unalloyed evil, and death from the air:

The Oligarchy have a large force of several thousands of [dirigible air-ships], sheathed with that light but strong metal, aluminum; in popular speech they are known as *The Demons*. Sailing over a hostile force, they drop into its midst great bombs, loaded with the most deadly explosives, mixed with bullets; and, where one of these strikes the ground, it looks like the crater of an extinct volcano; while leveled rows of dead are strewed in every direction around it. But this is not all. Some years since a French chemist discovered a dreadful preparation, a subtle poison, which, falling upon the ground, being heavier than the air and yet expansive, rolls, "like a slow blot that spreads," steadily over the earth in all directions, bringing sudden death to those that breathe it. The Frenchman sold the secret of its preparation to the Oligarchy for a large sum; but he did not long enjoy his ill-gotten wealth. He was found dead in his bed the next day, poisoned by the air from a few drops of his own invention; killed, it is supposed, by the governments, so that they would possess forever the exclusive monopoly of this terrible instrument of slaughter.

In a climate overheated by these paranoid reveries, it was inevitable that anti-Semitism, a European pathology that formerly had been comparatively mild in America, would become embedded in the populist creed. (Russian Jews, who were alleged to be agents of bolshevism, were seen as doubly suspect.) Full-blown Jew-hatred would remain a fixture of American political life until the 1940s, finding especially prominent expression in fascist street-marching groups, such as the German-American Bund and the Silver Legion of America; and the national radio broadcasts of Father Charles Coughlin, a Nazi sympathizer who blamed Jews for both the Depression and the Russian Revolution. Like the scattered anti-Semites who still pop up in today's conspiracist movements, Coughlin would sometimes couch his hatred in more particular attacks on the Rothschilds, whom he accused of having "re-established in modern capitalistic life the pagan principle of charging interest . . . The horrible, hated word spelled 'W-A-R' was the secret of their success." In 1941, no less an American hero than Charles Lindbergh publicly blamed American war fever on "the British, the Jewish and the Roosevelt administration," and fretted about the Jews' "large ownership and influence in our motion pictures, our press, our radio and our government." (When the United States *did* enter the war, many conspiracy theorists switched their focus to FDR himself, who, it was believed, had deliberately engineered or facilitated the Japanese strike on Pearl Harbor. As described later in this book, this belief has become embedded in Truther mythology as a false-flag precursor to the 9/11 attacks.)

To Americans' great credit, wartime anti-Semitic propaganda never led their country to the same barbarism that afflicted Europeans following the publication of the *Protocols*. Throughout the late nineteenth and early twentieth centuries, American populists groused noisily about the Jews and their imagined machinations, but for the most part, grousing is all they did: The United States has never once witnessed an anti-Semitic pogrom.*

Following World War II, anti-Semitism was fatally discredited as a mainstream middle-class creed in the United States. And it was the communist, not the Jew, who became the primary target of American conspiracists. "How can we account for our present situation unless we believe that men high in this government are concerting to deliver us to disaster?" thundered Senator Joseph McCarthy to the U.S. Senate in a famous June 14, 1951, speech.

---

* There is, however, at least one recorded instance of a Jewish man being lynched: Atlanta, Georgia, factory manager Leo Frank, who in 1915 was accused of murdering a girl in his employ.

"This must be the product of a great conspiracy, a conspiracy on a scale so immense as to dwarf any previous such venture in the history of man. A conspiracy of infamy so black that, when it is finally exposed, its principals shall be forever deserving of the maledictions of all honest men."

McCarthy's career was brief: He would flame out into political disgrace, alcoholism, and an early death in the space of just a few years. But his impact on American politics was immense. With his theatrics and accusations, he turned populist conspiracism into a major force within conservative politics, something no politician had managed to do in generations. "He was the conservatives' first insurrectionist," Sam Tanenhaus wrote in his 2009 book *The Death of Conservatism*. "His cry of '20 years of treason' drew on the banked passions of the Right, America First isolationists, small-business men, Catholic organizations." (Though one should not overlook the grain of truth in his assertions—despite the mendacity of his trumped-up charges, there were in fact Communist agents in the U.S. government, as later revelations would confirm.) This insurrectionist flame would dim during the latter part of the twentieth century. But like a pilot light in the gas oven of American politics, it never died out completely. Fifty years later, fed by the raw fuel of Barack Obama, the health care debate, a major recession, and the war on terror, conservative insurrectionists roared back to life in the form of Birthers, the Tea Party movement, and a rageaholic blogosphere.

McCarthy had help, however. If he was the insurrectionists' martyred Jesus, a retired candy manufacturer named Robert Welch was their Paul.

In December of 1958, a year after McCarthy's death, Welch invited eleven of his like-minded friends to a two-day meeting in Indianapolis, where he set out his vision for a new organization that would arrest the world's slide into "darkness, slavery and terror." Within two years, the group had a membership approaching one hundred thousand Americans, most of them the sort of suburban types who might otherwise spend their evenings at bridge clubs and bowling leagues. Welch named his group after John Birch, a Baptist missionary killed by Chinese communists in August 1945—a man widely claimed to be the first American victim of the Cold War.

In fairness to Welch and his John Birch Society (which is still around today, albeit in diminished form), the communist menace was very real in the late 1950s—and the Soviets truly *were* seeking to conquer the world with their totalitarian ideology. But as with McCarthy, fear turned into paranoid hallucination. "This octopus is so large that its tentacles now reach into all of the legislative halls, all of the union labor meetings, a majority of the religious gatherings, and most of the schools *of the whole world*," Welch wrote in *The Blue Book of The John Birch Society*, a volume given to all new JBS members. "It has a central nervous system which can make its tentacles in the labor unions of Bolivia, in the farmers' cooperatives of Saskatchewan, in the caucuses of the Social Democrats of West Germany, and in the class rooms of the Yale Law School, all retract or reach forward simultaneously. It can make all of these creeping tentacles turn either right or left, or a given percentage turn right while the others turn left at the same time, in accordance with the intentions of a central brain in Moscow or Ust' Kamenogorsk."

More than two decades after the fall of the Soviet Union, much of the material in Welch's *Blue Book* reads like dated Cold War propaganda—a trip down memory lane to a time when groups like the Committee to Investigate Communist Influences at Vassar College, and Women Against Labor Union Hoodlumism were still going concerns. Yet great swathes of it easily could be copied and pasted into modern conspiracist tracts, or used word for word as Glenn Beck talking points, without seeming in any way out of place. Multilateralism, for instance, is denounced in Welch's book as a plot "to induce the gradual surrender of American sovereignty, piece by piece and step by step, to various international organizations—of which the United Nations is the outstanding but far from the only example . . . until one day we shall gradually realize that we are already just a part of a world-wide government."

Over time, Welch's views became increasingly bizarre. He accused Dwight Eisenhower's brother Milton, for instance, of being the president's secret communist overlord—and came to believe that communism itself was just a front group for an even more sinister Master Conspiracy involving the Rothschilds, the Rockefellers, the Bilderbergers, and (of course) the Illuminati. But by that time, right-wing conspiracism already had attained a perch in respectable middle-class civil society—a significant achievement for the insurrectionists at a time before cable television and deregulated talk radio had opened up the airwaves to political radicals.

During the 1950s, the paranoid style Hofstadter described was most evident on the right side of the American political spectrum—a combined manifestation of Cold War hysteria, Americans' traditional fear of big government, and a lingering conservative backlash against the massive expansion of Washington's powers that had begun with the income tax amendment of 1913 and then crested with FDR's New Deal. The main focus of conspiracists was Soviet communism—though some right-wing groups, such as the John Birch Society, found innovative ways to graft on old crusades against freemasons, Illuminati, and "international bankers."

This would change in the space of seconds on November 22, 1963. The assassination of John F. Kennedy, in the succinct description of author Thomas Powers, was likely "the greatest single traumatic event" America had ever experienced. More than one million Americans were moved to write condolence letters to Jacqueline Kennedy in the months after the assassination. "Twenty-six years of escaping from Hitler—growing up in wartime China fleeing from communism—watching my father's futile struggle against cancer—seeing my roommate killed in an automobile accident—all these I deemed adequate preparation for some of life's bitter moments," wrote a typical letter writer named Gabriele Gidion. "Yet NEVER, until last Friday, have I felt such a desperate sense of loss and loneliness."

It was also the single-most-studied nonreligious instant in human history. By one estimate made in the early 1990s, two thousand books had been written about the killing. And to this day, new offerings still appear on bookshelves—including, most spectacularly, a 1,648-page doorstopper from former prosecutor Vincent Bugliosi that was more than two decades in the making. As James Piereson wrote in his 2007 book *Camelot and the Cultural Revolution: How the Assassination of John F. Kennedy Shattered American Liberalism*, Americans' enduring obsession with the event, their speculation about how history might have played out had JFK survived, and the mind-boggling array of theories put forward to explain the murder all serve to demonstrate that "the assassination was never fully digested by the generation that lived through it."

Given that JFK's killer was a Marxist and a vocal supporter of Fidel Castro, one might have expected that the president's assassination would have generated a backlash against socialism, and the Left more generally. But as Piereson notes, the opposite happened: "In the aftermath of the assassination, left-wing ideas and revolutionary leaders—Marx, Lenin, Mao, and Castro foremost among them—enjoyed a greater vogue in the United States than at any other time in our history . . . It is one of the ironies of recent history that many of those young people who filed in shocked grief past the president's coffin in 1963 would just a few years later embrace as political activists the very doctrines that drove Oswald to assassinate him."

In effect, many American leftists dealt with the emotional agony of JFK's murder—exacerbated as it was by the killings of Martin Luther King and Robert Kennedy five years later—by convincing themselves that, in some cosmic sense, it wasn't actually a fellow traveler who was responsible, but rather some fundamental defect in the United States itself. The *New York Times* editorial board, for instance, wrote of "the shame all America must bear for the spirit of madness and hate that struck down President John F. Kennedy." According to this strain of thinking, Oswald, though nominally a communist, was somehow channeling the spirit of bigotry, violence, and hatred of change typically harbored by the reactionary *Right*. New Orleans district attorney Jim Garrison, for instance, declared that "Oswald would have been more at home with *Mein Kampf* than *Das Kapital*."

Or was Oswald even the assassin? From the notion that the man was a spiritual stand-in for the conservative forces arrayed against liberalism, it was but a short jump to the notion that the assassination was just the last act of a conspiracy hatched by the CIA, big business, the U.S. military, or hawkish Cuban exiles— "an attempted coup d'état by the forces of political reaction, racism, and unbridled militarism" in the words of one Marxist quoted in the *New York Times*. And when Robert Kennedy and Martin Luther King were assassinated five years later, the radicalized Left viewed the events through the same distorted lens: Both murders generated their own elaborate conspiracist mythology—as did the attempted assassination of George Wallace in 1972, and the killing of Chicago Black Panther leader Fred Hampton in 1969. Many Americans came to believe that these events had all been set in motion by the same group of people. As Allard Lowenstein wrote in the classic 1976 conspiracist anthology *Government by Gunplay* (coedited by one-time Bill Clinton aide Sid Blumenthal), "The last three presidential elections were distorted by bullets. If somewhere there are groups and organizations that have aborted the electoral process for political purposes—and could do so again—the rest of us may be characters in a charade."

Naturally, these same murderous conspirators were assumed to be powerful enough to cover their tracks: Just as the 9/11 Commission Report has been dismissed by Truthers as a corrupt cover-up, so was the report of the Warren Commission denounced following its publication in 1964. By Bugliosi's estimate, 95 percent of the books about JFK's assassination that have appeared since his death allege some form of conspiracy to kill the president. Most of these also assumed the existence of a *second* conspiracy—to cover up the first one.

It is thanks to this second imagined conspiracy, as much as the first, that America's mania for conspiracism took off in the 1960s. For it is one thing to suppose that Oswald had help in killing JFK: Even the House Select Committee on Assassinations concluded as much (based primarily on a dubious analysis of a police audio recording, which suggested that a coconspirator had fired a gun from the grassy knoll). But it is another completely to suggest that some of the most influential and accomplished figures in America would conspire to sweep this epic crime under the carpet. In this theory, as Bugliosi writes, "such distinguished Americans as Chief Justice Earl Warren, Senator John Sherman Cooper and Richard B. Russell, Representatives Gerald Ford and Hale Boggs, former CIA director Allen Dulles and former president of the World Bank John J. McCloy . . . as well as the Commission's general counsel, J. Lee Rankin, a former solicitor general of the United States, and 14 prominent members of the American Bar . . . people of impeccable honor and reputation, got together in some smoky backroom and *all* of them agreed, for some ungodly reason, to do the most dishonorable deed imaginable—give [the assassins] a free pass in the murder of the president of the United States. And in the process, not only risk destroying everything they had worked for—their reputation and legacy to their families—but expose themselves to prosecution for the crime of accessory after the fact to murder."

Told in this way, it seems preposterous. And yet millions of Americans came to believe it—mostly for the simple reason that the idea of a lone extremist single-handedly bringing down the most powerful man in the world and changing the face of Cold War geopolitics was simply too astonishing to contemplate. Moreover, as with virtually all conspiracy theories, there was a grain of truth lodged within the dissidents' arguments: The shooting attributed to Oswald truly was a fantastic feat of marksmanship—even if not, strictly speaking, impossible. The single-bullet theory provided by the Warren Commission—according to which a single, serially deflected round from Oswald's rifle caused all the various wounds to Texas Governor John Connally, plus the nonfatal wounds to JFK—also seems odd. Both anomalies explain why surveys of ordinary Americans taken from the 1960s onward have showed that about two-thirds believe the killing was "part of a larger conspiracy."

It is impossible to overstate how influential the legacy of JFK's murder has been in the formation of the flourishing and variegated conspiracist subcultures of later decades: If government officials weren't going to tell us the truth about something as important as the assassination of JFK, what *wouldn't* they lie about?

JFK conspiracism, unlike many of its main historical precursors, was no mob phenomenon: It came to pervade the West's educated classes. In 1964, for example, no less acclaimed a philosopher and logician than Bertrand Russell, radicalized by his years of railing against nuclear weapons and American policy in Southeast Asia, published *16 Questions On the Assassination*, in which he asked the following:

1. Why were all the members of the Warren Commission closely connected with the U.S. Government?
2. If, as we are told, Lee Harvey Oswald was the lone assassin, where is the issue of national security?
3. If the Government is so certain of its case, why has it conducted all its inquiries in the strictest secrecy?
4. Why did the Warren Commission not establish a panel to deal with the question of who killed President John F. Kennedy?
5. Why have so many liberals abandoned their own responsibility to a Commission whose circumstances they refuse to examine?
6. Why did the authorities follow many persons as potential assassins and fail to observe Oswald's entry into the book depository building while allegedly carrying a rifle over three feet long?

7. Why was the President's route changed at the last minute to take him past Oswald's place of work?

8. Why has the medical evidence concerning the President's death been altered out of recognition?

9. What is the evidence to substantiate the allegation that the President was shot from behind?

10. Why has the FBI refused to publish what could be the most reliable piece of evidence in the whole case [photographs taken of JFK's vehicle just before and during the shooting]?

11. How is it that millions of people have been misled by complete forgeries [of photos of the murder weapon] in the press?

12. Why was the result of the paraffin test [on Oswald's face and hands] altered before being announced by the authorities?

13. Why was the only description of [Patrolman] Tippitt's killer deliberately omitted by the police from the affidavit of the sole eyewitness?

14. Why was Oswald's description in connection with the murder of Patrolman Tippitt broadcast over Dallas police radio at 12:43 p.m. on November 22, when Tippitt was not shot until 1:06 p.m.?

15. How was it possible for Earl Warren to forecast that [wife] Marina Oswald's evidence would be exactly the reverse of what she had previously testified?

16. How does a District Attorney of [Henry] Wade's great experience account for all the extraordinary changes in evidence and testimony which he has announced during the Oswald case?

Russell's JFK conspiracism reflected many of the broad intellectual trends that took flight in the 1960s—anti-Americanism fed by the war in Vietnam, distrust in government, and the merging of academia with left-wing activism. But it also reflects an important strain of delusional thinking that persistently has asserted itself following the demise* of celebrities and national leaders—particularly those who, like the slain American president, were cast in the popular imagination as the quasi-deific embodiment of some larger-than-life idea. "There's [an] instinctive notion that a king cannot be struck down by a peasant," Bugliosi writes. "Many Americans found it hard to accept that President Kennedy, the most powerful man in the free world—someone they perceived to occupy a position akin to a king—could be eliminated in a matter of seconds by someone they considered a nobody."

This same psychological reflex is at the root of most conspiracy theories involving public figures—even self-destructive celebrities whose manner of death is perfectly obvious. Something in the human mind rebels at the notion that famous people can be felled by lone assassins, accidents, a drug overdose, or suicide.

Surely, the death of Princess Diana could not be blamed on the drunk chauffeur who slammed Dodi Fayed's Mercedes into a concrete pillar; the act must have been orchestrated by MI6 in order to prevent the People's Princess from marrying a Muslim. *Nirvana* lead singer Kurt Cobain, pill-popping grunge hero to a generation of music fans, could not have died from a self-inflicted shotgun blast to his head—he must have been murdered by a jealous, Brutus-like Courtney Love. Marilyn Monroe could not have died from barbiturate poisoning—she must have been murdered by Robert Kennedy and the CIA. U.S. Senator Paul Wellstone

---

* The impulse toward conspiracism seems to be triggered only when the public figure in question actually *dies*. In 2003, Royal Holloway University of London researcher Patrick Leman reported a study in which people were read a story about a president being attacked by a would-be assassin. Leman found that people were far more likely to embrace conspiracy theories about the event if the president were presented as having died as opposed to having been merely injured—a phenomenon described as the "major event-major cause" heuristic.

couldn't have died in an accidental 2002 plane crash: Several prominent 9/11 Truthers have written essays arguing that the U.S. government murdered him (according to one theory, with an "electromagnetic pulse weapon") to advance their right-wing agenda. Michael Jackson's death in June 2009 elicited similar theories: His sister La Toya told reporters, "I believe Michael was murdered, I felt that from the start. Not just one person was involved, rather it was a conspiracy of people." As for Yasser Arafat, it goes without saying that Palestinian leaders reject the notion that his 2004 death could be attributed to natural medical causes: At a 2009 Fatah conference, delegates unanimously decreed that their former leader somehow was secretly murdered by Israel.

(As a sidebar, it should be noted that the psychic need to protect a revered figure from the indignity of meaningless death also often serves to convince followers that the fallen icon isn't actually dead at all. For decades, millions of Elvis fans clung to the belief that the King is still alive and occasionally popping up at convenience stores. Aging Nazis maintain the hope that Hitler made it to Latin America to fight again. A subcult of Lady Di conspiracy theorists believe that she faked her own death so that she and Dodi could resume a private life outside of the public eye. Even Dan Brown's Christian mythology—based on notion that Christ's bloodline did not perish on the Cross, but took root in France, where it survives to the present day—owes something to this reflex.)

This same species of magical thinking applies to 9/11 conspiracy theorists, even if the Twin Towers were made of steel and concrete instead of flesh and bone. These buildings were no ordinary structures. They were miracles of American engineering—embodiments of the wealth, ambition, and grandeur of the free world. The video footage of their collapse, which remains shocking to this day, seems to show a pair of Olympian gods being brought to their knees. "My feelings about the World Trade Center and just about everyone else's all became the same: the buildings became our first skyscraper martyrs," wrote *New Yorker* architecture critic

Paul Goldberger in his 2009 book *Why Architecture Matters*. "If you doubt it, think of how . . . sidewalk vendors all over New York were selling pictures of the twin towers for years after September 11, the way they used to sell pictures of Malcolm X and John F. Kennedy."

The more one studies the Left's reaction to the JFK assassination, the more striking is the similitude with the 9/11 Truth movement: In both cases, the actual crimes were committed by radical terrorists who pledged loyalty to totalitarian movements, and who were clearly motivated by their hatred of the United States and everything it stood for. Yet both acts were perversely reinvented in the minds of millions of conspiracy theorists as an indictment of the nation's own democratically accountable establishment.

Perhaps I shouldn't have been surprised that so many of the Truthers I interviewed also turned out to be avid JKF conspiracy buffs—and sometimes even interlaced the two subjects in bizarre ways. Ken Jenkins, the Bay Area flower child who is profiled in Chapter 3, segued from our interview about the 9/11 Truth movement to make the case that JFK's assassination was part of a larger conspiracy involving three separate shooters. Pilots for 9/11 Truth leader Rob Balsamo suggested to me in our interview that JFK might have been assassinated because of his refusal to implement Operation Northwoods. During my interview with Pennsylvania-based Truther Paul Thorns, he declared that 9/11 had been perpetrated by "Israel and the neocons"—and then casually mentioned, as an afterthought, that "the whole Muslim angle is just a Lee Harvey Oswald thing." When I asked him to elaborate about who killed JFK, he told me, "It was a lot of different factions working together—the Mob, the CIA, the money people, and the Israelis."

David Ray Griffin—probably the most influential Truther alive—was also full of elaborate notions about JFK's assassination. During our three-hour interview at his seaside California home, he told me, for instance, that Lee Harvey Oswald was in fact two people—one named

"Lee," and the other named "Harvey"—both of them well-groomed CIA assets since youth. Influential California-based conspiracy theorist Michael Ruppert wrote in his Truther opus *Crossing the Rubicon* that his 9/11 theories were influenced by his investigations into the murder of JFK, as well as his "verifiable knowledge that the murder of John's brother Robert was a CIA operation." Pasadena, California–based Truther James Fetzer published three books on JFK's assassination. His current theory, described in his 2000 book *Murder in Dealey Plaza*, has it that the conspirators who killed the former president not only altered JFK's x-rays and doctored the Zapruder film, but also substituted another man's brain prior to autopsy.

In fact, the death of JFK acts as a sort of universal hinge point for conspiracy theorists everywhere—even those who aren't American. As part of a bizarre JFK-themed *non sequitur* inserted into his 2009 speech to the United Nations General Assembly, for instance, Libyan leader Moammar Gaddafi asserted that Jack Ruby was "an Israeli," and declared, "The whole world should know that Kennedy wanted to investigate the nuclear reactor of the Israeli demon."

Then there is Paul Zarembka, a sixtysomething Marxist economics professor at the State University of New York at Buffalo. In his widely distributed 2006 Truther anthology, *The Hidden History of 9–11*, Zarembka includes Bertrand Russell's above-listed *16 Questions On the Assassination*—along with David Ray Griffin's *Sixteen Reasons to Question the Official Story About 9–11*. The anthology also includes a bizarre* contribution by Arizona-based freelance writer Jay Kolar titled *What We Know About the Alleged 9–11 Hijackers*, in which the author alleges that most of the 9/11 terrorists had "doubles." Hijacker Ziad Jarrah, a subject of special interest to Kolar, is described as having *many* doubles—Kolar isn't

---

* Kolar's various theories include the notion that 9/11 lead hijacker Mohammed Atta was actually "a pilot in a very lucrative heroin trafficking operation" involving all manner of celebrity arms dealers and criminals.

quite sure how many. In any event, he backs up his theory of clone CIA terrorists by casually arguing that the trick was borrowed from the JFK era: "If there was a 'Lee Harvey Oswald Award' for 9–11, it would certainly go to Ziad Jarrah (and his doubles(s))."

When I interviewed Zarembka in his SUNY Buffalo office in mid–2009, one of my first questions was whether he gave any credence to Kolar's doubles theory.

"Yes, I do," Zarembka told me. "Remember—the same kind of doubles issue came up with Oswald being in Mexico City. In fact, I'm reading a new book about the Bush family right now—it's called *Family of Secrets* [by Russ Baker]. And there is a mention of that very issue in the book . . . For instance, here's a question: What was [George H. W.] Bush doing on the day Kennedy was assassinated? If you ask him, he can't remember . . ."

Following that, Zarembka sketched out a detailed plot involving a confidante of the Bouvier family who would eventually become entangled with Oswald and then befriend the owner of the Texas School Book Depository. "Is it really possible that someone who knew Jackie Kennedy's family so intimately—who had Jackie sit on his lap like he was her uncle—that he would go on to become connected like that in Dallas, and we're supposed to believe this was a coincidence? What's the chance of that?"

I didn't know how to answer that question. But I did drive away from the interview with one lesson solidly in hand: Scratch the surface of a middle-aged 9/11 Truther, and you are almost guaranteed to find a JFK conspiracist.

The Men in Black: How Technology Shaped American Conspiracism

Outside of Russian-language literary circles, the name Yevgeny Zamyatin is little known. That's unfortunate, because his 1922 novel *We* may be the most influential novel in the history of the science-fiction genre. Without *We*, there would have been no *Brave New World*, no *Anthem*, no *Nineteen Eighty-Four*. George Orwell's dystopic masterpiece in particular hews so closely to *We* that parts of it descend almost into outright plagiarism. Orwell was the more gifted and accessible writer—which is why "Orwellian" appears in the dictionary instead of "Zamyatinian." But it was the Russian who first sketched the nightmarish implications of modern technology in the harness of totalitarian ideology. And amazingly, he did it while the Ford Model T was still on the production line.

The plot of *We* revolves around a scientist in the One State, a totalitarian society governed by a white-robed Big Brother–like figure known as the Benefactor. Citizens live in glass houses, their every movement visible to government observers. They are permitted to draw the shades only during lovemaking—which can be conducted only on state-approved days, with state-approved partners. The weather is controlled by "Accumulator Towers." Food is synthesized from petroleum. Music is confined to government-approved tunes, such as *The March of the One State* and *The Hymn of the One State*. Dreams are treated as a form of psychosis—as is ownership of a soul. The only forms of approved literature are tables of numbers. The only human right is the right to be executed by the Benefactor. The (Orwellian) state creed is that freedom is misery, slavery the ultimate joy. Or, in the Benefactor's words: "What did people—from their very infancy—pray for, dream about, long for? They longed for someone to tell them, once and for all, the meaning of happiness, and then to bind them to it with a chain."

As the melodramatic plot of *We* unfolds, the protagonist's faith in the Benefactor's totalitarian order begins to break down: He falls in love with a fellow citizen and has nonstate-approved sex. He ventures out behind the walls of the One State, and meets the happy savages who lie beyond. In time, he even develops a soul, and joins with others in conspiring to bring down the One State. They are on the brink of success when the Benefactor suddenly orders all citizens to report for brain cauterization, a surgery that leaves them "cured of imagination."

The result is an army of perfect robot citizens, stripped of the ability to think independently. In a scene that could have been ripped from any modern-day New World Order–themed conspiracist website, Zamyatin writes: "A slow, heavy column of some fifty people emerges. 'People'? No, that does not describe them. These are not feet—they are stiff, heavy wheels, moved by some invisible transmission belt. These are not people—they are humanoid tractors."

We was directly inspired by Zamyatin's experience under Lenin and the Bolsheviks. But as the totalitarian virus spread to Nazi Germany and other parts of the West in the 1920s and 1930s, so did the fears he expressed. While Orwell and Aldous Huxley wrote their novels from democratic England, they shared Zamyatin's vision of a coming age in which every aspect of human existence— including the basic chemistry of our bodies, and the inner workings of our minds—would be subordinated to a power-hungry elite armed with frightening new technologies.

In Western high schools, *Nineteen Eighty-Four* and *Brave New World* are presented as cautionary political tales. But they also document an important shift in the human condition that transcends mere politics. For the entirety of man's existence leading up to the twentieth century, what humans feared most wasn't the dictatorship of Zamyatin's One State—it was the blood-soaked anarchy of the jungle beyond its walls. Reality was, as Thucydides put it, "a human race that escaped chaos and barbarism by preserving with difficulty a thin layer of civilization." It was only with the rise of totalitarian ideologies, and their enabling technologies, that this fear was flipped on its head. The noble savages who live outside our gate are no longer the enemy—they are the salvation. The greatest threat to society is no longer that the flesh will be exterminated by war, disease, tribal warfare, or natural disaster; but that our *minds* will be lobotomized through state terror, propaganda, soma, or outright surgery. The publication of *We* marks the moment that basic fear switch was being toggled.

Because of their geographical isolation, Americans were insulated from these emerging fears to a certain extent. But as the century wore on, the rapid march of technology, the increasing bureaucratization of America's postwar society, and the rise to power of an anonymous, professional managerial class all conspired to create a generalized climate of anxiety. By the 1960s, Americans were confronted with a welter of agencies, think tanks, and international organizations that had popped into existence within the space of a generation—including, at the highest level, NATO, the Warsaw Pact, and the United Nations. Spies from both sides of the Iron Curtain—armed with hidden microphones and secret cameras—were believed to be everywhere. In 1958, the same year that the John Birch Society came into existence, J. Edgar Hoover was warning Americans that the communist "is in the market places of America: in organizations, on street corners, even at your front door. He is trying to influence and control your thoughts."

The resulting paranoia produced a collective vision drawn straight out of the brain-surgery scene in *We*. Miami University scholar Timothy Melley calls it "agency panic"—"the conviction that one's actions are being controlled by someone else, that one has been 'constructed' by powerful external agents . . . This fear sometimes manifests itself in a belief that the world is full of 'programmed' or 'brainwashed' subjects, addicts, automatons, or 'mass-produced' persons."

The CIA in particular, an organization whose MK-ULTRA mind-control and chemical-interrogation experiments truly were something out of a conspiracist's nightmare, seemed to symbolize a world in which average citizens were targeted by their own government. In 1974, the *New York Times* published a blockbuster story by Seymour Hersh under the headline "Huge CIA Operation Reported in U.S. Against Anti-War Forces," claiming that the agency had generated surveillance files on at least ten thousand

Americans. As author Arthur Herman wrote in the pages of *Commentary* magazine, describing the frenzied intellectual climate that resulted: "Once the process of blame and suspicion got underway, it was impossible to stop. If the CIA had killed Vietnamese citizens with impunity and without leaving a trace, then perhaps it had done the same to American citizens. If the CIA had been willing to plot to assassinate Fidel Castro, why not JFK? . . . For the New Left culture at its most feverish, there was no crime too heinous, no bugging too minor, no assassination too unjust, no Spanish Inquisition–style interrogation of some hapless prisoner too appalling that the CIA wasn't prepared to carry out at the behest of its corporate masters."

In the realm of science, meanwhile, the postwar period witnessed a bewildering proliferation of groundbreaking technologies. New public-health innovations, such as compulsory vaccination, psychiatric treatment, and water fluoridation seemed especially threatening—since they transferred control of a citizen's own bodily integrity to strangers. Like USAF Brigadier General Jack D. Ripper, the *Dr. Strangelove* character who attacks the Soviet Union out of fear that enemies were trying to contaminate Americans' "precious bodily fluids," millions of Americans reflexively connected such technological apprehensions to the Red menace. According to Dr. Charles Betts, president of the Anti-Cancer Club of America, fluoridation was "better than using the atom bomb [for the purposes of Communists] because the atom bomb has to be made, has to be transported to the place it is to be set off, while poisonous fluorine has been placed right beside the water supplies by the Americans themselves ready to be dumped into the water mains whenever a Communist desires!" (Antifluoridation activists no longer cite the communist menace, yet in municipal politics, they remain a force to be reckoned with in many North American jurisdictions. In late 2010, as this book was in its final edits, the Canadian city of Waterloo, Ontario, voted to end its water fluoridation program. When I criticized this decision in the *National*

Post, I was met with a storm of email that was extraordinary, even by the standards I had come to expect from writing about the 9/11 Truth movement. Many correspondents passionately advocated the same discredited theories that sprang to life in the days of Charles Betts, such as the idea that water fluoridation had been invented by the aluminum industry as a means to dispose of its toxic, fluorine-containing waste products.)

Medical imaging technology that permitted doctors to peer inside our bodies also became a prominent motif in conspiracist fantasies—a trend that found lurid expression in the UFO cults of the postwar period.

In the 1940s and 1950s, Americans who reported encounters with aliens typically were anxious about the possibility of the earth being invaded or destroyed by an extraterrestrial army, à la *War of the Worlds*. But in the late 1960s, the trend changed: Americans began reporting that aliens (who, not by coincidence, often looked just like the fetuses depicted in the ultrasound scans that pregnant mothers now saw in their doctors' offices) were taking them on board their spaceships, and subjecting them to invasive sexual and medical procedures, with the ultimate goal of involving them in an interspecies breeding project (possibly located at Area 51 in Nevada). As researcher Bridget Brown concluded after interviewing numerous alien abductees and closely studying their accounts, the phenomenon seemed to reflect a widespread, subconscious anxiety about body integrity in a high-tech age, with the alien taking the role "as part medical technician, part bureaucrat, part fetus."

The *Protocols* and the conspiracy theories that followed it in the early part of the twentieth century were elaborately extrapolated folk tales based on tribal, anti-Semitic hatred. But during the Cold War era, conspiracy theories became more complex and technocratic—mirroring the modern society they sought to explain. Byzantine, acronym-littered organizational diagrams setting out the imagined hierarchy of society's all-powerful overlords increasingly became a staple of what I have called "flowchart conspiracism."

The Emergence of "Flowchart Conspiracism"

This book cannot do justice to the bewildering range of flowchart conspiracy theories that have trafficked through the nether regions of American political culture in the postwar decades. But it is worth taking up at least one particular example from the genre as a case study—especially since its name tends to pop up often in conversations with Truthers: Daniel Estulin's breathless 2007 best seller, *The True Story of the Bilderberg Group.*

Even most educated readers are unlikely to know much about the Bilderberg Group. But in modern conspiracist lore, the organization ranks as nothing less than a modern-day Illuminati. And no one has done more to peddle Bilderbergian conspiracism than Estulin, a middle-aged Russian-born Canadian who's spent the last two decades stalking the group's organizers, skulking outside their meetings, and delivering paranoid reports on the proceedings, based on tidbits provided by people he calls "informants."

The Bilderberg Group is named after a Dutch hotel where a group of fifty European and eleven American worthies, including David Rockefeller and Prince Bernhard of the Netherlands, met in the spring of 1954 with the goal of strengthening trans-Atlantic understanding. By all available accounts, the event was a success, and follow-up meetings were organized. Over time, something called the "Bilderberg Group" evolved into a once-a-year, off-the-record talk shop for a rotating cast drawn from the world's foremost politicians, corporate leaders, and intellectuals—Davos without the cameras, essentially.

To no one's surprise, I have never received an invitation. But my *National Post* colleague Conrad Black has attended more than twenty Bilderberg conferences, and even sat on the group's Steering Committee for the better part of two decades. Through him, I've been able to form a fairly detailed picture of the annual proceedings. "In my time, starting at the end of the 70's, it had become a

Western Alliance meeting place—with a few others, i.e., Swedes, Finns, Irish, Austrians, Swiss, and an Icelander—where attendees discussed how to deal with the Soviets, how to organize and manage Western economies," he reported to me. "Beyond that, it was a meeting place for up and coming people from each of the countries, along with the venerable grandees who were among the founders and were then on the Advisory Council. There were also a bunch of wealthy Americans who did not participate too much in the discussions, but paid a lot and did socialize vigorously, such as Henry Kravis, Hank Greenberg, Dwayne Andreas, and Jack Heinz, and Evelyn de Rothschild from the UK. Rupert Murdoch came a few times . . . The atmosphere was very courteous, bonhomous, and open, and the social conversations were often very interesting, and the debates the best I have participated in, apart from the [British] House of Lords at its best. Some business arrangements were made there, including the beginning of my acquisition of [Britain's] *Daily Telegraph* [newspaper], but there was absolutely no continuous linkage or organizing principle. It was an atmosphere of earnest *hauts fonctionnaires*, altruistic businessmen, and self-important people, sufficient in what they fancied to be their influence and right-mindedness."

All lies, says Estulin. In fact, he claims, the Bilderbergers are the top cell in a centrally coordinated global conspiracy involving the Council on Foreign Relations, CIA, Mossad, Trilateral Commission, Aspen Institute, Freemasons, MI6, Royal Institute of International Affairs, Tavistock Institute for Behavioural Analysis, Brookings Institution, Institute for Policy Studies, RAND Corporation, European Union, United Nations, Gorbachev Foundation, Bill Gates Foundation, Club of Rome, the European monarchy, UNESCO, and (unnamed) drug-running aristocrats. "What today is called the Bilderberg Group already existed over 800 years ago," he writes. "Back then, they were called the Venetian Black Nobility. In fact, Bilderberg is the creation of the Synarchist Movement of Empire, who are the plenipotentiary founders and financiers of Hitler—and Synarchist International, they in turn were founded by [the] Freemason Secret Society back in the 1770s as a sort of counterattack on the principles on which the United States was built."

The Bilderbergers' true goal in orchestrating this *ne plus ultra* of flowchart conspiracies, Estulin argues, is to control the world money supply, create a single global currency, establish a "world army," use "mind control" to "direct all humanity to obey [Bilderbergian] wishes," eliminate economic growth, suppress "all scientific development," and create a "New World Order" in which obedient slaves will be rewarded and nonconformists targeted for "extermination."

Estulin sees himself as just such a "nonconformist," and spends much of his book reciting adventure stories about Bilderberg agents trying to assassinate him in downtown Toronto ("In front of me, a chilling spectacle . . . an empty elevator shaft with certain death awaiting me 800 feet below"), or draw him into a deadly firefight on the streets of Rome ("I know my guns, and it wasn't difficult to see by the non-metallic polymer frame that I was staring at a Glock semiautomatic pistol"). His efforts to discover the truth about the Bilderberg plot, he writes in one particularly purple passage, have sent him hurtling into a "parallel world . . . a cesspool of duplicity and lies and double-speak and innuendo and blackmail and bribery. It is a surreal world of double and triple agents, of changing loyalties, of professional psychotic assassins, brainwashed black ops agents, soldiers of fortunes and mercenaries . . . I converted into one of them, a spook, a specter, a shade . . . dancing between raindrops and disappearing at the first sign of danger: a shadow dancer. In America, they simply called me 'the Highlander.' "

It's easy to laugh off Estulin's pulp-fiction style and mixed metaphors. (One cringes, in particular, at the notion of Estulin "dancing between raindrops" spilling forth from the aforementioned "cesspool of duplicity.") Yet *The True Story of the Bilderberg Group* has become something of a sensation. As of 2010, the publisher claimed it had been translated into forty-eight languages and sold in sixty-seven countries. And in the best tradition of Dan Brown, it may soon be coming to the big screen: In 2009, rights to the book were purchased by the Los Angeles–based Halcyon Company, which also owns the *Terminator* franchise.

In regard to its political orientation, Estulin's theory betrays an interesting political shift on display in the conspiracist literature of the last two decades: Though he rails against the CIA, the RAND Corporation, the military-industrial complex, and all the traditional bugbears of post-JFK left-wing conspiracists, Estulin is— like Alex Jones, the Texas-based radio host profiled in the previous chapter—very much a libertarian conservative. And the dystopia he sketches out looks a lot like the communist USSR of his youth (not to mention the "Super-Government Administration" detailed in the *Protocols of the Elders of Zion*, the One State of *We*, and the Oligarchy of *Caesar's Column*—but more on this similitude in the next chapter).

Far from being enemies of communism, Estulin argues, today's corporate oligarchs are its admiring successors: "The fact is that members of the Establishment operating through 'private' organizations such as the Bilderbergers, the CFR and the Trilateral Commission understand socialism as the ultimate power system for control, and understand its psychology better than the Marxists do . . . Socialism to them . . . is not a system to redistribute wealth from the rich to the poor. Rather, it's a mechanism for gaining a greater and greater concentration of power and control."

Estulin and Jones are not alone: Beginning in the 1980s, and accelerating throughout the 1990s, the politics of conspiracism began to become an equal opportunity affair, as fringes on both sides of the ideological spectrum increasingly began promoting the same basic type of New World Order conspiracy theories. In 1991, for instance, no less a mainstream conservative than televangelist (and former presidential aspirant) Pat Robertson published an odd book arguing that a satanic network of Illuminati, Masons, and "international bankers" is conspiring to create an Antichrist-inspired world government that will rob Americans of their freedoms, promote pedophilia—and, of course, destroy Christianity.

Lurid as all this may sound, Robertson's book tapped into the deep resurgence in right-wing populism that had vaulted Ronald Reagan to power. The sexual revolution, on-demand abortion, the Equal Rights Amendment, gay rights, forced busing, and the end of school prayer all had a traumatizing effect on American social conservatives during the 1970s and 1980s. But during these battles, the bulk of their hostility was directed overseas—at the Soviet Union, whose godless creed was blamed for secular humanism and other evils afflicting the world. When the Berlin Wall fell, and George H. W. Bush declared a "new world order" (he actually did use those words), right-wing paranoia suddenly became directed inward, at an imagined conspiracy by America's elites to roll back basic liberties—especially regarding guns, and the loosely defined constellation of powers known as "states' rights"—while surrendering the nation's sovereignty to some global overlord. On the extreme fringes, Americans began organizing armed militias to fight back against a feared "occupation" of America—a movement centered in the tristate region of eastern Washington, Montana, and the Idaho Panhandle.

Like Robertson, many of the most influential conspiracists tied their theories directly to America's tradition of apocalyptic End Times millennialism. But even among purely secular conspiracy theorists, there was clearly a casting about for some epochal, Manichean struggle to replace the comforting, good-versus-evil organizing principle of the Cold War. The result was a hodgepodge of different groups and movements, embracing creeds as diverse as Christian Identity, Aryan Pride, militant libertarianism, states' rights, anti-Semitism, crank monetary theories, and nativist xenophobia.

During this transitional period, American conspiracist culture grew very dark. Linda Milligan, an Ohio-based researcher who had first studied UFO conspiracists in the 1980s, told me she was shocked at the transformation she observed when she revisited the same people a decade later. "Aquarian-age optimism has been transformed into a dark new-age despair," she reported in a 1994 essay. "Interest in the mind, for example, has shifted from speculation about the mind's as yet unrealized powers (ESP, for example) to absorption in the belief that evil beings, UFO aliens referred to as the Grays, are implanting mind control devices in the brains of thousands of Americans. And they are doing this, my informants believe, with the cooperation of elements of the U.S. government along with the internationalists bent on creating a one world government."

As another UFO-conspiracist expert, Michael Barkun, notes, the words "new world order" became a sort of "unifying conspiracy theory," drawing in a huge range of angry prophets with a narrative containing some or all of the following elements: "the systematic subversion of republican institutions by a federal government utilizing emergency powers; the gradual subordination of the United States to a world government operating through the United Nations; the creation of sinister new military and paramilitary forces . . . the permanent stationing of foreign troops on U.S. soil; the widespread use of black helicopters to transport the tyranny's operatives; the confiscation of privately owned guns; the incarceration of so-called patriots in concentration camps run by FEMA; the implantation of microchips and other advanced technology for surveillance and mind control; the replacement of Christianity with a New Age world religion; and, finally, the manipulation of the entire apparatus by a hidden hierarchy of conspirators."

The right-wing militia movements withered in the late 1990s—largely as a result of the stepped-up investigation and prosecution that came in the wake of the Oklahoma City bombing. But the radical habits of mind the movement epitomized—extreme hatred of government, hostility toward foreign and multilateral entities, and an expectation of an apocalyptic confrontation with the forces of evil—persisted, and have been taken up by a new generation of Internet-savvy activists—Alex Jones now being the most famous and influential.

Perhaps the most extraordinary aspect of this right-wing conspiracist movement is the manner in which its fantasies came to mesh almost exactly with those propagated on the opposite, university-educated, anti-American, left-wing side of the political spectrum.

Some articles of faith divide the two camps: Radical leftists believe that the totalitarian and cryptocratic forces plotting to take over the world are oil magnates, uniformed Dr. Strangeloves, CIA spooks, and the like, while radical rightists imagine a world run by the United Nations, the European Union, the International Criminal Court, and NAFTA tribunals. But at both poles, the vision of the totalitarian hell to come is otherwise identical—as are the 9/11 conspiracy theories the two camps came to embrace.

CHAPTER TWO

Warrant for Genocide, Blueprint for Paranoia

Since I entered politics, I have chiefly had men's views confided to me privately. Some of the biggest men in the U.S., in the field of commerce and manufacturing, are afraid of somebody, are afraid of something. They know that there is a power somewhere so organized, so subtle, so watchful, so interlocked, so complete, so pervasive, that they had better not speak above their breath when they speak in condemnation of it.

—*Woodrow Wilson*

There exists a subterranean world where psychological fantasies disguised as ideas are churned out by crooks and half-educated fanatics for the benefit of the ignorant and the superstitious. There are times when this underworld emerges from the depths and suddenly fascinates, captures and dominates multitudes of usually sane and responsible people, who thereupon take leave of sanity and responsibility. And it occasionally happens that this underworld becomes a historical power and changes the course of history.

—*Norman Cohn, preface to 1996 British edition of* Warrant for Genocide

In the previous chapter, I wrote about the broad political, religious, and technological trends that have shaped American conspiracism. In this chapter, I will focus on the actual mythology of the most popular conspiracy theories, especially the 9/11 Truth movement.

Nailing down this mythology proved surprisingly difficult. That's because few of the Truthers I interviewed presented any sort of coherent narrative about what they believe actually happened on 9/11. While almost all of them embraced the general idea that explosives brought down the World Trade Center, and that Dick Cheney and his CIA friends were in on it, that's generally as far as they'd go. None offered any kind of detailed theory about how such a massive plot might have been organized, financed, and executed, let alone the identity of the hundreds of demolitions experts, engineers, and spies who would be needed to staff it. "[This website] critically examines the official government explanation of the attack and concludes that many of its key assertions are impossible," asserts one typical Truther website, 9/11 Research. "We do not pretend to know exactly how the attack was carried out or exactly who the perpetrators are."

Following in the tradition of Bertrand Russell's famous essay about JFK, most Truthers prefer to focus on *questions*. Among the "10 reasons for starting a new 9/11 investigation" listed on the leaflets they distribute at Ground Zero, for instance, are such entries as, "What force pulverized most of the concrete and office material of the Twin Towers into dust, and was able to eject steel beams into buildings over 400 feet away?" and, "Why was there no mention in the 9/11 Commission Report of WTC Building 7?"

The result is that any author setting out to describe the Truthers' take on 9/11 has a difficult time putting together a coherent narrative. Instead, he has notebooks full of esoteric debating points about avionics, building demolition, NORAD flight-tracking procedures, and a dozen other scattered subjects. Though I will summarize some of this material in the next chapter, I don't believe it is the best way to introduce the uninitiated to the Truther worldview.

Instead, I will begin by taking a step back, and focusing on the broad undercurrents reflected in Truther literature. While the 9/11 conspiracists I met exhibited a wide range of different personalities and niche obsessions, their claims about the people who control our planet consistently fell into the same basic template—a template that governs not just the Truth movement, but almost every major systemic conspiracy theory dating back to Europe's Belle Époque.

And so that is where this chapter's investigation will begin.

A Dark Fairy Tale

In August 1897, Theodor Herzl and two hundred fellow activists convened at a concert hall in Basel, Switzerland, to attend the First Zionist Congress. The capstone of their deliberations was *The Basel Program*, a landmark manifesto aimed at "establishing for the Jewish people a publicly and legally assured home in Palestine." The delegates also officially adopted *Hatikvah*, a song that, six decades later, would become the national anthem for the country we call Israel.

But as legend has it, it was all an elaborate act—just a respectable set-piece to divert gentile journalists and spies from the real meeting taking place at a secret location nearby. There, Herzl delivered a clandestine twenty-four-part lecture series for Jewish ears only. In these speeches, "protocols" as Herzl called them, there was little talk of carving a small country out of the Middle Eastern desert. What he proposed was nothing less than a plan for total world domination.

Europe's gentiles—or *goyim*, as they were described in Yiddish—generally were a happy, earnest lot, Herzl told his audience. They worked their farms and small businesses assiduously, prayed to a benevolent Christian God, and prospered under the kindly, lawful aristocrats who rose up from among their ranks.

But they were also gullible, lustful, greedy, and unstable in their attitudes—human frailties that the calculating, ascetic Jew could exploit in order to rob them of their entitlements.

The Jewish strategy, Herzl explained, would target all strata of *goyim*. To corrupt the proles, Jewish smut merchants would provide pornography and "alcoholic liquors." To ensnare middle-class farmers and merchants, Jewish moneylenders would practice usury.

Ambitious gentile politicians would be co-opted through extortion and outright bribery; or else installed as quislings in Europe's Masonic lodges, which Jews secretly controlled.

Meanwhile, gentile intellectuals, such as they were, would be beguiled by democracy, liberalism, Marxism, socialism, communism, Darwinism, anarchism, "Nietzsche-ism," and all the other fangled creeds the Jew had created.

Ironically, the Jews' most powerful weapon in the campaign to enslave gentiles would be none other than the lure of sweet liberty itself: "The abstraction of freedom has enabled us to persuade the mob in all countries that . . . the steward may be replaced like a worn-out glove," Herzl explained to the assembled Elders. "It is this possibility of replacing the representatives of the people which has placed them at our disposal, and . . . given us the power of appointment."

Of course, God-fearing men would never willingly succumb to Jewish tyranny. But Herzl had an answer to that: Jews would not only annihilate Europe's earthly rulers, but also "the very principle of God-head and the spirit," whose presence in men's souls shielded them from the "arithmetical calculations and material needs" upon which the Jew preyed. No longer would the peoples of the world "walk contentedly and humbly under the guiding hand of [their] spiritual pastor submitting to the dispositions of God upon earth." Instead, "all nations will be swallowed up in the pursuit of gain, and in the race for it will not take note of their common foe [the Jew]."

As his plan played out, Herzl explained, Jews would cycle the world through an endless series of bloody wars and economic depressions, which would serve both to enrich Jewish war profiteers and speculators, and cast the rest of the globe into poverty. Traumatized to the point of total despair, the peoples of the world would have no choice but to succumb.

When Herzl was done with his twenty-four protocols, the conference disbanded, and the Jewish Elders returned to their homes in order to prepare their plots. The world might never have learned of the protocols' existence—but for a single Russian police agent who, through means unknown, intercepted one of Herzl's acolytes at a German Masonic lodge.

In exchange for what one must assume to have been an extravagant sum, the Jew agreed to turn over his handwritten transcription of Herzl's protocols—but only till the next morning. All through the night, a team of Russian scribes feverishly copied out the Hebrew text. When sunrise broke, the fruits of their labor were sent to translators in Moscow, who would go on to warn the world of the Jewish menace.

Thus ends the fairy tale, known to history as *The Protocols of the Learned Elders of Zion*—a document that would become the most influential conspiracist tract since the era of the French Revolution. Millions of readers were taken in by this poisonous fraud following its widespread publication in 1919. Adolf Hitler and other war criminals would be inspired to act on it, setting in motion a wave of anti-Semitic hatred so intense that, by the end of the Second World War, Central and Eastern Europe were left virtually *Judenrein*.

All this came to pass despite the fact the *Protocols* was debunked within months of its dissemination. As investigators revealed, the document was concocted by czarist anti-Semites who had not even taken the trouble to invent the lies themselves. Instead, they plagiarized *Protocols* from two sources: *Biarritz*, a lurid anti-Semitic novel published fifty years previously in Germany, and a French propaganda tract from the same era, *Dialogues in Hell between Machiavelli and Montesquieu*, written by a French lawyer named Maurice Joly. (The influence of Joly's book is particularly obvious: According to one scholar's analysis, a full 40 percent of *Protocols'* content is lifted word for word from *Dialogues*.)

The *Protocols* was a lie. But like all successful conspiracy theories, it was a lie that people wanted to hear. This was a moment when Europe had just endured not one, but two epic upheavals, neither of which had a simple, comprehensible cause. The Russian Revolution had been sparked by an artificial, untested, schismatic ideology created by an impoverished eccentric living in England. The First World War was an accidental product of Great Power paranoia, miscalculation, and jingoism—all sparked into deadly reaction by an assassination in one of Europe's most obscure back-waters (an event that is itself the subject of innumerable conspiracy theories). When it was over, the flower of European youth was dead, and two once-great empires had been destroyed. It's not hard to understand why millions of shell-shocked survivors could become convinced that the leaders who'd sent these men to their deaths had somehow been tricked by a hidden, demonic force.

For Europeans reading the *Protocols* in the 1920s and 1930s, the document offered something precious: the idea that only a *single* barrier—the Jewish race—blocked a return to the peaceful, pious, and socially ordered world that had been destroyed by war, revolution, mechanization, urbanization, radical political ideologies, secularization, and catastrophic inflation. The evil brilliance of the *Protocols* lay in the fact that it patched together a theory of Jewish conspiracy that covered every one of these upheavals—all the while enchanting the reader with backward glimpses of the noble, God-fearing milieu that the Jew allegedly had undermined.

The *Protocols* did not arise out of the ether. As Norman Cohn illustrated in his 1967 classic *Warrant for Genocide*, the period between 1850 and World War I was a golden age of apocalyptic Judeo-Masonic* propaganda. From France to Russia, all sorts of overlapping, mutually plagiarizing fraud manifestos became best

---

* Amazingly, many modern conspiracists remain obsessed with Masonry. To this day, I still get emails like this one, which I received in 2008: "Dear Mr. Kay, Show me a picture of an airplane in the Pentagon Building. Any part of a real airplane will be enough. When a picture of this kind can be shown I will take the trouble to admit I have been wrong about the Masons and their friends trying to manipulate the population. Masons, those lovable people who believe in SLAVERY. They are the problem. Finding surrogates like yourself to get paid to promote their dirty handiwork is easy for them. They have a history of understanding your kind."

sellers. Many of them even were structured like the *Protocols*, with a cackling rabbi instructing his Jewish brethren in his faith's plans for world domination. But thanks to a series of historical accidents, the *Protocols* became the document that definitively popularized the conspiracist spirit that seized Western civilization during the early decades of the twentieth century, and which has survived, in the same basic form—albeit with an ever-changing cast of villains—to the present day.

As noted in the previous chapter, ancient forms of conspiracism typically vilified one of two enemies: Jews and secret societies. The *Protocols* twisted these two venerable strands into one deadly skein: The Jews, by this hateful telling, were both a filthy religious sect seeking to exterminate Christendom *and* a secret society bent on adapting world trade, politics, media, and all the other secular pillars of civilization to their evil schemes.

Even when the Third Reich lay in ruins, and anti-Semitism became widely detested in its bald-faced Nazi-style form, the *Protocols* would remain ensconced as a sort of universal blueprint for all the successor conspiracist ideologies that would come to infect Western societies over the next nine decades—right up to the modern-day Truther and Birther fantasies of the twenty-first century. In these conspiracy theories, the imagined evildoing cabal would come by many names—communist, globalist, neocon. But in most cases, it would exhibit the same five recurring traits that the *Protocols* fastened upon the Jewish elders in the shadow of World War I: singularity, evil, incumbency, greed, and hypercompetence.

Singularity

Oliver Stone calls it the Beast—a single overarching power that controls history and punishes those who swim against its currents. "What I see from 1963, with Kennedy's murder at high noon in Dallas, to 1974, with Nixon's removal, is a pattern," the filmmaker told an interviewer in 1996. "Call me wrong, but we have John Kennedy suspiciously killed, we have Robert Kennedy suspiciously killed, we have Martin Luther King suspiciously killed, and we have Nixon suspiciously 'falling on his sword.' These four men came from different political perspectives, but they were pushing the envelope, trying to lead America to new levels. We posit that, in some way, they pissed off what we call 'the Beast,' the Beast being a force, or forces, greater than the presidency . . . Between 1963 and 1974, these four men all ran up against the Beast and were removed or killed as a consequence."

It's not clear who or what the Beast is. (Based on my reading of the full interview, I'd say Stone himself hadn't quite figured it out.) But the details are beside the point. What is crucial to Stone is his conviction that Nixon, MLK, and the two Kennedys were somehow done in *by the same people*. As with the *Protocols'* fixation on a few dozen Jewish Elders (a collective sometimes called "All-Judaan" by Henry Ford and other anti-Semites) the conspiracist mind unfailingly compresses life's many random evils into a single, identifiable point-source of malign power. As discussed in Chapters 5 and 6, this tendency is one of conspiracism's main psychological consolations.

The label placed on this evil font varies. Modern conspiracist movements fixate on the Council on Foreign Relations, the Bilderberg Group, the Trilateral Commission or—in the case of the 9/11 Truth movement—some sort of Cheney-led "neocon" Star Chamber. Old-school conspiracists insist the real demons are the Illuminati, Freemasons, Jesuits, Opus Dei, Knights Templar, *Philosophes*, Carbonari, Prieuré de Sion, Rosicrucians, or the like. In extreme cases, the supposed evil masterminds aren't even human: Influential British Truther David Icke, for instance, claims that ultimate power lies with extraterrestrial "Prison Warders"—who control events on earth (including 9/11) through a human clique known as "the Global Elite." But insofar as a conspiracist's psychic appetites are concerned, the evildoers' actual identities are interchangeable.

In some cases, quite *literally* interchangeable: Deceased right-wing UFO conspiracy theorist Milton William Cooper, author of the apocalyptic 1991 tract *Behold a Pale Horse*, explicitly endorsed the *Protocols of the Elders of Zion*, and reprinted it for his readers . . . but warned them that the document "has been written intentionally to deceive people. For clear understanding, the word 'Zion' should be 'Sion'; any reference to Jews should be replaced with the word 'Illuminati'; and the word 'goyim' should be replaced with the word 'cattle.'" Michael Baigent, Richard Leigh, and Henry Lincoln—the three pseudohistorians whose theories about Jesus Christ traveling to France as a husband and father became the basis for much of Dan Brown's conspiracy fiction—have a similar theory about the *Protocols*: "There was an original text [of the *Protocols*] that was not a forgery. On the contrary, it was authentic. But it had nothing whatever to do with Judaism or an 'international Jewish conspiracy.' It issued, rather, from some Masonic organization or masonically oriented secret society that incorporated the word 'Sion.'" (Icke, incidentally, believes the *Protocols* were written by lizard people as part of an intergalactic plan to impose reptilian control over Planet Earth.)

This psychic need to impute all evil to a lone, omnipotent source inevitably requires the conspiracist to create larger and larger meta-conspiracies that sweep together seemingly unconnected power centers. This is why, as discussed in the previous chapter, modern conspiracy theorists are so fond of flowcharts—in which all of society's actors can systematically be grouped into cascading hierarchies that soar upwards to a single, ultimate puppetmaster.

Anti-Semitic conspiracy theorists couldn't explain the origins of the First World War, which began when control of Europe was split up between a half-dozen major European powers—except by somehow imagining that all of them secretly answered to some common Jewish overlord. Likewise has the John Birch Society (JBS) declared Hillary Clinton and the world's communists to be partners in an Illuminati-driven plot to conquer the world—along with coconspirators Dick Cheney and Wall Street. In his

1991 book *New World Order*, Pat Robertson pulled the same trick, arguing that America's political and economic elites were in league with Bolsheviks to engineer a Soviet takeover of the United States. Intergalactic conspiracy theorist David Icke explained the power struggle between Israel and the Arab world this way: "Have you ever wondered why the 'home' of Islam, Saudi Arabia, says and does nothing in the face of what is being visited upon the Arab world? There is a reason for this. The House of Saud is a fake front for the House of Rothschild, and they are not 'Arabs' or 'Muslims' at all. They are Rothschild Zionists who can be traced back to a Jewish man called Mordakhai bin Ibrahim bin Moshe. Researchers say this was in the year AD 851."

One leading 9/11 Truther, Washington, D.C.–based career conspiracist Webster Tarpley (profiled later in this book), provides a helpful flowchart on page 77 of his epic 2005 tract *9/11 Synthetic Terror: Made in U.S.A.* demonstrating the hierarchical relationship between "paramilitary terror pros," "big business," and "corrupt private networks"—with everyone in the chart answering to the top cell, a cartoon octopus labeled with the single word "oligarchy." Who this oligarchy is, Tarpley doesn't tell us—except to hypothesize vaguely that it probably consists of "financier factions." But again, the oligarchy's exact identity isn't the point. What matters is that it exists as a unified, malign presence.

Many conspiracists will even project their fantasies backward through history—so that time itself does not compromise their protagonists' monopoly on evil. Some 9/11 conspiracists implicate the Bush family in the murder of JFK and (as noted in Chapter 1) the Nazi war machine. Alex Jones goes back further—viewing 9/11 as just the latest barbarism inflicted by a satanic network that has been "steering planetary affairs for hundreds of years." Lyndon LaRouche's publishing house has promoted the theory that Jewish bankers and religious leaders have been involved in a massive conspiracy stretching back to ancient times—with an especially creepy emphasis on the role played by Shylockian "Venetian bankers" of the Renaissance era. Sergei Nilus, the original Russian publisher of the *Protocols*, went even further, tracing the Jewish conspiracy back three thousand years: "According to the records of secret Jewish Zionism, Solomon and other Jewish learned men already, in 929 B.C., thought out a scheme in theory for a peaceful conquest of the whole universe by Zion." In an introduction to the *Protocols*, the author sketches the historical path of the "Symbolic Snake of Zion" through the great crises of Western civilization—Greece in 429 B.C., Augustan Rome, Madrid in the age of Charles V, and, of course, that singular obsession of anti-Semites for more than two centuries, the French Revolution.

The onset of this sort of obsessive historical monomania is often the canary in the intellectual coal mine when sober-minded pundits transmute into conspiracists. A good contemporary example is left-wing crusader Naomi Klein, who became a superstar of the antiglobalization circuit in 2000 with her anticorporate manifesto *No Logo*. Over the next seven years, Klein's increasingly radicalized hunt for corporate demons launched her into the realm of full-fledged conspiratorial fantasy. By the time she'd published her 2007 book *The Shock Doctrine: The Rise of Disaster Capitalism*, Klein had convinced herself that the world was controlled by a cabal of hypercapitalists who'd been personally recruited and indoctrinated by U.S. economist Milton Friedman. Like the European anti-Semites who believed that Jews supported both sides in Europe's great wars, Klein casts her Friedmanite villains as equal-opportunity architects, enablers, and cheerleaders of all manner of human misery—from the 2005 Asian tsunami, to Hurricane Katrina, to slaughter in Iraq—motivated by the single goal of intimidating societies into accepting free trade and globalization. In one particularly far-fetched section, Klein even suggests that the state of Israel is a willing promoter of the terrorism campaign against its Jewish civilians—because the "continual and continuously expanding war on terror" helps inflate the profits of the country's "high-tech security" industries.

The 9/11 Truthers follow this reductionist tradition faithfully—theorizing that Washington and al-Qaeda's jihadis secretly play on the same team. British-based Truther Nafeez Mosaddeq Ahmed—whose early published work set the stage for many of the American conspiracy theorists who emerged in the years after 9/11—argued that the term "al-Qaeda" was real, but only to the extent that it referred to "a database of [CIA-controlled] pseudo-Islamist covert operations recruits." California-based Michael Ruppert, similarly argues that "there is a compelling case to be made that Osama bin Laden has long been a well-cultivated, protected, and valued asset of U.S. and British intelligence."

And why didn't Barack Obama spill the beans about all this when he took power in 2010? The answer is obvious: America's major parties are both bought-and-paid subsidiaries of the same all-controlling Beast.

Boundless Evil

Right-wing conspiracists traditionally have railed against the international campaign to reduce global warming, which they regard as a pretext to destroy national sovereignty and impose a world government. Even so, the 2009 Copenhagen conference on climate change stood out as a subject of special agitation. This time, the world leaders meeting in Denmark weren't seeking merely to create a hyperenvironmentalist UN dictatorship, conspiracist websites claimed: They actually were plotting to annihilate whole swathes of humanity.

Texas-based syndicated radio host Alex Jones led the charge on his December 11 broadcast:

Do you understand how diabolical this is? It isn't a bunch of idiot tree-huggers that mean well and just got their science wrong. These are vicious *Nazis*—it's the only way to describe them. But in truth, they're *worse* than the Nazis . . . They [the Malthusians] came up with this idea to exterminate, and re- duce births . . . It is life and death! These people are taking over right now! . . . Did you get the memo not to drink the water. Did you get the memo not to take the inoculations . . . ? Do you *like* being sterilized? Do you like being *killed*?! You better grow up, ladies and gentlemen. You better realize that we're facing a threat far more dangerous than Mao Tse Tung and Adolf Hitler and Joseph Stalin and Vladimir Lenin! . . . This is the New World Order crashing the gates. They're spilling over the wall. If this was the Alamo . . . Those of us fighting the globalists, we're like Davey Crockett, we're out of ammo, we're swinging our muskets. A lot of us are going to get killed, we're going to get imprisoned. This is only going to get worse in the years to come. But, you take my life, I take yours, too.

This tirade captures many of the modern conspiracist obses- sions—vaccines, mass sterilization, apocalyptic confrontation. But the aspect that jumps out more immediately is the manner in which Jones describes his imagined "globalist" enemies: as foes who are not merely as evil as the totalitarian monsters of the twen- tieth century, but somehow worse. What Jones has in mind isn't just evil on the scale of a mass murderer or a terrorist, or even a genocidal sociopath, but rather on the science-fiction scale of Sau- ron from *Lord of the Rings*, Darth Vader (*Star Wars*), or SkyNet (*The Terminator*). In his 2007 film *Endgame*, Jones claims that "a world government is just the beginning. Once in place, [the New World Order] can engage their plan to exterminate 80 percent of the world's population, while enabling the 'elites' to live forever with the aid of advanced technology."

In support of such claims, Truthers tick off a long list of ep- isodes in which the U.S. government has killed innocents on a large scale: Hiroshima and Nagasaki, Vietnam, the proxy wars of Central America, sanctions in Iraq. The death toll of 9/11, by this telling, is a mere rounding error for our utterly amoral leaders. Toronto-based conspiracy theorists Terry Burrows and Ian Woods explain the elites' mindset this way:

> Such perpetrators are not normal. They are psychopaths—individuals lacking both empathy and conscience, self-centered to the extreme, driven by their insatiable lust for power and control. [Their] New World Order is intended to be a totalitarian feudal dictatorship where a super-wealthy and over-privileged few will completely dominate and control an entire planet of impoverished serfs, imprisoned by a high-tech global surveillance matrix . . . This 'Diaboligarchy' uses wars and catastrophes (which the members themselves instigate) to break down natural human resistance to their corrupt enterprise, which is now approaching its endgame. The predominance of individuals devoid of empathy for the feelings and sufferings of others—operating without conscience at the very centers of corrupt power and intending to dominate the human race totally—makes them mankind's greatest natural predators.

The notion of some sort of "diaboligarchy" pops up in almost every corner of the conspiracist universe, dating back all the way to the earliest forms of Christian anti-Jewish propaganda, in which unconverted Jews were portrayed as demonic servants of the Antichrist; and the campaign of extermination against them, by corollary, a form of existential human obligation that became the jihad of the Nazi religion. "The Jewish world-conspiracy was seen as the product of an ineradicable destructiveness, a will to evil which was believed to be inborn in every Jew," Norman Cohn wrote. "A peculiar breed of sub-human beings, dark, earthbound, was working conspiratorially to destroy these sons of light, the 'Aryan' or Germanic 'race,' and the *Protocols* contained their plan of campaign . . . When the *Protocols* came into contact with the *völkisch*-racist outlook the result was an apocalyptic vision not only of contemporary politics but all history and indeed of all human existence on the planet."

As Jones' rant shows, modern conspiracy theorists have picked up this theme of "ineradicable destructiveness," but placed it in a secular context. In describing the motives of the imagined evil-doers, the one word that constantly pops up is "control"—of oil, gold, money, blood (as described in more detail later in this chapter). The villain is portrayed as the ultimate control freak, so pathologically freakish, in fact, that he slips the bindings of human morality. (In this regard, the villains may be a projection of con-spiracy theorists' own frustrated drive to impose order on a chaotic world—but I'll admit that this is merely pop-psychological specu-lation on my part.)

In Truther mythology, it is assumed that the CIA and Pentagon will do literally anything to advance their dark plots—even the wholesale massacre of schoolchildren: Thierry Meyssan, the French Truther whose 2002 *Pentagate* kicked off the conspiracy theory that no plane hit the Pentagon on 9/11, told me in a phone inter-view from his home in Lebanon that the terrorists who attacked an elementary school in Beslan, North Ossetia, were drugged dupes deployed by the CIA. As noted elsewhere, influential Truther Mi-chael Ruppert believes the 9/11 plot is part of a long-term con-spiracy aimed at exterminating most of humankind: "Who among us cannot picture the war criminal Henry Kissinger—protégé of David Rockefeller—sitting back in his chair and muttering with his German accent, 'The problem is not that there is too little oil. The problem is just that there are too many people.'"

On this point, Ruppert quotes CIA deputy director Higgins from the 1975 film *Three Days of the Condor*: "It's simple eco-nomics. Today it's oil. In 10 or 15 years . . . food. Maybe even sooner. Now what do you think the people are gonna want us to do then? . . . Ask them when there's no heat in their homes and they're cold. Ask them when their engines stop. Ask them when people who've never known hunger start going hungry." (Like a surprisingly large number of conspiracy theorists, Ruppert likes to prove his point by reference to Hollywood movies.) He also footnotes fellow conspiracy theorist Jay Hanson, who similarly sees the end of oil as the beginning of the apocalypse:

> In less than 20 years, the self-regulating market system will have "run out of gas" and vanished. With the market system gone, the ruling elites will fall back on the good old-fashioned means of control: a police state. In the United States alone, 200 million guns in private ownership guarantee that this police state will quickly devolve into rebellion and anarchy. If the anarchy scenario were to reach its natural conclusion, the global elites would be eliminated by the angry masses. Those who managed to escape would die more miserably than the poor since they are unsuited for day-to-day survival because they lived their lives like queen bees. But when the above scenario seems inevitable, the elites will simply depopulate most of the planet with a bioweapon. When the time comes, it will be the only logical solution to their problem. It's a first-strike tactic that leaves the built-infrastructure and other species in place and allows the elites to perpetuate their own genes into the foreseeable future . . . The global genocide will be rationalized as a second chance for humanity—a new Garden of Eden—a new Genesis. The temptation will prove irresistible.

A prominent corollary to this line of thinking is the notion that our overlords are, even today, using the medical system to systematically "cull the herd" with exotic diseases and infected medications. One of the most famous AIDS conspiracy tracts of the 1980s—the so-called *Strecker Memorandum*—argued that the AIDS virus was developed jointly by the National Cancer Institute, World Health Organization, and U.S. military as part of a plot "to exhaust America with hatred, struggle, want, confusion, and inoculation of disease," and thereby "speed the Soviet Union toward its goal of world domination."

Many UFO conspiracists believe that AIDS is part of "the gray alien agenda," whose goal is to clear away humankind in order to make way for a terrestrial alien colony. Other conspiracists believe that the H1N1 virus is a man-made disease, and that the vaccines we've been offered for it are actually poisons that will do nothing but increase the death toll. In the Arab world, conspiracy theorists imagine great legions of Mengele-like Jewish doctors roaming the world, committing an endless list of vile plots. Following Haiti's 2010 earthquake, for instance, a Syrian television feature about Israel's humanitarian mission to Port au Prince told viewers that the mission's real purpose was "to steal organs from the corpses of the Haitian dead."

In all of these claims, one finds echoes of the *Protocols*, in which the mythical Herzl stalks Basel like a crazed sociopath, rhapsodizing about "the complete wrecking of that Christian religion," and urging Jews to harness their "burning greediness, merciless vengeance, hatred and malice" to expedite "the killing out of the *Goyim*." Like the conspiracy theories it inspired, the *Protocols* reads more like a satire of human evil than a catalog.

Incumbency

In Spring 1918, the end of the First World War was just months away. But in the United States, Washington's first Red Scare—which would climax with the infamous Palmer Raids of 1919 and 1920—was just heating up. One target was former Minnesota congressman Charles August Lindbergh, a conspiracist firebrand who'd immigrated to the United States in the 1850s as the infant child of a Swedish bank embezzler on the lam.

In 1913, Lindbergh wrote *Banking and Currency and the Money*

Trust, a tract denouncing Wall Street as "a man-made god that controls [America's] social and industrial system." Four years later, he produced *Why is your Country At War?*, an equally radical book arguing that America's soldiers were fighting in support of a corrupt international financial order, and that Washington needed to take back the commanding heights of the U.S. economy from Wall Street's clutches. The same year, Lindbergh brought articles of impeachment against members of the Federal Reserve Board, whom he accused of conspiring "to violate the Constitution and laws of the United States." All this attracted the attention of U.S. Attorney General A. Mitchell Palmer, who branded *Why is your Country At War?* seditious. In June 1918 federal agents raided Lindbergh's Washington, D.C. printer, where they had the plates for the book destroyed.

Lindbergh *père* has lapsed into obscurity. (He died of brain cancer in 1924, three years before his more famous son, also named Charles, made his famous solo flight from Long Island to Paris.) But his story is worth dusting off: As University of California historian Kathryn Olmsted argued in her 2008 book *Real Enemies*, it contains a crucial lesson about the evolution of American conspiracism.

In 1913, when Lindbergh published *Banking and Currency and the Money Trust*, the federal government was tiny—with a budget of less than $1 billion. The FBI was smaller than the constabularies of many American towns, and largely confined itself to investigating prostitution. Its agents had neither the mandate nor manpower to police the nation's political literature. Likewise, conspiracists like Lindbergh tended to be less fearful of Washington than of Wall Street, international financial speculators, and other nongovernment actors.

The massive expansion of government that took place during World War I changed perceptions on both sides. By 1918, the federal government suddenly controlled a budget worth almost $13 billion and a network of agencies charged with fighting political subversion. "In the process, these federal agents elevated Charles

Lindbergh from harmless critic to Enemy of the State," Olmsted writes. Lindbergh and other conspiracy theorists immediately returned the favor: "Some Americans had worried for decades that malign forces might take over the government. Now, with the birth of the modern state, they worried that the government itself might be the most dangerous force of all."

A similar phenomenon was taking place across the Atlantic. Prior to the twentieth century, most European conspiracy theories focused on the plots of Freemasons, Illuminati, Jews and the like to seize power from society's rightful aristocratic stewards. But in the radical conspiracist mythology of the *Protocols*, this changed: The evildoer was no longer the outsider, sneaking into villages under cover of darkness to poison wells and steal babies. He was now entrenched in the banks, the trading houses, the salons, the Masonic lodges, and all the rest of society's nerve centers.

As discussed in the next chapter, Truthers take a similar view about the "neocon" cabal that gained influence in George W. Bush's administration—a process of political infiltration that they claim began decades before 9/11.

Greed

Some historians consider it the greatest speech in the history of American politics. Certainly, it was among the most rapturously received. Audience members screamed and cheered "like one great burst of artillery," wrote a journalist who covered the event. Others waved their arms in the air, flailing about "like demented things." A day later, the man who'd thrilled the audience was nominated as the Democratic Party's candidate for president. The year was 1896, and the burning populist issue on which William Jennings Bryan had staked his political fortune was . . . the free coinage of silver to gold at a conversion rate of 16 to 1. Strange as it may seem to modern readers, the word "bimetallism" then stood among populists for "hope" and "change" rolled into one.

On the surface, the debate was about monetary policy: The coinage of silver would have inflated the money supply, and thereby permitted indebted farmers and other rural businessmen to repay their loans on more advantageous terms. But the undercurrent was far broader: To Bryan and other bimetallists, the word gold was a stand-in for the upper classes—the fat land speculators, urban businessmen, and financiers who counted out their fortunes in the currency of bullion. Silver, on the other hand, was imagined to be the currency of the farmer, the miner, and the rural yeoman.

There was an international dimension as well: In Bryan's conception, the gold standard was an English institution, and so America's continued reliance on it symbolized a shameful, quasicolonial continuation of American subservience toward a European master. "It is the issue of 1776 over again," he declared in his closing flourish on July 9, 1896 (according to a surviving copy). "Our ancestors, when but 3 million, had the courage to declare their political independence of every other nation upon earth. Shall we, their descendants, when we have grown to 70 million, declare that we are less independent than our forefathers? . . . We shall answer their demands for a gold standard by saying to them, you shall not press down upon the brow of labor this crown of thorns. You shall not crucify mankind upon a cross of gold."

At the heart of Bryan's vision is the standard rural populist's division of the world between (in his words) "the farmer who goes forth in the morning and toils all day, begins in the spring and toils all summer, and by the application of brain and muscle to the natural resources of this country creates wealth"; and, on the other hand, the "financial magnates who in a backroom corner the money of the world." But his special obsession with gold also captures an aspect of conspiracist thought that has remained timeless: the notion that evildoers' plots revolve around a campaign to control some crucial *substance.*

In many cases, that substance is in our bodies. Hitler believed Jews were conspiring to pollute the Aryan bloodline; modern European conspiracists claim Israel is harvesting the internal organs of murdered Palestinians; in the late 1980s and early 1990s, Latin American conspiracy theorists alleged that Westerners were abducting local children to steal their innards for transplant. Many UFO buffs believe cosmic visitors have created a subterranean human-farming operation somewhere in the western United States so that they may harvest our vital fluids. Vaccine and AIDS conspiracy theorists imagine a global plot to contaminate us with infected blood. In most of these narratives, it is imagined that the evildoers have a special fondness for the life force of *children*. For instance, David Icke describes the secret plot hatched by humankind's Reptilian overlords this way: "Humans have a particular type of energy, and the Reptilians have structured human society to trawl that energy, especially from children when it is at its most 'pure.' "

From the nineteenth century onward, the hoarding of gold was an especially common theme in conspiracist tracts. References to the precious metal litter the *Protocols*, always in the context of the Jew as a greedy monopolist: "In our hands is the greatest power of our day—gold: In two days we can procure from our storehouses any quantity we may please." By this period in history, the idea that a gold syndicate was behind the misfortune of farmers and laborers already had become a prominent theme in American conspiracist tracts, especially those authored by Greenbackers and free-silverites. A Populist manifesto circulated in 1895, a year before Bryan's speech, declared that "[in] 1865–66, a conspiracy was entered into between the gold gamblers of Europe and America . . . Every device of treachery, every resource of statecraft, and every artifice known to the secret cabals of the international gold ring are being made use of to deal a blow to the prosperity of the people." As late as 1934, amid the battle over silver remonentization in the United States, fascist radio host Charles Coughlin denounced (Jewish) Treasury Secretary Henry Morgenthau Jr., and sang the praises of silver, which, he claimed, was a more "gentile" substance.

Since the rise of the automobile, and the Teapot Dome Scandal of the early 1920s—an instance in which petro-conspirators truly *did* seek to secretly commandeer America's ship of state—oil gradually has replaced gold as the mythical object of the conspirators' obsessions; just as, more recently, "neocons" have replaced Jews, "bankers," and "gamblers" as a description for the conspirators themselves. In the case of the 9/11 Truth movement, certainly, it is hard to find any conspiracy theorist who does not put oil smack at the center of his mythology.

"Although the apparent crisis is about terrorism, the real one is about energy scarcity," career conspiracist Michael Ruppert wrote in *Crossing the Rubicon: The Decline of the American Empire At The End of the Age of Oil.* "In order to prevent the extinction of the human race [due to a lack of oil], the world's population must be reduced by as many as four billion people. [This] constitute[s] the ultimate motives for the attacks of 9/11."

Interestingly, the market crash of 2008, and the attendant rise of the price of precious metals, has led to a modest comeback for gold-based conspiracy theories. One widely circulated conspiracist email that began landing in my inbox in 2009 informed me that: "The biggest gold crime story of the century might be soon coming to full light. Evidence is accumulating that the Clinton administration . . . replaced perhaps the entire contents of the Fort Knox gold with tungsten bars plated by gold." On conspiracist websites, such stories often appear side by side with advertisements from gold-coin wholesalers who, along with peddlers of wind-up radios and other survivalist gear, have carved out a profitable niche as conspiracism's piggyback profiteers.

Moreover, gold does figure prominently in one significant "retro" strand of the Truth movement: In the original version of the influential Truther film *Loose Change* (described in Chapter 7), director Dylan Avery spends several minutes making the case that the destruction of WTC 2 may have been part of an elaborate plot to steal no less than $167 billion in gold using a "10-wheel truck."

The claim was removed from subsequent versions—after it was pointed out that $167 billion in gold, valued in Sept. 2001, would weigh more than 19,000 tons, thus requiring a fleet of about 485 semitrailer trucks.

Cui Bono?

As noted already, early conspiracy theories about the French Revolution focused in large part on the Illuminati, Freemasons, and anti-Catholics. It wasn't till several years later that Jews were added to Abbé Augustin Barruel's list of suspects, almost as an afterthought. What convinced many Frenchmen of Jewish involvement? The French National Assembly abolished special restrictions on Jews in 1791, and Napoleon Bonaparte convened a high-profile meeting of Jewish notables in Paris sixteen years later. Then, as now, conspiracy theorists acted on the logic of *cui bono*—"who benefits?"

The authors of the *Protocols* recited the logic of *cui bono* on every page, intertwining it with the related theme of insatiable Jewish greed: The Jews, it was imagined, would happily engineer any form of human tragedy to make a buck. Nazi propagandists applied this theme relentlessly in their propaganda. The 1943 Polish edition of the *Protocols*, for instance, depicted a fat Jew grasping two large bags of money as he sits atop a big pile of skulls.

In our own era, the logic of *cui bono* has been trotted out by conspiracists when Halliburton, Blackwater, or some other American conglomerate is awarded a contract in Iraq or Afghanistan. Assassination-related conspiracy theories, in particular, tend to emphasize the logic of *cui bono*—since the death of any public figure (JFK is a good example) always produces hundreds of indirect beneficiaries. Career conspiracy theorist and leading Truther Webster Tarpley, for instance, argues that the likely suspect behind the assassination attempt on Ronald Reagan was none other than "Freemason George Bush," for whom "the vice presidency was not an end in itself, but merely another stage in the ascent towards the pinnacle of the federal bureaucracy, the White House.

"The Roman common sense of Lucius Annaeus Seneca (who had seen so many of Nero's intrigues, and who would eventually fall victim to one of them) would have dictated that the person who would have profited most from Reagan's death be scrutinized as the prime suspect," Tarpley has explained. "That was obviously Bush, since Bush would have assumed the presidency if Reagan had succumbed to his wounds."

Under the logic of *cui bono*, Truthers see today's neocons—like the Jews of the *Protocols*—as both architects and profiteers of perpetual war. To quote John McMurtry, an influential Truther who teaches at the University of Guelph in Ontario:

One would be naive to think the Bush Jr. faction and its oil, military-industrial and Wall Street backers who had stolen an election with its man rated in office by the majority of Americans as poor on the economy . . . and more deplored by the rest of the world as a deep danger to the global environment and the international rule of law, do not benefit astronomically from this mass-kill explosion. If there was a wish-list, it is all granted by this numbing turn of events. Americans are diverted from a free-falling economy to attack another foreign Satan, while the Bush regime's popularity climbs. The military, the CIA and every satellite armed security apparatus have more money and power than ever, and become as dominant as they can over civilians in 'the whole new era' already being declared by the White House. The anti-missile plan to rule the skies is now exonerated (if irrelevantly so), and Israel's apartheid civil war is vindicated at the same time. Even the surgingly popular "anti world-trade" movement is now associated with foreign terrorists blowing up the World Trade Center . . . The more you review the connections and the sweeping lapse of security across so many co-ordinates, the more the lines point backwards.

Hypercompetence

In September 2001, the World Trade Centre was attacked allegedly by terrorists. I am not sure now that Muslim terrorists carried out these attacks. There is strong evidence that the attacks were staged. If they can make Avatar, they can make anything.

—*Former Malaysian prime minister Mahathir Mohamad, January 2010*

Of all the 9/11 conspiracy theories I've encountered, perhaps the most elaborate is that of Alexander Keewatin Dewdney, a retired Canadian mathematician who believes there were no Arab hijackers on September 11, 2001: The passengers of the four planes were killed using sarin gas, and the planes were flown into their targets by government-programmed computers.

Among the many inconvenient facts casting doubt on Dewdney's thesis are the various telephone calls from passengers on the hijacked 9/11 aircraft to their loved ones. And so, Dewdney has made it his life's work to prove that the people who originated these phone calls actually were actors and actresses pretending to be hijack victims. Dewdney has even gone up in rented aircraft with a bag full of cell phones so that he can prove to the world that the alleged phone calls never took place.

In his forty-page essay on the subject, "Ghost Riders In The Sky," Dewdney describes how he thinks U.S. government agents stage-managed the desperate phone calls, in real time, on 9/11:

Imagine then an operations room (of which every intelligence agency has several) with a screen on which the events appear as text, keeping all operatives on the same page, so to speak. An operations director would have much the same role as a symphony conductor, cueing various operators as the script unfolds. An audio engineer would have several tapes already made in a sound studio. The tapes, which portray mumbled conferences among passengers or muffled struggles, replete with shouts and curses, can be played over any of the phone lines, as determined by the script, or simply fed as ambient sound into the control room. Trained operators with headsets make the actual calls. Each operator has studied tapes for several of the individuals, as recorded on prior occasions of Flight 93, as well as profiles of the individuals, including a great deal of personal information, some of it obtained 'on the ground,' as they say. As soon as the passenger lists become available, each operator scans his or her own copy, searching for the names that he or she will special-ize in, discarding the rest. The introductory sentence, some-what fuzzily transmitted, would carry the hook: 'Honey, we've been hijacked!' Thereafter, with the belief framework installed, a similar live voice could react to questions, literally playing the situation by ear, but being sure to include pertinent details such as 'Arab-looking guys,' 'boxcutters,' and all the rest. If the contact has been made successfully in the operator's opinion, with the essential information conveyed, it is always possible to terminate the call more or less gracefully, depending on what portion of the script is under execution. 'Okay. We're going to do something. I'll call you back.' Click. Each operator has a voice that is somewhat similar to that of the person he or she is pretending to be. It is not particularly difficult to do this. For example, it is far easier to find someone with a voice that can be mistaken for mine (especially over a telephone line) than it is to find someone who looks like me (even in a blurred pho-tograph). Moreover, most people can learn to mimic voices, an art well-illustrated by comedians who mimic well-known per-sonalities. Operators would have received general instructions about what do to in the course of a call. Although each has been supplied with at least some 'intimate' details of the tar-get's life, there would be techniques in place for temporizing or for avoiding long conversations where basic lack of knowledge

might threaten to become suddenly obvious, and so on. Three
such techniques are praying (from text, if necessary), crying, or
discussing the other attacks.

This fantasy encapsulates what *Popular Mechanics* editor James
Meigs calls "the myth of hypercompetence." Even as the conspiracy theorist imagines a world-controlling cabal that is subhuman
in its lack of pity, morality, honesty, and empathy, he is simultaneously awestruck by their superhuman intelligence, ambition, guile,
discipline, and singularity of purpose.

Given the evildoer's massive intellect, it is imagined that he has
access to—or seeks to perfect—doomsday machines and other
science-fiction technologies worthy of Dr. No. Truther David Ray
Griffin, for instance, warns readers in his many books that 9/11 is
in fact a "Space Pearl Harbor" that somehow will lead to the wea-
ponization of the cosmos. Prominent British Truther David Icke (a
man widely quoted within the movement, notwithstanding his odd
claims that the world is controlled by intergalactic lizards) believes
the CIA has developed microchips so small that they can be injected into humans through hypodermic vaccine needles. Michael
Ruppert writes at great length about an all-knowing, all-powerful
U.S. government computer program called PROMIS: "Having inspired four new computer languages, [the software] had made possible the positioning of satellites so far out in space that they were
untouchable. At the same time the progeny had improved video
quality to the point where the same satellite could focus on a single
human hair. The ultimate big picture. PROMIS progeny had also
evolved to the point where neural pads could be attached to plugs
in the back of the human head and thought could be translated
into electrical impulses that would be equally capable of flying a
plane or wire-transferring money . . . Data, such as satellite recon-
naissance, could also now be downloaded from a satellite directly
into a human brain. The evolution of the artificial intelligence had
progressed to a point where animal behavior and thought were be-

ing decoded. Mechanical humans were being tested. Animals were being controlled by computer."

During my years interviewing conspiracy theorists, I often felt like I was entering a science-fiction convention—a world of wide-eyed boy-men talking excitedly about remote-controlled jet airliners, paint-on explosives, undetectable electronic communications, and doomsday pathogens concocted in government weapons labs. Millions of conspiracy theorists—including Venezuelan leader Hugo Chavez—even believe that the United States possesses "tectonic weapons" that can cause massive earthquakes, such as the one that struck Haiti in January 2010. Another popular theory is that the High Frequency Active Auroral Research Program (HAARP) ionospheric research facility in Gakona, Alaska, is a superweapon that can rain instant death (or, in the alternate view, control people's minds) anywhere on earth. One correspondent even informed me that the 9/11 attacks were the work of time travelers: "A key whistleblower, Andrew D. Basiago, has emerged with evidence that secret U.S. time travel technologies were used as early as 1971 to acquire first-hand documentary knowledge about September 11, 2001—fully three decades before the horrific events of that fateful day. Mr. Basiago, a child participant in DARPA's time travel program, Project Pegasus, has publicly stated how in 1971 he viewed moving images of the attack on the Twin Towers on September 11, 2001 that had been obtained from the future and brought back to the early 1970's."

This is one of the reasons why conspiracist movements tend to be so overwhelmingly male in their core membership. (Another is that the male mind tends to become more easily obsessed with abstract logic puzzles and eccentric ideological systems that are disconnected from the reality of day-to-day human existence—a subject to which I shall return in Chapter 5.) For all their pretensions to sophisticated truth-seeking, conspiracists often seem stuck in the suburban-basement universe of secret decoder rings and Star Wars action figures. As Meigs put it, many conspiracists have seen "too many movies"—particularly in the action genre. Like James Bond, freshly equipped at the beginning of each film with the latest gadgets from MI6's weapons lab, the government agents of conspiracists' imaginations have access to every sort of weapon ever invented—as well as many that are still imaginary. They possess Bond's skill and savvy, as well. How else could they constantly avoid detection and capture?

The *Protocols*—which cast the Jews as full-fledged evil geniuses, far superior in intellect to their gentile victims—once more provides the perfect case study. But the evil superman is a staple of all forms of conspiracism. In the anti-Soviet mythology of Cold War America, he was imagined to be a sort of emotionally neutered robot—as I.F. Stone put it, "some supernatural breed of men, led by diabolic master minds in the distant Kremlin, engaged in a satanic conspiracy to take over the world and enslave mankind." When the Cold War ended, the evil superman moved to Turtle Bay, and took up residence in the executive suites of the United Nations, where he developed the power to control fleets of undetectable black helicopters. "When the troops come in, they'll come in such force it will be incredible," Militia of Montana leader David Trochmann told journalist Michael Kelly back in 1995, near the height of the so-called patriot paramilitary militia movement. "In 48 hours, they can have one hundred million troops here. They'll come out of the ground! They'll come from submarines! They'll come from air drops! They'll come from everywhere."

Covering Their Tracks

In the introduction to this book, I explained that my initial interest in the 9/11 Truth movement had an inward-looking aspect: Many of the conspiracy theorists I communicated with reminded me, in some way, of my own obsessional self. But there was another factor, too: Just about every conspiracy theorist I spoke with believed that my own industry—the corporate media—is deeply complicit with the government agents who destroy buildings and spread disease; that we know (or at least suspect) the awful truth, but refuse to report on it. Like all journalists, I regard myself as one of the good guys, as a force acting *against* unchecked government power. So why does my profession arouse such intense suspicion and hostility—not only among hard-core paranoiacs, but also among legitimate political activists spanning the political spectrum from left-wing student groups to right-wing Tea Partiers?

The fact is that there is a grain of truth to the claim that the media creates its own "invented reality" (to cite the words of influential Canadian Truther Barrie Zwicker)—just not in the way that conspiracy theorists believe. No, we aren't privy to shocking, otherworldly state secrets: If we were, there would be a mad rush among my colleagues to publish them, become sainted stars on par with Bernstein and Woodward, and then sign seven-figure book deals. Rather, the reality we journalists "invent" is very much based on the mundane happenings in the world around us, but it is selected, packaged, and sold according to our own editorial and ideological biases, as well as our commercial understanding of what interests our readers, listeners, and viewers. As a result, the news that appears in the media often is dumbed down, sensationalized, slanted left or right in a way that can make people think we are making it all up out of whole cloth.

In the three-channel universe of the postwar years, the variance between corporate media sources was so small that most people could imagine that the reported world and the world they knew were one and the same. Now that media choice has expanded by several orders of magnitude; people can switch realities merely by changing the channel—including an option now known as "reality television." In describing the day's news, for instance, FOX and NPR provide such different points of view that they might as well be broadcasting from different planets. In the current political environment, the usual practice among ordinary media consumers is that they "trust" one side and accuse the other of dishonesty. On this score, conspiracy theorists distinguish themselves only by their even-handedness: They accuse all sides of lying.

Gregg Roberts describes himself as a freelance writer, business analyst, and lifelong peace activist. From the moment the Twin Towers collapsed, Roberts tells his readers, he was "surprised" by "the apparent completeness of the collapses, and the huge amount of dust that was produced." In time, he came to conclude that the tragedy actually was the result of controlled demolition. "I spent the next couple of weeks appropriately depressed," he reports. "I had known even before I knew all the facts that *if* the facts showed US officials were behind the attack, my life would never be the same. I would not be able to live my life in the same leisurely, typical American way. I would be compelled by my sense of integrity to try to do something about this attack, to try to bring the perpetrators to justice."

But when Roberts tried to spread the message to his friends, he got a frustrating response. "In many personal discussions I have had about the issue, I am often interrupted long before I can describe much of the evidence, with the objection that such a large conspiracy could not have been covered up," he writes. "[A] whisteblowing exposé would be published by a 'reputable' news outlet, the story would be picked up by other mainstream news organizations [and] widely known among Americans." Why wasn't any of this happening?

Finally, Roberts stumbled on the "chilling explanation"—that the media organizations we trust to give us the news are actually in cahoots with the military-industrial complex. "[Even] the Left media are largely controlled by elites tied to the very national security state that the Left media pretend to oppose," Roberts writes, referring readers to a bewildering flowchart that includes entries for "George Soros," "Skull & Bones," and "Mother Jones." "Even the venerable Left magazine *The Nation* seems to have significant ties to the Central Intelligence Agency." In his lengthy 2006 essay, "Where are the 9/11 Whistleblowers?" Roberts concludes that the insiders who conspired to blow up the World Trade Center also were able to ensure that none of the conspirators would share their story with the outside world.

The idea that the 9/11 masterminds are sufficiently powerful to control the reporting of thousands of different American news outlets, as well as stifle after-the-fact disclosures from hundreds of active conspirators, is far-fetched. But it isn't much more far-fetched than the notion that they could execute the 9/11 plot in the first place, which always is explained by reference to the evildoers' allegedly superhuman powers of organization, discipline, and self-control.

A variation of Roberts' argument is made within all conspiracy movements. Just as America's early nineteenth-century anti-Masonic conspiracists claimed the Masons' diabolical plots were being covered up by Masonic editors and newspaper owners, so do modern-day anti-Bilderberg conspiracists like Daniel Estulin claim that "Bilderberg meetings are never mentioned in the media, since the mainstream press is fully owned by the Bilderbergers."

Likewise, in protocol twelve, the fake Herzl is made to go into minute detail about Jewish control of the media. "Our government," he says, "will become proprietor of the majority of the journals. This will neutralize the injurious influence of the privately-owned press and will put us in possession of a tremendous influence upon the public mind . . . . If we give permits for ten journals, we shall ourselves found thirty, and so on in the same proportion." At the same, Herzl provides elaborate instructions on how to concoct bogus rifts among newspapers and other publications, so as to convince the broad public that the marketplace of ideas is genuinely free. And if, by chance, some renegade journalist might try to spill the beans about the Jewish menace, he would be silenced with extortion: "Not one [journalist] is ever admitted to practice literature unless his whole past has some disgraceful sore or other . . . These sores would be immediately revealed."

Since 9/11, the idea that the mainstream media is too corrupt and timid to report the real facts about the Sept. 11, 2001, terrorist attacks has become a cliché in Truther culture. " 'The news' consumed by most people in North America and Europe is a cocoon of manufactured facts, distractions and personalities forming an almost seamless web of invented reality—including invented history—obscuring the power of money and other resources in the hands of the few, even while cleverly masking its own unreality," wrote Barrie Zwicker in the influential 2006 Truther book *Towers of Deception: The Media Cover-Up of 9/11.* "Fake events are a key component of the illusion, a *Truman Show* writ large. The mainstream media remain mute in the face of mounting evidence that Western covert operators were behind Bali, Madrid, London 7/7, mosque bombings in Iraq and elsewhere and, of course, 9/11. Because the mainstream media are integral to the Industrial Military Academic Intelligence Media complex (IMAIM), the cold-blooded technicians of death face no journalistic scrutiny. Without moral, legal, technical or financial constraints, the black operators range freely, executing the orders of the global oligarchies—what I call the Invisible Government."

One of the reasons that this book likely will do little to change the mind of anyone who is already a Truther is that I am a mainstream newspaper editor and columnist—which makes me a presumptive accomplice to government lies. Like the *Protocols* and so many other conspiracist and faith-based phenomena, the 9/11 Truth movement has embedded within its dogmas an airtight means for defending itself from outside critics.

And just like everything else, they borrowed the trick—without knowing it—from a cabal of plagiarist anti-Semites working for the Russian czar.

CHAPTER THREE

False Flags and Lava Lamps: The Birth of a Conspiracy Movement

Fortune, especially when she desires to make a new prince great, who has a greater necessity to earn renown than an hereditary one, causes enemies to arise and form designs against him, in order that he may have the opportunity of overcoming them, and by them to mount higher, as by a ladder which his enemies have raised. For this reason many consider that a wise prince, when he has the opportunity, ought with craft to foster some animosity against himself, so that, having crushed it, his renown may rise higher.

—*Machiavelli,* The Prince

I can surely understand your reluctance to believe that the leaders of the United States could perpetrate such a crime against humanity. History, however, would seem to disagree with you. When you look at the history of false flag attacks performed by the American intelligence agencies, military and government you get a very different view of history . . . Create a problem, gauge the reaction of the public then provide the solution to soothe the people that fits the goals that the folks in charge had to begin with.

—*Oregon-based blogger and conspiracy theorist Greg Hoggatt, in an Oct. 28, 2008, email sent to the author*

Ken Jenkins: Videographer, Flower Child, Truther

If you want to meet the gentle giant who embodies the sixties soul of the 9/11 Truth movement's older members, you will find him, living and working alone, in a split-level wood-frame walk-up apartment on the fringes of a medium-sized town twenty minutes north of San Francisco.

He's easy to find: Ken Jenkins makes no secret of his radical politics. A poster declaring "9/11 WAS AN INSIDE JOB" fills one of his windows. A similar bumper sticker festoons the car parked outside. The freelance video editor will talk to anybody about his cause—even a nosey nonbeliever like myself, traveling through the Bay Area and seeking an interview on short notice.

The Truther who had introduced me to Jenkins via email—a conservative, buttoned-down architect named Richard Gage (profiled in Chapter 5)—warned me not to judge the man based on first impressions. "He might come off as a bit of a flower child," Gage told me. "But never mind that. He has an extremely sharp mind."

And Gage was right. As soon as I walked into his apartment—a mishmash of sixties-era psychedelic posters, Ankhs, and lava lamps alongside banks of state-of-the-art computers and video gear—I knew I'd hit on a lively interview. New-age spiritualist, electrical engineer, video producer, psychologist, computer expert: Of all the Truthers I've met, the pony-tailed, six-feet-three Jenkins is easily the most intellectually multifaceted.

He also happens to be a charming fellow. During the hours we spent together in his apartment, our conversation was wide-ranging and open. He exhibited none of the brittleness that conspiracy theorists sometimes display if you challenge them on their dogmas.

Slightly bewildered by the riot of spiritual symbols decorating the four walls, I asked Jenkins about his religious faith. He paused thoughtfully, then said: "It's a little hard to define unless you've seen a movie called *What the #$*! Do We Know!?* (which, upon subsequent googling, turned out to be a 2004 documentary about the spiritual links between quantum theory and living consciousness). Part of his belief system, he told me, involves categorizing personalities according to a nine-pointed psychospiritual "Enneagram" that he's pinned up in his kitchen. (Ken describes himself as a "Peacemaker," which aligns to node number nine. But he is quick to point out that the Truth movement contains all manner of personalities, including more aggressive types, such as radio host Alex Jones, whom Jenkins describes as a "Challenger," placing him squarely on node number eight.) The man has not eaten meat since the 1960s—though he confesses to "a little fish now and then"—and pursues a lifestyle program he calls "intentional longevity." It is clearly working: A baby boomer born in 1947, Jenkins could pass for midforties.

A Silicon Valley native, Jenkins ventured east in the 1960s to study electrical engineering at Pittsburgh's Carnegie Mellon University. Following graduation, he returned to California, where he pursued a career in video production. For a while, he worked as a technical director at Hewlett-Packard's in-house film studio, then left in 1989 to pursue freelance projects—including a phantasmagoric, avant-garde title called *Illumination: Visual Music.*

Then came 9/11. "On the day itself, I'll admit I was somewhat blasé," he tells me. "It was horrible, of course. But I assumed it was blowback from U.S. foreign policy—well, finally someone did something about everything the United States had inflicted on the world. So many thousands of people die awful deaths every day from starvation, et cetera—so I didn't find those particular three thousand deaths themselves particularly upsetting."

But in the weeks that followed, Jenkins began asking questions—especially about NORAD's slow response to the hijackings. To this day, he remembers the period as one of intense struggle and self-examination.

"My initial resistance to the truth had to do with what is commonly called 'the Big Lie'—an idea that Hitler and J. Edgar Hoover talked about quite specifically," Jenkins told me. "Normal people are not accustomed to thinking of great, audacious lies. They think about small white lies. The idea that something as vast as 9/11 could be explained by anything other than the official story is outside a lot of people's reality. That's why I was skeptical myself during almost two months of daily research."

As the weeks went by in the fall of 2001, a handful of conspiracist pioneers began to post their theories on the Internet. One of the most influential was author Michael Ruppert, a charismatic former L.A. narcotics investigator who'd originally gained fame in the 1970s for his allegations that the CIA was involved in the drug trade. In his previous writings, Ruppert already had developed an unusually well-textured conspiracist mythology linking the government to a variety of smuggling plots. After 9/11, he extended his theories to the world of Islamic terrorism on his *From the Wilderness* blog. And in late 2001, he took his act on the road, delivering speeches at various West Coast venues, including universities. While Ruppert identifies himself as a conservative, his radical message appealed to left-wing campus activists—the type who had constructed their image of America from books written by Noam Chomsky and Howard Zinn. This "Truth and Lies of 9/11" speaking tour helped define the first stirrings of what we now call the Truth movement.

According to Ruppert's view, the seeds of 9/11 were planted in the Caspian Basin "sometime during the period between late 1998 and early 2000." Global elites had been expecting that the oil deposits from that region would forestall "the pending calamity of Peak Oil," he argued. When they saw the first exploration and drilling results, they grew desperate. It was then that "Dick Cheney and the neo-cons stepped up with a plan"—the first stage of which was the election of George W. Bush with the connivance of the U.S. Supreme Court.

"An irrevocable decision had been made to cross the Rubicon, that bloody line between an ailing republic and the empire that irreversibly supervened," Ruppert later wrote. "In May 2001 President Bush placed Dick Cheney in charge of all planning for a terror attack, effectively giving him complete control over FEMA, the military, everything. In June 2001 the NORAD scramble protocols that had worked efficiently since 1976 were rewritten to take most decision-making power out of the hands of Air Force field commanders. Although minor exceptions in those protocols still allowed commanders to act on their own in certain cases . . . the change itself provided deniability for elements of the confusion that Dick Cheney was going to deliberately engineer and control . . . These men, led by Dick Cheney, chose what they thought was their only logical option. I believe it seemed to them the 'right' thing to do; after all, it was only a few thousand lives. Other rulers have made similar choices in the past."

Ruppert also helped develop Truther mythology, vague as it is, in regard to the actual mechanics of the 9/11 operation. Osama bin Laden, he theorized, was a "CIA/U.S. government/Wall Street asset" who had been groomed under the Clinton administration for exactly this sort of assignment. The "so-called hijackers" were probably "part of an ultra-secret U.S. military and intelligence joint operation 'Opposition Force,' or OPFOR, which routinely played bad guys in hijack exercises around the world." The World Trade Center was an attractive target because "it housed not only the vast archives of criminal investigative records of agencies like the SEC but also an unknown-sized paper trail of financial crimes, cooked books, inflated profits, and sundry other offenses. There were large amounts of gold and negotiables in a number of vaults, many belonging to foreign central banks, that could be secretly removed and later claimed destroyed."

After Jenkins saw Ruppert speak at a Sacramento event during his "Truth and Lies of 9/11" speaking tour, he came away impressed. "It took a lot of courage to do that in those days," Jenkins told me. "The Patriot Act had been passed. Once you accepted that 9/11 was an inside job—that these people were so ruthless that they would mass-murder three thousand people—it seemed pretty dangerous. But I thought to myself, 'If someone doesn't stand up and say something, they're going to get away with it. I don't want to live in that sort of world.'"

Using his skills with computers and video editing, Jenkins became the Truth movement's unofficial multimedia coordinator—helping fellow conspiracists adapt their theories into slick video montages and PowerPoint presentations. He also partnered in the creation of 911tv.org, a website that archived footage of Truther conferences, and packaged it for distribution to local-access television stations. As with every full-time Truther I've met, his funding is meager—a few hundred dollars here and there from donors and video sales. But it's clear from my visit to his home office that the man's material needs are modest.

In the years following 9/11, the Truth movement gained traction through blogs such as *From the Wilderness* and left-wing campus activist networks. In 2003 and 2004, major Truther conferences were held in Lucerne, San Francisco, Toronto, and New York. Michael Ruppert's massive book on the subject, *Crossing the Rubicon*, appeared in 2004, and became the Truth movement's bible. In the same year, Claremont School of Theology professor David Ray Griffin published *The New Pearl Harbor*: *Disturbing Questions About the Bush Administration and 9/11*. Another major Truther milestone came in 2005, when twenty-one-year-old director Dylan Avery released *Loose Change*, which helped spread the Truther message through the then-emerging medium of web-streaming video. In 2006, the ranks of elite Truthers were joined by professional architect Richard Gage, who used his expertise in structural engineering to create detailed technical presentations alleging that the Twin Towers could have been brought down only through internal demolition. Increasingly, members of the Truth movement began presenting themselves as scientists as much as activists.

During these years, Jenkins began gearing his own 9/11 presentations to a recruitment strategy. He eventually published an article summarizing his approach, entitled "The Truth is Not Enough: How to Overcome Emotional Barriers to 9/11 Truth." Among those barriers, Jenkins argues, are "blind nationalist faith"; our desire to look up to governmental authorities as parent figures; shame at our longstanding gullibility; enduring "post-traumatic stress disorder" in the wake of the Twin Towers' destruction; and "apathy and complacency." Regarding the latter, Jenkins quoted radio talk-show host Mike Rivero to the effect that "most propaganda is not designed to fool the critical thinker, but only to give moral cowards an excuse not to think at all."

As a 1960s-vintage student of human spirituality and consciousness, Jenkins takes the long view when it comes to changing American minds. "The implications of 9/11 Truth are so big that for society as a whole to accept it is not something that can happen overnight. In fact, you would not even *want* it to happen overnight—it would cause chaos. Even if somehow we could magically get on all the networks and instantly prove that 9/11 was an inside job, on one level it would be nice, but it would do damage . . . Richard [Gage] is always saying 'We're going to *break* the story.' And my attitude is: 'I don't think it's going to happen that way.' It's going to continue to be a gradual process. And as I said, I think that's for the best."

Looking back at his own conversion process, Jenkins told me, the decisive factor was the realization that 9/11 was hardly a one-off crime: History was repeating itself.

"What got me from 97 percent sure to 100 percent sure was the revisionist account of Pearl Harbor," he explained. "In that case, too, I bought into the official history. But the more I studied it, the more I realized it wasn't true. The U.S. government had broken the codes. We knew just what the Japanese were doing. And that's when it clicked—because of the similarity in scale.

"Pearl Harbor wasn't the same as 9/11," he adds. "It was *allowed* to happen [by the American government], not *made* to happen. But it was similar in that our normal military defenses should certainly have detected those planes and ships. There was information kept from the military in Hawaii to allow that to happen. And then there's the fact that all of our best ships were taken out of the harbor before the attack, and a bunch of old clunkers were put in . . ."

With that, Jenkins was off and running about an event that took place sixty years before 9/11. Over the next two hours, more diversions were to follow—about the assassination of JFK, the Gulf of Tonkin, Iraq, and a slew of other alleged precedents. As anyone who's talked to conspiracy theorists can testify, such exercises in historical hopscotch are common: A conversation about the present inevitably turns into a conversation about the past.

Amid the swirling tangents, it's easy to lose the thread and drift off. But if you want to understand the Truth movement, it pays to listen closely.

Operation Northwoods and Its Legacy

In March of 1962 Operation Mongoose—the plan to depose Fidel Castro—was dead in the water. The previous year, on the heels of the CIA's disastrous Bay of Pigs adventure, John F. Kennedy had authorized a campaign of aggressive covert operations to destabilize Cuba's communist government. But none had borne fruit, and time was slipping away: Operation Mongoose was viable "only as long as there can be reasonable certainty that U.S. military intervention in Cuba would not directly involve the Soviet Union," wrote the Joint Chiefs of Staff in an infamous "Top Secret" March 13, 1962, memorandum to Secretary of Defense Robert McNamara. "All projects are suggested within the time frame of the next few months."

But while the Kennedy administration was desperate to be rid of Castro, it couldn't afford to be seen as a naked aggressor. What was needed, the Joint Chiefs concluded, was a pretext for war that put "the United States in the position of suffering justifiable grievances. World opinion and the United Nations forum should be favorably affected by developing the international image of the Cuban government as rash and irresponsible, and as an alarming and unpredictable threat to the peace of the Western hemisphere."

In other words, the Joint Chiefs were urging a "false flag" attack—a shocking U.S.-staged incident that would be falsely blamed on Fidel Castro, and thereby offer Washington a pretext for "defensive" action. (The term originates in an earlier age of military history, when fighting ships on the high seas identified one another by the flags on their masts.)

The plan contained in the March 13, 1962, memorandum—codenamed "Northwoods" and set out on six typed pages—delivered to McNamara a long menu of false-flag options. Some were vague and set out in single lines of point-form notation, such as: "Start rumors (many). Use clandestine radio. Land friendly Cubans in uniform 'over-the-fence' to stage attack on [the Guantanamo Bay Naval Base]. Capture Cuban (friendly) saboteurs inside the base. Start riots near the base main gate (friendly Cubans). Blow up ammunition inside the base; start fires. Burn aircraft on air base (sabotage). Lob mortar shells from outside of base into base. Some damage to installations." But others seemed like elevator pitches for Hollywood action films—such as a plan to "Sink ship near harbor entrance. Conduct funerals for mock-victims." An even stranger plan, contained in a separate memorandum, suggested something called Operation Dirty Trick: "The objective is to provide irrevocable proof that, should the Mercury manned orbital flight fail, the fault lies with the Communists et al."

Operation Northwoods never materialized: Days after the Northwoods memo was drafted, Kennedy rejected the plan, signaling to the Pentagon that he had no appetite for new military adventures in Cuba. Though the CIA would continue to engage in covert operations against Castro's regime following the 1962 Cuban Missile Crisis, the Northwoods memo would become a mere footnote to the larger sweep of Cold War history—albeit one that offers a fascinating glimpse into the hawkish mindset of military leaders at the height of the Cold War.

But to conspiracy theorists, Northwoods is anything but a footnote. The Vietnam War often is held up as a definitive event that, along with Watergate, caused Americans to break faith with their government. But in conspiracist lore, the JFK era actually has proven to be an equally dominant influence. As Truthers see it, the 1962 Northwoods memo—references to which are sprinkled casually throughout Truther speeches and articles, like biblical citations at a prayer meeting—is essentially an early blueprint* for the even more diabolical plot that would unfold thirty-nine years after the memo was written.

What makes Northwoods particularly tantalizing to modern conspiracists is that several of the more ambitious schemes contained in the 1962 memo share key elements of the Truther narrative: (1) the intentional destruction of airplanes; (2) fake terrorism stage-managed by Washington; and (3) the wanton killing of innocent civilians; (4) all with the goal of furthering America's geostrategic interests. While most strategies got only vague mention in the Northwoods memo, these more elaborate plots were described in minute detail:

- We could sink a boatload of Cubans en route to Florida (real or simulated) . . .
- Harassment of civil air, attacks on surface shipping and destruction of U.S. military drone aircraft by MIG type

---

* It's worth noting that—despite the superficial similarities between Northwoods and the supposed neocon conspiracy to blow up the World Trade Center—the 1962 episode actually helps demonstrate why Truther theories are so far-fetched. Northwoods was conceived in a climate of perceived urgency: Fidel Castro's regime was an obsession in Washington, and preventing the spread of communism on America's doorstep was properly seen as an urgent, life-and-death foreign policy challenge. Yet even under these conditions, the plan was rejected as unnecessarily risky by JFK—despite the fact that the schemes contained in the Northwoods memorandum were orders of magnitude less complex and deadly than bringing down three Manhattan skyscrapers.

planes would be useful as complementary actions. An F–86 properly painted would convince air passengers that they saw a Cuban MIG, especially if the pilot of the transport were to announce such fact . . .

- It is possible to create an incident which will demonstrate convincingly that a Cuban aircraft has attacked and shot down a chartered civil airliner en route from the United States to Jamaica, Guatemala, Panama or Venezuela. The destination would be chosen only to cause the flight plan route to cross Cuba. The passengers could be a group of college students off on a holiday or any grouping of persons with a common interest to support chartering a non-scheduled flight. An aircraft at Eglin [Air Force Base] would be painted and numbered as an exact duplicate for a civil registered aircraft belonging to a CIA proprietary organization in the Miami area. At a designated time the duplicate would be substituted for the actual civil aircraft and would be loaded with the selected passengers, all boarded under carefully prepared aliases. The actual registered aircraft would be converted to a drone.*

During the course of my interviews with Jenkins and others, Northwoods consistently served as Exhibit A in the Truther argument that American leaders would be willing to lie to their own citizens, and even kill innocent people, as a means toward sparking a military conflict. Many described the 1962 memorandum as

---

* The convoluted nature of the Northwoods schemes—involving drone planes, passengers shuffled from one plane to another, and repainted airplane tail numbers—may help explain some of the especially otherworldly "no-planer" Truther theories of 9/11, which suggest the four passenger aircraft that crashed that day were somehow not what they seemed, but instead were drones, or had been emptied of passengers at some indeterminate location in the northeast United States, or even that they were not real aircraft at all.

the crucial piece of evidence that originally tipped them into the Truther camp.

That includes Robert Balsamo, a middle-aged commercial pilot who now helps lead a group called Pilots For 9/11 Truth.

By Balsamo's description, he was a loyal, even jingoistic, American patriot until he found out about the Joint Chiefs' plans for Castro. "Being a New Yorker and a pilot, 9/11 was like a double-whammy for me," he told me during a phone interview from his new home office in Tennessee. "And I wanted to go get the big bad terrorists. I called every military branch to offer my services—but they told me they were all set with pilots in the military, and I would be better serving my country as a civilian pilot to get Americans back in the air."

His attitude changed in 2006 when he turned on CNN and saw Glenn Beck interviewing David von Kleist, a Missouri-based Truther who attacks the notion that American Airlines Flight 77 ever hit the Pentagon.

"The Department of Defense had just released a video of the Pentagon getting hit, and Beck showed it on his program," Balsamo tells me. "Then Beck said that this should put all those 'conspiracy theories' to rest. And I was thinking, 'Oh, that's great. This'll clear everything up.' But then the video rolls, and I'm sitting there, and I'm looking at the footage, and I'm thinking—wait a minute—I can't *see* any 757.

"And as a professional pilot, I know what I'm looking for," he adds. "The 757 is a very sexy airplane to pilots. Excuse my language, but pilots call it 'big tits, long legs, and a tight ass,' because that's what it looks like. It's got two huge engines, long landing gear and a tight rear. It's very distinctive."

So Balsamo started poking around on the Internet, seeing if he could find a clearer version of the video. Instead, what he found were Truther sites—and a copy of the famous Northwoods memo. From then on, there was no turning back.

"[The 9/11 commission] came out and said that our biggest

failure regarding 9/11 was our lack of imagination—imagining that some people could get some planes and fly them into buildings, and terrorists hijacking airliners and what not," Balsamo told me. "But just forty years prior—this was exactly what people in our own government, the people trying to invade Cuba, were proposing. It blew me away when I read that. It blew me away that these elements could get that high within our government, could get to that level of power."

But the history lessons don't end at Northwoods. In the Truther worldview, false-flag conspiracies can be read into most modern wars—all the way back to World War I. Or even further: Webster Tarpley—a prominent Washington, D.C.–based 9/11 conspiracy theorist—traces the false-flag roots of 9/11 to the Gunpowder Plot of 1605, in which a group of English Catholics sought to blow up the Houses of Parliament with a massive bomb, and thereby slaughter King James I of England and VI of Scotland, and much of the Protestant ruling class besides. (Tarpley believes the event was staged as an excuse to persecute papists.) In their presentations to 9/11 Truth conferences, Canadian conspiracy theorists Ian Woods and Terry Burrows go back even farther: to the Greeks' use of a Trojan Horse three thousand years ago, and Nero's move to pin the Great Fire of Rome on the Christians.

In some historical cases, the Truthers have a point—or, at least, an arguable debating position. Almost as frequently cited as Northwoods in Truther literature, for instance, is the 1933 Reichstag fire, which gave the Nazis a pretext to purge Germany's communists from public life—notwithstanding suspicions that the mentally disturbed communist convicted of the crime was a Nazi pawn. Two years after the Reichstag fire, Stalin seized on the death of popular Politburo moderate Sergey Kirov and the machinations of the invented "Trotskyite-Zinovievite Terrorist Center" to usher in his Great Purge. Five years after that, Stalin executed another bona fide false-flag operation: As Finnish Truther Vesa Raiskila noted to me in an interview, the Soviet Union's 1939 invasion of Finland was justified by Finland's alleged shelling of the Russian village of Mainila—despite the fact that not a single Finnish artillery unit was in range.

The 1964 Tonkin Gulf Resolution, which gave Lyndon B. Johnson authorization to use military force in Southeast Asia without a formal congressional declaration of war, was secured in the aftermath of a pair of naval engagements that many legitimate historians believe were the result of American provocations and blunders. And then there's the 2003 invasion of Iraq, which was justified in large part by Saddam Hussein's possession of (nonexistent) weapons of mass destruction. Many Truthers I spoke with told me that their latent suspicions about 9/11 didn't mature into full-blown Trutherdom until the spring and summer of 2003, when the search for Iraqi WMD turned up nothing of significance.

Other examples of historical false-flag conspiracies cited by Truthers are more dubious. As part of the historical analysis she embeds in her speeches at Truther events, for instance, former MI5 Intelligence Officer Annie Machon, who now lives in Germany, alleges false-flag connivance between the British government and IRA bombers. She also suggests that the July 26, 1994, bombing of the Israeli embassy in London was a false-flag Mossad operation; and, far more plausibly, that Alexander Litvinenko's 2006 assassination by polonium in London resulted from his blowing the whistle on what Machon alleges to be the Kremlin-orchestrated 1999 bombing of Russian apartment blocks as a pretext for full-scale war in Chechnya.

Like Ken Jenkins, many American conspiracists have lapped up Robert Stinnett's controversial 1999 blockbuster *Day of Deceit: The Truth About FDR and Pearl Harbor*—which is itself based on a Northwoods-type 1940 document known as "The McCollum memo"—suggesting that FDR engaged in a deliberate campaign aimed at provoking Japan into attacking Pearl Harbor so that he would have an excuse to drag a reluctant America into the war against the Axis powers.* Others allege NATO was complicit in a whole range of false-flag terrorist plots on European soil during the Cold War (allegations inevitably sourced to a single eccentric 2004 book written by Daniele Ganser, *NATO's Secret Armies: Operation Gladio and Terrorism in Western Europe*).

Radio host Alex Jones likewise claims the 1915 sinking of the RMS *Lusitania* was a false-flag operation designed to get the United States into World War I. (Jones admits that the ship was sunk by a German torpedo, but adds that "[the *Lusitania's* commander] sailed it back and forth in front of submarines to get a false-flag attack.") Other alleged false-flag attacks that have become Truther talking points are the 1995 bombing of the Alfred P. Murrah Federal Building in Oklahoma City; and Israel's attack on an American intelligence-gathering ship called the USS *Liberty* during the Six Day War of 1967. (The plan, according to one typical theorist, "was for Israel to attack and sink an American ship, kill the crew and the U.S. would blame Egypt, invade and oust Soviets from the Middle East, and control the world's oil supply.") According to this

---

* The notion that FDR knew about—or knowingly provoked—the Pearl Harbor attacks is refuted in chapter 15 of Conrad Black's definitive 2003 FDR biography, *Franklin Delano Roosevelt: Champion of Freedom*. When I asked the author (who happens to be a *National Post* colleague) what he thought of Stinnett's thesis, he had this to say: "The idea that Roosevelt would have been aware of an attack on the Pacific Fleet and under-warned his local commanders is outrageous. He loved the navy, and he would have had just as much anger and unanimity behind his war policy from the US public if the torpedo nets [around the harbor] had been out, the air force airborne, and the damage had only been 2 percent of what it was. This is one of the dumbest conspiracy theories [I've ever heard].

"I don't buy any of the conspiracy theories about 9/11 either," Black added. "It was another intelligence bungle by the United States, but God knows we are accustomed to those, such as unawareness that there were already 140,000 Red Chinese troops in North Korea while Truman and MacArthur were meeting at Wake Island; and of the presence of nuclear, immediately attachable warheads and 40,000 Russian soldiers in Cuba before Kennedy made his speech and imposed his quarantine in 1962."

view of history, there is no such thing as an honest *casus belli*: Just about every conflict in the history of human civilization has been caused by a warmongering conspirator killing his own kind and blaming it on an innocent enemy.

Many conspiracy theorists who embrace this radical understanding of history readily draw on their own bloodlines and personal histories to justify their claims. Some, like former football player Lubo Zizakovic, are Slavs who believe NATO hatched a plot to humiliate Serbia in the 1990s.* A conspiracy-minded Canadian civil-rights lawyer I've crossed paths with, Rocco Galati, sees current events through the lens of his Italian ancestors—whom he believes were stereotyped as Mafia members in the postwar decades. Daniel Estulin, whose elaborate conspiracy theories about the Bilderberg Group already have been discussed, was raised in the USSR, and claims his father was jailed and tortured by the KGB. Luke Rudkowski, the twentysomething firebrand who's emerged as New York City's noisiest, most aggressive Truther in recent years, is the son of Polish immigrants who imparted to their son an evident hatred—and fear—of totalitarianism. Both of these men follow faithfully in the tradition of Ayn Rand, whose radicalized fear of government seems to have taken root when the Soviets took over her father's pharmacy in St. Petersburg.

The aforementioned Webster Tarpley—an avuncular, fast-talking charmer who has been spinning conspiracy theories for the last three

---

* In 2008, an email correspondent sent me this anecdote, in response to a column I'd written about 9/11 Truthers: "While at dinner with a well educated (lawyer and building contractor) Serbian immigrant couple we befriended in the late 90's, I mentioned the surreal experience of watching the initial attack on Dubrovnik live on a BBC feed to Canadian television, a man walking his dog down a path alongside the seaside hotels as Serbian naval missiles slammed into them with the trailing wires visible on the screen. They immediately informed me that this, and all the other TV coverage of atrocities like the market mortar attack, was faked in Hollywood. We remained friends but never discussed politics and I concluded that there are simply limits to what one can believe evil about one's [own] group."

decades—presents another interesting example. Following his graduation from Princeton in 1966, the Fulbright Scholar moved to Rome,
where he found work as a journalist. When former Italian prime minister Aldo Moro was kidnapped and killed in 1978—his body found
in a car just two blocks from Tarpley's downtown Rome office—Tarpley found his life's work. The murder, he concluded, was a false-flag
operation conducted by NATO intelligence officers under the guise
of the Red Brigades. ("The Red Brigades are now widely recognized
as CIA agents," he told me in our interview. "The only question is
whether they were *originally* agents of the CIA or whether they were
[co-opted] later on. I tend to believe the former scenario.")

As the years rolled on, Tarpley transformed into a professional
conspiracy theorist, gaining international exposure through Lyndon LaRouche's cable television programs and book publishing
outlets. In 2005, he set out his Truther views in a book by the name
of *9/11 Synthetic Terror: Made in USA*, which he followed up with
a weekly online radio show.

Interviewing Tarpley is an adventure: As with Alex Jones, he
is a machine-gun talkaholic whose conspiracy theories extend to
pretty much every world event you can name. (As already noted,
he even has a detailed theory about George H. W. Bush's role in
the 1981 shooting of Ronald Reagan, an event that has inspired
relatively sparse attention from conspiracists.) But unlike Jones, he
has an Ivy League pedigree, and a genuinely impressive knowledge
of world history. He is also more methodical, having spent years
developing a sort of universal typology of false-flag terrorism—one
that's been adopted by countless Truther acolytes.

Essential to any false-flag enterprise, he says, are three distinct
groups of people—the "patsies," the "moles," and the "technicians."

The patsies, he tells me, are "the lone assassins, the [Lee Harvey]
Oswalds, the [Mohamed] Attas, and so forth. These are the ones
who get caught. Their characteristics are then used as the sorting
principle to go after whatever group you're looking to [vilify]. If you
want to go target Russians, get a Russian national to commit an act

of 'terrorism.' The giveaway is that these people are physically incapable of carrying out the act in question. Oswald couldn't have shot that many bullets with the required accuracy. The Red Brigades—the people who were supposed to have killed Moro—were wild student leftists and anarchists who didn't know what they were doing. Yet what they did [kidnapping Moro on Rome's Via Fani, after killing his five escort agents] would have done the special services proud. The Baader-Meinhof gang were a bunch of psychotics. And the 9/11 hijackers—to the extent any of them actually set foot on those airplanes—could never have done those feats of flying. Any fool can see it. These guys are the clown show in the foreground—that's it."

The next group up, according to Tarpley, are the "moles"—a "private intelligence network that is embedded in the government, cutting across agencies transversally . . . They look like government, but they're not. A typical example is the FBI guys who made sure the 9/11 hijackers weren't arrested—but then when the deed is done, they immediately swoop in and give the public all the answers."

Finally, Tarpley says, come the "technicians"—the professional Hollywood-style supervillains who actually do the dirty work. These include, he says, the "two or three pro marksmen" who shot JFK in Dallas, and the network of "retired military and CIA old boys" who likely hatched 9/11. But private actors are part of the technician team, too: "I believe the [9/11] command center was probably in some kind of private firm," he tells me. "A lot of the 9/11 books say Dick Cheney ran everything. That's absurd. He's had four heart attacks—on 9/11 the guy was sitting in a bunker with one phone getting [harassed] by his wife."

Project for the New American Century: A Modern Northwoods

When did conservatives begin plotting to create their own false flag as a pretext to invade the Middle East and Central Asia? It depends on which Truther you ask. Many trace it back to University of Chicago political philosopher Leo Strauss (1899–1973)—a figure of epic myth among neoconservatives and their most fevered critics alike—who wrestled (ambiguously) with the question of whether a guileless politician could ever hope to solve society's problems. Others cite the work of hawkish RAND Corporation analyst Albert Wohlstetter (1913–1997), one of the real-life inspirations for Dr. Strangelove in Stanley Kubrick's 1964 film of the same name.

Henry Kissinger also figures prominently in Truther mythology. In particular, conspiracists point to an article entitled "Seizing Arab Oil: How the U.S. Can Break the Oil Cartel's Stranglehold on the World," which appeared in the March 1975 issue of *Harper's* magazine under the byline "Miles Ignotus" (described in the magazine as "a pseudonym of a Washington-based professor and defense consultant with intimate links to high-level U.S. policy makers"). In the article, the unknown author argues that the United States should exploit the next "crisis" to launch a full-fledged 40,000–man military invasion of Saudi Arabia—the goal being to force OPEC nations to bring oil prices to two dollars per barrel, and to turn the nations of the Persian Gulf into virtual colonies: "An occupation of 10 years and probably much less would suffice. Once the dust of the invasion settled, once every evidence of permanent intent became apparent, the remaining members of OPEC would see reason, and accept a binding commitment to maintain supplies at agreed prices in exchange for American withdrawal." There is no evidence the author of these words was Kissinger. (The prevailing speculation points to conservative intellectual Edward Luttwak.) Yet the idea has become an article of faith among many conspiracists.

Some Truthers focus on another former national security advisor, Zbigniew Brzezinski—who served (of all presidents) Jimmy Carter. In his 1998 book, *The Grand Chessboard: American Primacy and Its Geostrategic Imperatives*, Brzezinski declared: "It is imperative that no Eurasian challenger emerges capable of dominating Eurasia and thus of also challenging America," and that "a power that dominates Eurasia would control two of the world's three most advanced and economically productive regions [including] three-fourths of the world's known energy resources."

Then, in language that seems precisely calculated to set the hairs on a conspiracy theorist's neck on end, he lamented: "Never before has a populist democracy attained international supremacy. But the pursuit of power is not a goal that commands popular passion, except in conditions of a sudden threat or challenge to the public's sense of domestic well being. The economic self-denial (that is, defense spending) and the human sacrifice (casualties, even among professional soldiers) required in the effort are uncongenial to democratic instincts. Democracy is inimical to imperial mobilization."

And finally, many chapters later, this oft-quoted gem: "As America becomes an increasingly multi-cultural society, it may find it more difficult to fashion a consensus on foreign policy issues, except in the circumstance of a truly massive and widely perceived direct external threat."

But though Brzezinski's theories may sound sinister when recited in a certain way, he gets distinctly secondary billing compared to the Project for the New American Century (PNAC), a group whose membership reads like a *Who's Who* of the group now commonly lumped together as "neoconservatives."

Formed in 1997 by Washington hawks William Kristol and Robert Kagan, PNAC was composed of conservatives who felt that America had lost its sense of purpose during the Clinton years, and that both America and the world would profit from a more assertive American foreign policy. One founder was former Florida governor Jeb Bush. Others—such as Donald Rumsfeld, Dick Cheney, Zalmay Khalilzad, I. Lewis Libby, and Paul Wolfowitz—would go on to create the nucleus of the Bush foreign policy brain trust. On June 3, 1997, they announced PNAC's presence to the world with these soaring words:

American foreign and defense policy is adrift . . . As the 20th century draws to a close, the United States stands as the world's preeminent power. Having led the West to victory in the Cold War, America faces an opportunity and a challenge: Does the United States have the vision to build upon the achievements of past decades? . . . America has a vital role in maintaining peace and security in Europe, Asia, and the Middle East. If we shirk our responsibilities, we invite challenges to our fundamental interests. The history of the 20th century should have taught us that it is important to shape circumstances before crises emerge, and to meet threats before they become dire.

From the beginning, PNAC advocated regime change in Iraq, successfully pushing Bill Clinton to sign the Iraq Liberation Act of 1998, committing the United States to regime change in Baghdad. On September 20, 2001, nine days after 9/11, the group sent a letter to George W. Bush, urging the White House to exploit the opportunity to wage war in the Middle East "even if evidence does not link Iraq directly to the attack."

But the true smoking gun, cited again and again in the Truther literature, was the group's 2000 report, "Rebuilding America's Defenses," in which the authors observe that "the [desired] process of [military] transformation, even if it brings revolutionary change, is likely to be a long one, absent some catastrophic and catalyzing event—like a new Pearl Harbor."

That single noun phrase, "new Pearl Harbor," has become one of the most popular tag lines of the Truth movement—one that, in just three words, captures the historical pedigree, sinister motives, deadly means, and epic consequences of the 9/11 conspiracy, as Truthers imagine it to have unfolded. It also became the title of what would become a foundational text of the Truther movement, David Ray Griffin's 2004 book *The New Pearl Harbor: Disturbing Questions About the Bush Administration and 9/11.*

Connecting the dots between 1941, 1962, and 2001, Truthers

have constructed not only an alternative vision of modern American history, but also an alternative vision of America itself. Gone is the image of a free nation, spreading liberty and human rights around the globe. In its place is an imperialist faux-democracy ruled by deep-state oil barons, weapons dealers, intelligence officers, and Pentagon warmongers.

"I don't know what to believe anymore," Balsamo tells me, after summarizing his discoveries. "I feel like I'm an infant again, relearning life—because everything that I've learned before is being questioned. I look up to the guys who were called hippies in the sixties now. They've been dealing with this kind of thing for decades.

"History was one of my worst subjects in school," he adds. "I was more interested in the other stuff—math, science, physics—because I wanted to be a pilot. Looking back, I really wish I'd paid a little bit more attention."

CHAPTER FOUR

"Show Me the Birth Certificate": Conspiracism in the Age of Obama

Joseph Farah: Birther Extraordinaire

A concise way to describe WorldNetDaily is that it defines the exact inflection point on the spectrum of right-wing punditry where legitimate journalism ends and out-and-out conspiracism begins. On one hand, the popular website employs a staff of professional reporters who cover real stories. But it also pushes discredited conspiracy theories about Barack Obama, and has become a clearinghouse for litigious extremists challenging the constitutional legitimacy of his presidency.

The brain behind WorldNetDaily is Joseph Farah, a middle-aged Arab American Christian Evangelical who originally made a name for himself two decades ago as editor of the *Sacramento Union* (where he picked a then-obscure pundit named Rush Limbaugh to be his daily front-page columnist). He began WorldNetDaily on a shoestring in 1997, in the days before many news websites even had advertisements, growing it into a profitable agglomeration of right-wing columns, original investigative articles, oddball medical product pitches, gold-buggery, an affiliated book-selling business, and, more recently, the sort of face-of-Jesus-revealed-in-oil-stain hokum usually found on the covers of supermarket tabloids. The ideology on display roughly coincides with the nativist, homophobic, socially conservative right-wing fringe of the Republican Party, but with an even heavier dose of paranoia and freaked-out America-gone-to-Gomorrah sensationalism. One mass emailing sent out in April 2010, for instance, asked readers to congregate at the Lincoln Memorial on May 1 to "cry 'May Day!' to God for our nation in distress . . . The elections are seven long months away and if God doesn't intervene now, there may not be freedom left to meet like this again." The next month, Farah said that his preferred 2012 presidential candidate was Senator Jim DeMint, a South Carolina politician who once declared that openly gay people and unwed mothers shouldn't be permitted to teach in public schools.

It wasn't always this way for Farah. "In high school, I was a revolutionary communist, a Che Guevera type," he told me during a 2009 interview in the lobby of an upscale Virginia hotel. (The meeting spot was a compromise: I'd pestered him to show me WorldNetDaily's Washington, D.C. offices, but he refused.) "I didn't know anyone who had a more radical viewpoint than me." Only later in life did Farah follow the example of *Radical Son* author David Horowitz: drifting rightward across the full breadth of the American political spectrum to the opposite pole, then spending his middle-aged years denouncing the fellow travelers he left behind.

As with many of today's middle-aged Road-to-Damascus conservatives, it was the Gipper who changed Farah's perspective. "Within a year of watching [Ronald] Reagan, I started reading everything he read, and I started thinking *this makes perfect sense!* During that first year—1981—my views changed dramatically. I saw [an ideology] that worked. The more I studied Reagan, and Margaret Thatcher, too, I thought, 'I don't know how anyone can dispute any of this.' " In time, Reagan's famous line from his first inaugural address—that "government is not the solution to our problem; government is the problem"—became Farah's political mantra.

Needless to say, Farah finds Barack Obama's policies appalling. But he also sees Obama as a possible blessing in disguise—as someone so offensive to American values that his presidency could provoke a revolutionary, rightward shift in the political landscape on a scale even greater than Ronald Reagan's 1980 election victory: "Americans aren't political. But with Obama, that's changed. I haven't seen anything like this in my life. This is bigger than the 1960s. That was just kids on campus. What we're seeing now are ordinary Americans. This anger is finally clicking."

The next time I saw Farah, in early 2010, he was standing behind a podium delivering a keynote address to the inaugural Tea Party National Convention in Nashville, Tennessee. The six hundred activists in attendance comprised a friendly audience: Many of them, including the conference organizer who introduced Farah, described WorldNetDaily as their primary source for news.

Farah warmed up the audience with a joke about a medical conference where doctors are bragging about their nation's technological prowess. "A French MD says, 'Medicine in my country is so advanced that we can take a kidney from one man, put it in another, and have him looking for work in six weeks,'" Farah told the crowd. "A German doctor says, 'That's nothing. We can take a lung out of one person, put it in another, and have him looking for work in *four* weeks.' To that, a Russian doctor said, 'In my country, medicine is so advanced that we can take half a heart out of one person, put it in another person, and have him looking for work in *two* weeks.' Then the American physician gets up and says, 'You guys are *way* behind. We recently took a guy with no birth certificate, no brain, and put him in the White House—and now half the country is looking for work!'"

After waiting for the applause to die down, Farah launched into a lengthy dissertation challenging the idea that Barack Obama is a natural-born citizen who is constitutionally eligible to be president of the United States—a Birther conspiracy riff, in other words—every word of it carried to a national audience on C-SPAN.

"I'm a Christian, and I make no apologies about that," Farah declared. "I'm a follower of Jesus Christ . . . I want to share with you briefly how the most important birth in history, that of Jesus of Nazareth was so well documented, unlike Barack Obama's. Jesus established himself as the Messiah and savior of the world by providing not one but two separate and distinct genealogical records, one gong all the way back to Adam, and another tracing his kingly lineage back to Abraham . . . There's no doubt about where he was born, when, and his parentage. Jesus recognized those qualifications were essential to establishing his right to his earthly throne as king of the Jews. In fact, look at your Bibles. The first seventeen verses of *Matthew* are devoted to his genealogy through the line of Mary . . . That's because God didn't want there to be any doubts about Jesus' eligibility or qualifications to be the King of Kings. There's a lesson in this story for Barack Obama. His nativity story is much less known!"

As Farah went on with his conspiracism, I looked around the room for signs of skepticism. If there were any, I didn't see them. In fact, Farah's speech earned a series of healthy ovations.

Obama's August 4, 1961, birth in a Honolulu hospital is documented by birth announcements in not one, but two, Hawaii newspapers. He has released a certified 2007 copy of his birth certificate, disproving the Birther thesis that he was born in Kenya or Indonesia. Every litigant who has tried to make an issue of Obama's presidential eligibility in the courts has been decisively rebuffed. And yet this crowd of political activists was willing to put their hands together for a speaker citing the Bible to support his contention that the president of the United States is some sort of illegal alien. Why?

Drinking Tea in Nashville

"I voted for Jimmy Carter, I'll admit that," the middle-aged New Jersey pediatrician with a George Carlin hairstyle tells me over

breakfast at the Gaylord Opryland Hotel in Nashville, as we wait for the 2010 Tea Party National Convention to commence. "And then the years passed, and I watched as the United States diminished in stature. The low point came when our helicopters crashed in the Iranian desert. We couldn't even rescue our own people. That's when I knew something was wrong."

Since then, he told me, things have only gotten worse. Over the Christmas holidays, he'd traveled to mainland China, visiting factories now being run by an old family friend. "The places were beautiful—air-conditioned and all that. Everywhere I looked, buildings were springing up. Cranes and construction as far as the eye could see. It reminded me of the United States back in the 1950s, my parents' time. Then I go back home to New Jersey, and I look around, and things are dead."

When quoted in the media, Tea Party activists usually are heard railing against health care reform, cap-and-trade carbon abatement, or some other national policy that piques the interest of reporters at CNN and Politico. But when you get them in a small group, away from the cameras, they spend a lot of time talking about state and local issues. Dan, for instance, went on for a long time about double-dipping—New Jersey public servants who end up getting two pensions because they work at two different state jobs.

"I'm a doctor. I make a pretty good living on paper," he tells me. "But New Jersey has a 12 percent state tax. By the time I'm done paying all the governments, my tax load is around 60 percent. I've got two kids in college. After paying the government, I've got nothing left to put away."

Another middle-aged fellow at our breakfast table, a former Marine who'd worked for two decades with the Los Angeles Police Department, pipes up with similar complaints. "The way the LAPD works, you can get most of your pension even if you quit in your forties, after just twenty years on the force—then they hire you back the next day as a 'consultant.' This is why governments are going bankrupt."

A common theme in my conversations was the bias of the media—which most Tea Partiers believe, with some justification, has bent over backwards to give Barack Obama an easy ride. (Indeed, one of the most striking moments of the whole convention came when blogger Andrew Breitbart delivered a particularly vicious fulmination against the liberal bias of the major networks and broadsheet newspapers, prompting literally everyone in the room to get up, turn toward the media section at the back of the conference room, and scream, "U-S-A! U-S-A! U-S-A!")

Tea Party organizers tend to describe their agenda with five bullet points: Lower taxes, less government spending, greater liberty, state's rights, national security. But that quintet—which also summarizes the major planks of the Republican Party—is misleading. The Tea Party movement is mostly made up of refugees from the mainstream GOP. They rail hard against RINOs (Republicans In Name Only). Bipartisanship—"kumbaya politics," as it's derisively called—is dismissed as a sell-out. Many of them are protectionists, in violation of Republican free-trade dogma. Their stance on immigration often flirts with xenophobia. Unlike buttoned-down corporate conservatives, they also tend to go in for oddball practices—do-it-yourself solar power generation, backyard food farming, Internet-peddled herbal medications, homeschooling, dubious tax-avoidance schemes—that hold out the promise of disentanglement from government regulators and their infrastructural grids.

Like all populists, Tea Partiers are suspicious of power and influence, and anyone who wields them. Their villain list includes the big banks; bailed-out corporations; James Cameron (whose *Avatar* is seen as a veiled denunciation of the U.S. military); colleges and universities (the more prestigious, the more evil). Their ideological heroes, meanwhile, tend to be people who are either criticizing Washington from beyond its gates (Sarah Palin), or dead (Ronald Reagan), and thus protected from the taint of power.

The economic tribulations that began in the last year of Bush's presidency hang heavy over the Tea Party and its events: Virtually every conversation comes back to joblessness in some way. In an echo of the populist fervor that arose amidst the economic ruts of the late nineteenth century—when Greenbackers, Free Silver types, and bimetallists all railed at the gold-hoarders in New York City and London—there is much dark talk about the banking system and those who run it.

The analogy between the populist movements of the nineteenth century and the Tea Party phenomenon holds up in some ways: Both championed a constitutionally inspired counterrevolution that would empower ordinary working people by casting off the deadening hand of society's parasitic plutocrats. Yet there are also many major differences. The late nineteenth-century populists of the Great Plains and the Southern states cast their movement as a campaign by rural yeomen, who produced real things like timber, ore, and food, against the city folk who did nothing but count gold and trade stocks—a populist subphilosophy described by American historians as "producerism," and encapsulated in William Jennings Bryan's "cross of gold" speech at the 1896 Democratic National Convention: "Burn down your cities, and leave our farms, and your cities will spring up again as if by magic; but destroy our farms and the grass will grow in the street of every city in the country."

As recently as the recession of the 1980s and 1990s, producerism took expression in anti-Japanese protectionism, Ross Perot, and pick-up-truck-commercial imagery that depicted proud, unionized American workers facing off against foreign sweatshops. There are thin wisps of this in the Tea Party movement: Sarah Palin, in particular, tends to fill her speeches with homages to the common workingman that would not have been out of place a century ago. (It isn't a coincidence that the greatest populist figure of our generation comes from Alaska, one of the few places in America that still relies on dirt-under-the-fingernails industries such as oil and fish.) But for the most part, such appeals are outdated: America doesn't really produce much out of steel and wood anymore. And a lot of what it does produce tends to be welded by robots or plucked out of the ground by illegal immigrants. Most Tea Partiers, like most other Americans these days, tend to be well-educated urban desk jockeys—consultants, health care administrators, mortgage brokers. Unlike farming and other rugged pursuits, these are hard professions to romanticize.

Another major difference comes in the prevalent attitude toward capitalism. In the 1890s, populists typically demanded government intervention to protect the rural way of life from the predations of monopolists and bankers. The Populist Party platform of 1892, in particular, declared "that the power of government—in other words, of the people—should be expanded." The manifesto called for more powerful unions, a state takeover of the railroads, and an increase in the money supply.

Tea Partiers, on the other hand, tend to embrace capitalism unreservedly. They agree with the preamble to the 1892 Populist Party platform, which declares that "the fruits of the toil of millions are badly stolen to build up colossal fortunes [by those who] despise the Republic and endanger liberty." But they identify the thieves as Washington tax collectors, not railway barons. One telling moment, for instance, came in April 2010, when the SEC charged Goldman Sachs with civil fraud relating to its marketing of securitized mortgages—exactly the sort of move that would have caused populists of old to cheer. Instead, many Tea Party types denounced the move as another instance of Obama-style socialism. According to one WorldNetDaily writer, "The SEC action is part of a populist campaign to demonize banks and Wall Street as Democrats try to regain independent voters and the far left." In May 2010, likewise, when many Americans were railing against BP following the Deepwater Horizon fire and oil spill, then-newly nominated Republican U.S. Senate candidate Rand Paul declared such criticism "un-American."

The smug left-wing take on the Tea Party movement is that its members are nothing but shell-shocked racists. (In the words of Janeane Garofalo: "It's not about taxes. They have no idea what the Boston Tea Party was about. They don't know their history at all.

It's about hating a black man in the White House.") But I saw little evidence of that in Nashville.

True, the conference floor was an almost unbroken six hundred-strong sea of white, middle-aged faces: I counted just four black people at the entire conference. But two of those people ended up speaking from the podium—including Washington, D.C. media personality Angela McGlowan, who received a series of massive ovations for her barnburner speech.

Most Tea Party activists do indeed distrust Barack Obama, but not because he's black. Instead, they've latched on to him as a living, breathing symbol of the expansion of government that's taken place in America since the New Deal, and of the decline of American influence on the world stage—the anti–Sarah Palin, in other words. Federal spending, they correctly note, has spiked radically upward in the years since he's come into office—moving America toward a European-style tax-and-spend model, complete with universal health care.

Many Tea Partiers in Nashville went further, and told me that Obama is a Marxist who hates capitalism, that he is deliberately trying to sabotage America's position as a superpower, that he has a secret plan to sell out Israel to the Arabs, or even that he is a closet Muslim in league with Iran. In building their case, they often focused on small, symbolic gestures: Obama's decision to bow to Saudi King Abdullah and Emperor Akihito of Japan, his lack of an American flag lapel pin at a 2008 campaign event, his failure to hold his hand over his chest during the playing of the national anthem in 2007—all of which they take as proof of a secret hatred of America and its values.

It would be entirely wrong to call Tea Partiers a straightforward conspiracist movement—and I don't want to stand accused of doing so here. Many of their political gripes about big government are shared by tens of millions of mainstream Americans: In a September 2010 survey, 71 percent of Republican respondents said they have a "positive opinion" of the Tea Party movement.

But as with all populist uprisings, it has attracted a fringe of angry extremists who will swallow just about any accusation launched against the nation's elite. Like the John Birch Society types who came a half-century before them, some Tea Party radicals believe Washington is packed with fifth columnists seeking to undermine the country's Christian character and its will to fight enemies abroad. The most obvious difference is that the word "Russian" has been replaced with "Muslim" in the accusatory lexicon.

This conspiracist fringe had a sizable presence at the Nashville conference. Roy Moore—the former Alabama chief justice who was fired for refusing to remove a five-thousand-pound sculpture of the Ten Commandments from his courthouse—gave a blistering Sodom-and-Gomorrah speech in which he warned of a "UN guard being stationed in every house." There was also an "emergency preparedness" seminar in which we learned what to do when Armageddon comes. During one meal, I sat next to a conference attendee from Clearwater, Florida—an accomplished and well-spoken computer programmer who worked for a major American technology company—who suggested to me that the American government had deliberately sparked the financial crisis of 2008 so they could devalue the currency to zero, pay off the nation's debts with worthless currency, and then create a new currency—the "Amero"—in monetary union with Mexico and Canada. At first, I dismissed him as an outlier. But later on, the entire conference was subjected to a screening of *Generation Zero*, a conspiracist film arguing a similar theme.

Steve Malloy, the author of *Green Hell: How Environmentalists Plan to Ruin Your Life*, told the crowd that America is controlled by the "three-headed totalitarian monster of Barack Obama, Nancy Pelosi, and Harry Reid." Hitting on what would become a major conference theme, he warned that Obama and his minions are conspiring to control every aspect of Americans' lives—the color of their cars, the kind of toilet paper they use, how much time they spend in the shower, the temperature of their homes—all under the guise of UN greenhouse-gas-reduction schemes. (Every single person I spoke to in Nashville took it for granted that global warming is a scam.) "Obama isn't a U.S. socialist," Malloy thundered. "He's an international socialist. He envisions a one-world government." Everyone applauded wildly.

The next speaker, Memphis Tea Party founder Mark Skoda, put up a dramatic slideshow depicting heroes who'd risen up against tyranny around the world—the anonymous figure blocking tanks at Tiananmen Square, Lech Walesa, Iranian political martyrs . . . and then concluding with images from a Tea Party demonstration.

Is the situation in America really that desperate? Apparently so. The election of Barack Obama, Skoda said, was "the Pearl Harbor moment" of our time.

Then came celebrity Texas preacher and self-described "Christocrat" Rick Scarborough—one of the many overtly religious figures to appear at this convention. In a fiery speech that sounded like a Sunday sermon, he portrayed Obama's America as a sinful hellhole now facing one last chance for salvation: "America has forsaken God. But the good news is that God has not yet forsaken America. And the Tea Party movement is the evidence, I believe, of that reality."

In between speeches, we would all file out of the main conference room and into a wide hallway area where various conservative groups had set up kiosks. There were also small businesses selling Tea Party–themed jewelry, T-shirts, and books. Inevitably, though, the center of attention was a middle-aged man from Brunswick, Georgia, named William Temple—a sort of unofficial Tea Party mascot who crisscrosses the country, appearing at events dressed in his trademark three-cornered hat and authentic Revolutionary garb. When journalists interview him (which is often—his outfit draws them in like a magnet), he cheerfully holds forth, flecking his speech with antique turns of phrase drawn from the days of Thomas Paine.

It's a charming shtick, and one that puts a great face on the movement for the uninitiated. At best, one supposes, these folks are proud patriots standing up for the original values of the Founding Fathers. At worst, they are merely libertarian oddballs—the political equivalent of the high school teachers who spend their weekends recreating the Civil War. But as the weekend convention progressed, it became clear to me that the movement's most radical activists really do imagine themselves to be protagonists in an existential struggle against a malign despot, just like their eighteenth-century forebears.

"We're in a crisis, a crisis as profound [as that] of the [American] Revolution, the Civil War, the Great Depression, or World War II," filmmaker Stephen K. Bannon told the crowd on Friday night. "You just have to ask the Kaiser, you have to ask the military junta that ran Japan in World War II, or the Nazis, or the fascists—no power on earth has ever stood against the common workingman part of this country." This statement seemed like a massive exaggeration—as extreme as anything I'd heard from the Iraq War–era activists who compared George W. Bush to Hitler. Yet, as with Farah's conspiracism, everyone around me nodded their head and applauded, confident in the notion that they were the appointed vanguard who would protect America from Barack Obama's "three-headed totalitarian monster."

Sarah Palin's speech the next day—which attracted more mainstream media attention than the rest of the conference put together—was actually quite moderate and sensible by comparison: Most of what she said about the war on terrorism, spendthrift Washington policies, and Barack Obama's lobbyist cronies sounded like talking points borrowed from a stack of clipped *Wall Street Journal* editorials. (To her credit, she even had a kind word for some of Barack Obama's policies—promoting nuclear power, and staying the course in Afghanistan, for instance—something no other speaker at the conference had provided.) Nevertheless, she was received rapturously by the Tea Party faithful, especially when she dropped allusions to her son in the infantry and the plight of "special-needs children."

A common image evoked by Palin, and by many other speakers, was that of decent, godly people awoken from a long political slumber by Washington's steady drumbeat of liberal outrages. "For too long, we stayed at home, taking care of our families, going to work, paying our taxes, going to church, taking our kids to school," Skoda told the crowd. "We expected the government to do what was right. But they chose to do otherwise, while we remained silent. Well, we are silent no more!" A delirious standing ovation duly ensued—one of many that Skoda and the others received as they shouted slogans to the crowd.

The theme of uplift and revival was much in keeping with the evangelical tone that was everywhere in evidence—something I hadn't expected. Virtually every keynote speaker appealed directly to America's Christian character, and specifically identified the Tea Party project as a direct manifestation of divine will.

"This event is a miracle from you [God]," declared a preacher, brought on stage to bless the food on Friday night. "Because we know it is beyond [the organizers'] human strength to have done what they have done. We thank you for using them—and we ask you to continue using them—and use *us* in this great battle. [May] these festivities be pleasing in your sight, in order that we may gather together one day, again, and celebrate the fact that we have gotten our nation back in Jesus' name." One scheduled speaker, who missed the conference because of illness, sent in a letter, which was read aloud to deafening applause, claiming that her ailment was divinely ordained, since God knew that the woman replacing her at the podium was the more effective speaker. Hosannas to God's will also rang forth spontaneously from the conference floor. At Rick Scarborough's speech, a pamphlet titled "Mandate to Save America" was distributed, in which a coalition of social conservatives enunciated a ten-point agenda to "break the bonds of tyranny." The first one was: "Acknowledge the centrality of faith in America." After Scarborough spoke, a middle-aged woman rose from her chair and declared: "Everyone wants to know why we're here. I say to them, 'We're here for some R&R—revival and revolt.' If you're not a Christian, a person of faith and principle, you can't understand what we're doing!"

For anyone looking to neatly categorize Tea Partiers using conventional poli-sci typology, their odd combination of extreme libertarianism with social conservatism appears confusing: On one hand, they are deeply suspicious of any government effort to redistribute wealth and manage the U.S. economy. On the other hand, they demand that this same government muscularly assert itself in the social sphere, and remake America in a Christian image. What binds these two strands of the movement is not any single notion of government, but a generalized nostalgia for America's past.

There's something deeper at play, too—something that explains not only the linkage between the Tea Party movement, Evangelical Christianity, and Barack Obama conspiracy theories, but also Joseph Farah's seemingly odd comparison between Obama and Jesus Christ.

Throughout recorded history, crisis, conspiracism, and millenarianism all have tended to flare up at once, following a script first set out no fewer than 2,500 years ago in the book of Daniel. Norman Cohn called this script "revolutionary eschatology." In his classic study of eschatology in the Middle Ages, *The Pursuit of the Millennium*, he summarized its main plot elements this way: "The world is dominated by an evil, tyrannous power of boundless destructiveness—a power moreover which is imagined not as simply human but as demonic. The tyranny of that power will become more and more outrageous, the sufferings of its victims more and more intolerable—until suddenly the hour will strike when the Saints of God are able to rise up and overthrow it. Then the Saints themselves, the chosen, holy people who hitherto have groaned under the oppressor's heel, shall in their turn inherit dominion over the whole earth."

According to this narrative, the Tea Party's radicalized activists are the self-appointed Saints. As for Barack Obama, he might not be the "tyrannous power of boundless destructiveness"—but he's the next worst thing.

Enter the False Prophet

The book of the Revelation of John—known simply as Revelation—almost didn't make it into the Bible. Many early Christian scholars believed the text's lurid, phantasmagoric images were simply too disturbing. In his preface to Revelation in the first edition of his New Testament, published in 1522, Martin Luther declared, "I can in no way detect that the Holy Spirit produced it" and, "My spirit cannot accommodate itself to this book." Even for a modern lay reader, it's easy to understand Luther's thinking: Revelation reads like a treatment for a full-on horror movie, a sort of *Cujo* meets *2012* for the age of Domitian.

In the popular imagination, Revelation is known primarily for its climax—in which the forces of God and Satan engage in an epic battle, after which Satan is cast into a lake of fire, and the righteous live on forevermore in a perfect, deathless world known as the New Jerusalem. But Revelation—which many scholars believe was inspired by Rome's intense persecution of the faithful during the reign of the Emperor Domitian—is far more complicated than that. The opening chapters, in particular, are full of obscure Church propaganda, numerology, bizarre animal behavior, an edible book, and a succession of random apocalypses—including the destruction of a third of the Earth's population by a two-hundred-million-strong army. There is also a fantastic menagerie of divine beings and creatures. On Satan's side, for instance, there is a beast who arises, Godzilla-like, from the ocean "having seven heads and ten horns, and upon his horns ten crowns, and upon his heads the name of blasphemy"; a "great red dragon, having seven heads"; and a great harlot of Babylon, "arrayed in purple and scarlet color, and decked with gold and precious stones and pearls, having a golden cup in her hand full of abominations and filthiness of her fornication."

Amid this science-fiction carnival, Revelation describes, almost in passing, a more mysterious figure who also fights on the dark side—a "false prophet" who "deceived those who had received the mark of the beast and those who worshiped his image." His role in Revelation is brief: He is barely introduced before being flung into the Lake of Fire along with Satan. Yet somehow, he has attained a starring role in many of the secular conspiracy theories that have grown out of America's Evangelical Christian tradition, including the conspiracist mythology currently at play on the extreme right wing of American politics.

False prophets pop up elsewhere in the Bible. Deuteronomy, for instance, warns the faithful of polygamous confidence men who pretend to predict the future, and commands death for one who "speaks in the name of other gods." But the false prophet in Revelation is not just some wandering nuisance, tempting villagers with hocus pocus: He is a singular creature, the seductive scout of the Antichrist himself. It is this image of the false prophet that has embedded itself in America's Evangelical Christian culture over the years; and from there, into the country's conspiracist literature, as a biblical prototype to describe any charming, smooth-talking politician suspected of selling America out to some Satan or other—be it communism, militant Islam, or green one-worldism. In fiction, the false prophet is epitomized by Leonardo Fortunato, the preening right-hand man to Antichrist Nicolae Carpathia in the massively popular *Left Behind* series of Christian novels. But in the real world of politics, he is now known as Barack Obama.

Some right-wing Christians are willing to go all the way, and declare Obama to be Satan himself. One popular parlor game on religio-conspiracist websites, for instance, is to prove this linkage by torturing the words of no less an authority than Jesus. A common starting point is Luke 10:18, which has Jesus state: "I beheld Satan as Lightning fall from Heaven." ("How does a Jewish rabbi, which Jesus is credited with being, say in Hebrew, that Satan is like *lightning* from heaven?" one site informs us. "Barack, also transliterated as *Baraq* in Hebrew, is *lightning* . . . The only way a Jewish rabbi can say in Hebrew that Satan is lightning is, 'Satan Barack!'") But the more common tactic is to instead present Obama as the front man for satanic forces that lie outside the United States. Pennsylvania-based conspiracy theorist Victor Thorn provides a typical specimen in his 2009 book *Barack Obama: Devil.* "Obama is the weak little man in front of the curtain, while the booming voice of his Oz-like globalist controllers looms through blips on an electronic screen. They pull the levers, and he dangles by their strings. He is the puppet of hope, a marionette Pied Piper leading us to a financial and spiritual Golgotha."

Whatever the details, the overarching thesis hews to the same False Prophecy myth: That Obama is not an ordinary politician, or, indeed, on some cosmic level, an ordinary *human being.* Rather, he is *counterfeit* in some fundamental and very dangerous way—a Manchurian Candidate—an unholy replicant who has come from beyond American shores (metaphorically or otherwise) to tempt Americans along some demonic path.

As with all conspiracy theories, there is a sliver of truth to the Birthers' anti-Obama mythology: America's forty-fourth president truly does have an unusual background, one full of genuinely radical influences. In his teenage years, Obama took cocaine and flirted with extreme leftist ideologies. While climbing the ladder of influence in Chicago, he made his bed with a menagerie that included a crook, a former terrorist, and a black-power preacher who spouted toxic anti-American conspiracy theories. For a brief period during his childhood, moreover, Obama was raised as a Muslim in Indonesia, and received a standard Islamic-themed education at a public school in that country—not damming facts in and of themselves, but unprecedented for someone who would become president of the most religious Christian nation on the planet.

Moreover—and this is the fact that truly sticks most painfully in the craw of many Birthers I've interviewed—the mainstream media has seemed entirely uninterested in investigating any of this. Worse: It heaps abuse and accusations of racism on those who do, suggesting that their inquiries can be explained by nothing except bigotry. (And yet this is the same media that went after George W. Bush's past so ferociously that a veteran CBS anchor was willing to sacrifice his entire career for the sake of a dubious tidbit about the President's wartime discharge records.) If the mainstream media isn't willing to investigate the dirt about Obama we *do* know to be true—the theory goes—who knows what other dirt is out there?

None of this is to excuse the wild Birther extrapolations detailed in the paragraphs below. But it does go some way to show that their accusations don't exactly rise out of the ether: In a way, Birthers are a product of the liberal media that now heaps abuse on them.

Glenn Beck and the New Populism

On October 30, 2010, nine months after I'd attended the inaugural Tea Party National Convention in Nashville, I spent time with another, equally fed-up voting bloc. But these people weren't angry. They were just . . . bemused. The event was Jon Stewart's "Rally to Restore Sanity and/or Fear," a comedy and music jamboree on the National Mall in Washington, D.C. It was billed as nonpartisan—with Jon Stewart playing the role of "sane" centrist jousting with faux-blowhard faux-fearmongering Stephen Colbert. But when I spoke to people in the crowd, it became clear that this was a solidly left-wing event. Not so much pro-Democrat—these folks are too jaded for party politics—as anti–Tea Party.

Like Tea Partiers, the Jon Stewart brigade has a narrative about a country that has been hijacked by extremists. For the Tea Partiers, those extremists are Barack Obama and his big-spending "socialist" allies in Congress. For the Stewart-ites, the hijackers are the Tea Partiers themselves, along with the enabling hard-right media culture spawned by FOX News.

The signs I saw on the Mall that day said it all. One trio at the rally dressed up in an Alice-in-Wonderland motif, and had a placard that read "I stopped having Tea Parties when I was 17!" There also was "Palin/Voldemort 2012," "I like tea—and you're kind of ruining it," and "Free hugs! (from a militant atheist with a gay agenda)." A major theme on the signage was the idea that taxes aren't the menace to society that Glenn Beck claims. Examples included: "Raise my taxes (please)," "I have no problem paying taxes because I'm an adult, and that's part of the deal," and "Who needs health care—just say 'no' to illness!" Another read: "CUT SPENDING NOW! BUT DON'T YOU DARE TOUCH MY: Social security, Medicare, Medicaid, Defense spending, Home ownership interest deduction, Home buyer tax credit, Farm subsidies, Children's health insurance fund, Retirement benefits, Disability benefits, Federal education subsidies, National Institutes of Health, Department of Agriculture, Appalachian Regional Commission, Department of Commerce . . ."

Walking among these people, it was almost hard to believe that they shared the same country with the activists I'd met in Nashville. It wasn't just that they urged their government to support different political priorities. They disagreed on the far more fundamental issue of whether the very concept of government itself is a presumptive force for good or evil.

How did the United States become so profoundly divided on such a basic question?

America's most exalted ideal is liberal individualism—the belief that each person's fate should be limited only by their God-given talents, the breadth of their imagination, and the strength of their character. From the Declaration of Independence, to the Bill of Rights, to the Emancipation Proclamation, to Martin Luther

King's "I have a dream" speech, the notion has continued to sit at the very foundation of America's national self-conception.

It's an inspiring vision. But also an emotionally exhausting one—for it makes every American the master of his own failures.

In every society preceding the American Revolution (and in many non-Western societies, still), a man's life largely was governed by factors beyond his control—by birth order, ancestry, caste, guild, religious edicts, and the feast-or-famine vicissitudes of nature. Every major decision in his life—whom he would marry, where he would live, what profession he would follow—was decided by others: parents, priests, clan patriarchs.

The modern Western mind recoils at such strictures. But it is important to remember that they at least served to confer some measure of dignity upon society's bottom rungs. A low-caste nineteenth-century Indian latrine cleaner or corpse handler may have had every reason to curse his fate as an "untouchable"—but he could not feel *responsible* for his own failure to rise up in society: The rules precluding him from advancing in life were explicitly articulated and enforced by a very real conspiracy of high-caste elites. In America, on the other hand, life's losers have no one to blame but themselves. And so the conceit that they are up against some all-powerful corporate or governmental conspiracy comes as a relief: It removes the stigma of failure, and replaces it with the more psychologically manageable feeling of anger.

America's culture of individualism can drive even the most successful Americans to conspiratorial social fantasy—though for reasons connected more with politics than personal achievement.

On parchment, the United States may be the land of freedom. Yet, as discussed in Chapter 1, the reality of twenty-first-century America is a place where citizens are constrained in virtually every sphere of human activity. A libertarian social contract—a realistic option in the pastoral frontier society of America's formative years—is an anachronism in today's industrialized, high-density consumer society, in which government is expected to regulate trillions of dollars' worth of trade between strangers, protect more than three hundred million people from crime, ensure universal literacy, prevent epidemics, save endangered species, police the airwaves, prop up failing banks, take care of the poor and old, and maintain a continental network of public roads and airports. From the very moment of America's creation, the march of technology and the growing complexity of society have given politicians no choice but to systematically prune the individual freedoms the proud American yeomen of yore took for granted—a process that's put much of life in the hands of government, corporations, and even machines.

Populist conspiracism flourishes in America in part because it helps resolve the cognitive dissonance generated by this gulf between liberalism's theory and practice—between the ideals embedded in America's national myths, and everyday reality. (In this respect, it follows the pattern of the "failed historian" conspiracist type discussed in the next chapter's typology.) But not for the evil machinations of this or that cabal, the fantasy goes, we'd be able to dial back the national time machine to a golden age of frontier libertarianism.

In the economic sphere, populist conspiracism also serves as an outlet when popular frustration boils over in the face of gross wealth inequality, abusive corporate practices, and cataclysmic economic busts—the populist uprising of the 1890s and the most extreme elements of today's Tea Party movement being the most obvious bookends.

Across Europe and other parts of the world, this type of frustration typically is channeled through Marxism and its various revolutionary offshoots. But as Michael Kazin noted in *The Populist Persuasion*, Americans already had their revolution at the act of creation. And so they channel their class antagonism through a reactionary lens. As Kazin writes, "There have, of course, been populisms in the history of other nations . . . But populism in the United States has made the unique claim that the powers that be are transgressing the nation's founding creed, which every permanent resident should honor . . . Radical transformations undertaken in other societies under such banners as socialism, fascism and anti-colonialism are thus impossible in the United States—at once the most idealistic and the most conservative nation on earth."

In broad strokes, American-style populism (especially the left-wing strain that predominated till the late 1940s) shares some attributes of Marxism in the sense that both presume an epic conflict between society's elites and its toiling masses. But while Marxists cast the fight between rigidly defined classes as an eternal, defining aspect of capitalism, populists do not. True to the evangelical spirit, they regard even the worst abuses as a function of a particular *kind* of predatory capitalist (and his political enablers) whose perverting effect upon the economy can be purged through spiritually infused collective action, thereby restoring American capitalism to its original state of grace. Unlike many Europeans, who retain vestiges of a precapitalist class mentality, even the poorest American believes he can become rich—if only Big Government and corrupt corporations get out of the way.

To quote one of my correspondents, Rick Hydrick of Penryn, California: "[Ours] is not the populism of the past, which often looked for socialistic remedies. It is a new populism, looking for its lost, constitutional liberties. Liberalism has resulted in a bloated, desensitized government. Obama's antidote is hyperliberalism. His natural instinct during a recession is to create government jobs, not to move out of the way of people trying to live by their own wits. He is incapable of thinking otherwise, having never tested those waters. Progressive liberalism and constitutional conservatism are antithetical to each other—oil and water. They cannot be mixed, though the majority of people in this country struggle in vain to do so, blinded by a basic lack of understanding of these political philosophies, severely handicapped by decades of neglect. They are awakening to the atrophying and unsustainable effects of progressive liberalism, wherein they allowed themselves to be duped by the counterfeits of liberty and freedom—social justice and entitlements."

Perhaps the purest example of this brand of populism to be found on the modern American stage is FOX News host Glenn Beck. In the summer of 2010, Beck published a conspiracist novel, *The Overton Window*, in which an evil cabal of government officials, Wall Street tycoons, and multinational corporations seek to sow the seeds of one-world corporate tyranny by staging a false-flag nuclear attack in Las Vegas. In a telling speech, one of the novel's heroines tells an assembled crowd that their mission is to "restore what's been forgotten [in America]. Restore. Not adapt, not transform . . . restore.

"Don't be fooled," she goes on. "'Transformation' is simply a nice way of saying that you don't like something! If you live in an old house that you adore, do you talk about 'restoring' that home or 'transforming' it into a modern-day McMansion? . . . I don't know about you, but I happen to believe that the America our Founders created is still worth preserving."

American populism is not, strictly speaking, a utopian creed, like Marxism or fascism: It does not imagine society being driven toward some purified paradise. It acknowledges that capitalism produces winners and losers, and merely demands something resembling a fair playing field. But it does share with utopian ideologies and religious faiths the idea of returning society to some original state of grace—the sparsely populated, lightly taxed, barely regulated nation of self-reliant farmers, prospectors, craftsmen, and rural yeomen that existed in the decades following independence. In its Tea Party manifestation, it also urges rigid fidelity to a foundational text—the U.S. Constitution—that is imagined to provide ancient answers to our modern problems.

Some conservative Christian activists even blur the line between the Constitution and the Bible by claiming that the latter inspired the former—this being the thesis of a 1981 book, *The 5,000 Year Leap*, which Glenn Beck, among others, have credited with forming their political philosophy. In this telling, the Founding Fathers are transformed into something resembling religious saints, and policy questions are settled by speculating about what view those men would have taken. Following her interviews with Tea Party supporters, Harvard historian Jill Lepore channeled their outlook this way: "That the Constitution speaks to us the way Jesus speaks to us in the Gospels. That it comes alive when we read it today. That it is our form of scripture. And that all the intervening years between the drafting of the U.S. Constitution in 1787 and the present don't matter. That those years represent a corruption from a state of purity . . . It's a particular form of Protestantism and a kind of understanding of the Bible as literal truth that has a really strong hold on America and in American religious culture."

The idea that an eighteenth-century-style social contract can cure America of its twentieth-century ills is attractive in the way that all romantic political ideologies seem attractive in turbulent times. But as several generations of conservative populists can attest, the romance always ends in heartbreak: Once elected, every modern politician, no matter how ostensibly conservative, eventually will have to hang up his tricorner hat, sit down at his desk, and confront the same modern-world realities that greeted his predecessor. Ronald Reagan is the greatest hero in the history of American conservatism. But even he couldn't find a way to eliminate a single major spending program during his presidency. George W. Bush, denounced by liberals as a heartless "neocon" during his two terms in office, actually *added* a major spending program—the Medicare drug benefit.

Such hypocrisy is old news among American political pollsters. As far back as 1964, two scholars—Lloyd Free and Hadley Cantril—used Gallup Poll data to cross-index American attitudes toward government programs and respondents' professed ideological beliefs. What they found was that overlapping majorities of Americans expressed support both for small government in principle, *and* big-government programs in practice—a paradox

Cantril identified in an influential book, *Political Beliefs of Americans*, as nothing less than "mildly schizoid." The same phenomenon manifests itself today among conservatives who make radical claims about the need to scale back the size of government, but also express satisfaction with classic welfare-state programs such as Medicare and Social Security. In late 2010, a poll conducted by the *Washington Post*, the Henry J. Kaiser Family Foundation, and Harvard University revealed that a majority of Americans who say they want more-limited government also believe that Medicare and Social Security are "very important." Likewise, more than half of self-declared Tea Party supporters said the government should maintain or increase its involvement in poverty eradication.

Since the New Deal era, America has been ravaged by a noisy on-and-off culture war, waged, in part, between those who are at peace with the need for bigger government, and those who are not. The "mildly schizoid" quality of American political life means that this culture war is fought not only between two camps of political partisans, but often within Americans' own dissonance-wracked minds.

This explains why the war is not only shrill, but endless: Since most American conservatives would never actually accept the much smaller government they claim as their goal, their war demands will never be met—even when their legislative armies conquer Washington.

So, instead, populist conservatives send waves of culture warriors into an unending series of symbolic proxy battles—"death panels," liberal media bias, border fences, evolution, gay marriage, don't ask/don't tell—that allow them to express their "schizoid" frustration through angry rhetoric, partisan attacks, and sometimes outright conspiracism, all without much changing the size of government, or preventing it from performing the functions on which we have come to depend.

This aspect of the American intellectual landscape has pathologized political debate—turning every discussion about legitimate policy areas into a screaming match about which of the Founding Fathers are being made to spin in their graves, and by whom. Yet it is also an aspect that most Americans seem to take utterly for granted, not realizing how strange it all seems to an outsider.

Perhaps that is why the book you are reading was written by a Canadian.

| **PART II** |

Meet the Truthers

Why They Believe: A Psychological Field Guide to Conspiracists

For the truth is that life on the face of it is a chaos in which one finds oneself lost. The individual suspects as much, but is terrified to encounter this frightening reality face to face, and so attempts to conceal it by drawing a curtain of fantasy over it, behind which he can make believe that everything is clear.

—*Jose Ortega y Gasset*

There are three infallible signs of the crank—that oddball, goofball sort of person who mutters, as he walks along, about how he's grasped the key to everything. The first is that he has a theory about the Jews. The second is that he has a theory about money. And the third is that he has a theory about Shakespeare.

—*Joseph Bottum*

The first four chapters of this book focused largely on conspiracism as a historical phenomenon. Conspiracy theories, I've shown, are more likely to blossom when great tragedies or national traumas—the French Revolution, World War I, the assassination of JFK, 9/11, the 2008 financial crisis—rupture a society's intellectual foundations, and shatter citizens' faith in traditional authority figures. I have also described the three major influences on American conspiracism—apocalyptic religiosity, faith in small government, and the rapid onset of invasive technology; and described the structure of most popular conspiracy theories by reference to the *Protocols of the Elders of Zion*.

But this big-picture approach tells us little about what motivates flesh-and-blood individuals to join conspiracist movements. Even in an intellectually traumatized society such as post-9/11 America, most people manage to resist the lure of conspiracism. This chapter will profile the characteristics of those who don't.

Surprisingly little research has been done on the psychology of conspiracy theorists. The few, scattered academic papers there are on the subject tend to be free-form essays by intellectual dabblers in the fields of philosophy, psychology, and political science. Even the few social-sciences researchers who've systematically surveyed the views of conspiracy theorists generally have been unable to identify any universal causative factors: Among survey respondents, the only characteristic that strongly correlates with belief in any particular conspiracy theory is a belief in *other* conspiracy theories.

That's because—as I've learned from my interviews—conspiracists tend to come to their beliefs for many different reasons. On a personal level, conspiracism is not so much a psychological ailment in and of itself as it is a symptom of a mind in flight from reality. That flight can be induced by any number of causes—including radical nationalism, tribalistic hatred, midlife ennui, narcissism, profound psychic trauma, spiritual longing, or even experimental drug use.

This chapter will offer readers a typology of the different varieties of conspiracist, along with sketches of a few typical specimens. In the next chapter, I will explain how and why their systems of belief often coalesce into something resembling a religious faith.

A wide range of conspiracy theories are represented in this material—from 9/11 Trutherism to ultraradical feminism to antivaccine activism. Some of the profiled theories are full-fledged conspiracist narratives in the tradition of the *Protocols*. Others are more limited in scope. But these details are of secondary importance: The organizing principle in this chapter is not the type of conspiracy theory being embraced, but rather the underlying psychological function that conspiracism performs for the affected individual.

The Midlife Crisis Case

Richard Gage: Truther Extraordinaire

After spending months taking in Truthers' messianic fervor on the Internet in 2008, my first visits to their real-world conferences proved to be something of a let-down. Truth movement propaganda comes off as slick and impressive when it's broadcast as web video, wherein arcane talking points can be packaged with glossy multimedia effects, ominous narration, and a catchy soundtrack. But once Truthers deploy to a real-world community center or academic lecture hall, the varnish of professionalism washes away, and the underlying crank conspiracism rises to the surface.

A typical 9/11 Truth event features about a half-dozen speakers. A local organizer or two will urge audience members to raise awareness in the community. Then a liberal arts professor or alternative journalist will lecture the audience about American state terrorism and neoimperialism. This might be followed by a speaker who focuses on some loosely related niche subject or other—media bias, Islamophobia, or Israel.

These speakers will attract polite applause. But they're just warming up the crowd for the main attraction: the celebrity mega-Truther who's been flown in to headline. These are the high priests of the 9/11 Truth movement—men (they're almost always men) who've dedicated their lives to preaching the gospel at congregations across North America.

Unlike the warm-up acts, the headliner recites his speech entirely from memory. He's given this talk dozens—perhaps hundreds—of times. The presentation is full of detailed references to airplane trajectories and chemical analyses. From experience, the headliner knows what buttons to push, what topics to emphasize and avoid, when to pause for laugh lines. When the time comes for Q&A, the headliner smoothly parries questions offered up by doubters in the audience (if any remain). As the event ends, fans cluster around him to continue the discussion. On their way out, they stop to buy a DVD copy of his lecture so they can share the Truth with friends and family.

Of all the Truther headliners I've seen, the very best is Richard Gage, a balding, mild-mannered, middle-aged architect who heads up a California-based group called Architects & Engineers for 9/11 Truth. I've heard Gage speak three times in three different cities. At each event, the response was rapturous. At a 2009 lecture in Montreal, his crowd sat mesmerized as he spoke for three straight hours—on a night when the Montreal Canadiens were contesting a playoff game, no less. At a speech in New York City a few months later, the audience burst into a spontaneous chant of "Ri-*chard*! Ri-*chard*!" Blushing and grinning like an earnest, overgrown schoolboy, Gage blurted out: "Your enthusiasm knocks my socks off!"

Truthers often are prone to rambling: Your average amateur might take the podium with an overflowing sheaf of Internet printouts, and cycle disjointedly through a half dozen sub-topics. Not Gage. His singular focus—laboriously examined in a six-hundred-slide PowerPoint presentation he trots out at every opportunity—is the precise sequence of events leading to the collapse of the World Trade Center buildings. Avoiding speculation on the Pentagon attacks and the machinations of the Bush White House is critical to the mission of Architects & Engineers for 9/11 Truth, he says. "We're building and technical professionals," Gage tells his audiences. "We're not conspiracy theorists."

Thanks to his bookish style and suit-and-tie wardrobe, Gage has become a unique property among Truthers: a quasi-respectable media pundit. In recent years, he's been featured in mainstream documentaries, and spoken at the Commonwealth Club. Some local television stations have broadcast the film version of his slideshow *Blueprint for Truth*. Colorado Public Television (KBDI-TV/12) even featured it during a 2009 fundraising drive.

Gage inevitably elicits emotional gasps and shouts with his slideshow. In Montreal, a couple sitting behind me seemed particularly moved. "How can those murderers sleep at night after what they've done?" one exclaimed. (She wasn't talking about al-Qaeda.) Even my own guest on that evening, a conservative-minded sixty-five-year-old woman, seemed transfixed, falling silent at points where I expected she'd be chortling and rolling her eyes.

In one particularly effective segment during his stump presentation, Gage puts up shots of the localized fires that broke out in the lower floors of WTC Building 7 hours before it collapsed. Seconds later, he shows footage of Beijing's Mandarin Oriental hotel—which suffered an epic top-to-bottom conflagration in 2009, yet remained standing. It's a cinematic juxtaposition that plays to the Truthers' strongest card: Even many architects and structural engineers who've never heard of Richard Gage will concede that the collapse of WTC 7, a fairly typical 1980s-era structure located about a football field away from WTC 1, was unusual.

Before beginning his presentation in Montreal, Gage had polled the crowd on their views. Five people, including me and my guest, said they believed the "official theory" of 9/11. Ten others said they were "unsure." Everyone else—about two hundred people—said they believed the WTC came down through "controlled demolition." Once Gage had finished, he conducted a second poll. This time, when he asked how many people supported the "official theory," mine was the only hand raised. Shocked, I cast a glance at the friend sitting beside me.

After three hours in a room with Richard Gage, she'd changed her vote to "not sure."

A few months later, when I sat down with Gage at a Starbucks in the upscale bedroom community of Lafayette, California, I wasn't sure what to expect. Gage is affable and disarming when surrounded by admirers. But like many cultish true believers, he can become emotionally erratic when his views are probed. At one point during our preceding email exchange, he'd interpreted one of my questions as an "indirect threat" on his life—and furiously threatened to cancel our interview.

But Gage arrived in a calm, friendly mood. After buying himself a soy latte, he sat with me on a bench outside the café for two hours, patiently describing his transformation from workaday commercial architect to 9/11 Truth evangelist.

It was in March 2006 that his life changed, Gage tells me. He was in his car just after lunch, fighting traffic en route to a construction meeting. Bored, he flipped on KPFA 94.1 FM, a listener-supported station out of Berkeley—"to hear what the communists were talking about."

Up to that point in life, Gage recalls, he'd been just your average workaday architect, with a wife, child, and a strong Republican voting record. "I believed strongly in America," he tells me. "I believed everything was okay. When Colin Powell was giving his Iraq evidence at the United Nations [in March 2003], I was cheering him on. I wanted us to go to war in Iraq. I wanted to find the WMD. I was completely on board. I was the poster child for George W. Bush's foreign policy."

But all that would change.

The voice he heard on KPFA's airwaves belonged to David Ray Griffin, a retired Claremont School of Theology professor who's since become a full-time 9/11 Truth activist. "Griffin was logical and methodical—almost grandfatherly," Gage remembers. "He was talking about the 118 [World Trade Center] first-responders—information that had just come out in 2005—who said they'd heard explosions and flashes of light, beams dripping with molten metal, all amid the collapse of 80,000 tons of structural steel. It hit me like a two-by-four. How come I'd never *heard* of any of this? I was shocked. I had to pull my car to the side of the road to absorb it all. I knew I'd be late for the meeting. But I didn't care."

Within days, Gage was prosletyzing the Truth to everyone who would listen—his family, his friends, even his architectural colleagues at the Walnut Creek firm of Akol & Yoshii. He even began setting up booths at American Institute of Architects meetings, where he'd play video footage of the World Trade Center buildings coming down, and invite skeptical onlookers to sign his AE-911Truth petition, which demands a "truly independent investigation" of the 9/11 attacks. Catcalls and mockery were common, Gage remembers—but he didn't care.

In 2007, Gage cut back on his day job—designing the Summerlin Center Mall in Las Vegas—so that he could spend more time on his activism. Then, in 2008, the project went bankrupt amid the nosediving real estate market, and Gage suddenly was unemployed. Looking back, he says, it was a blessing in disguise: "Making money for large corporations like General Growth was a lot less fulfilling than bringing the truth to people." Since then, he's become a full-time Truther, just like Griffin, delivering 9/11 sermons at events across North America.

Gage will admit that he's paid a price. Friends who failed to embrace his missionary zeal have drifted away. So has his wife, who he said had difficulty accepting his "dark" vision. Gage now lives by himself in a home office near Berkeley, paying his bills with the modest amounts he earns through donations.

Yet when Gage discusses all this, he seems curiously upbeat—almost euphoric—like a Benedictine monk who's happily renounced the material encumbrances of secular life. Although he doesn't talk much about his world before 9/11 Truth, he clearly remembers it as empty and unsatisfying.

"I would rather die speaking the truth than live in a police state, which is what 9/11 set the groundwork for," he tells me in a final, slightly manic flourish. "I can't have my son—or grandchildren—ask me, 'What did you do to stop it?'—and I say, 'I tried to talk to some architects but they wouldn't listen.'

"I've never been happier. I feel blessed, in fact. This is my destiny, my mission. I've lost my career. I've lost my marriage. I've lost my house. But I'm working with patriots, spreading the truth about what's happened to their country. What more could I ask?"

David Solway: *Born-Again Culture Warrior*

It was September 12, 2001, by the time David Solway learned that planes had hit the World Trade Center and Pentagon. At the time, the award-winning Canadian writer, then sixty years old, was on the tiny, picturesque Greek island of Tilos (population 350), finishing a book of poems, and watching the local birds circle over the island's spectacular seascapes.

The next day, he walked into one of the island's portside *kafeneia* for breakfast, and looked up at footage of the attacks on the café's flickering television set. In an instant, he became a different man: "I spent the rest of the day wandering aimlessly about, sensing that the world had changed irrevocably and that there were no more enclaves of safety and recreation, no more 'Greek islands' where one could enjoy time out of time," he later recollected. "I submitted myself, perhaps for the first time in my life, to a kind of Cartesian interrogation, a relentless scrutiny of the values and beliefs I accepted as gospel."

Until that point in this life, Solway's political attitudes had hewn faithfully to the left-wing cant expected of a man who makes his living with poetry. He was anti-American, anti-Israeli, antiglobalization. He read Chomsky with approval, railed against George W. Bush, expressed solidarity with the Palestinians, smoked pot, went to demonstrations, lived off government grants. As a young man, he'd even spent time at Berkeley with Mario Savio during the Free Speech Movement.

As the weeks passed, and the images of the World Trade Center flitted again and again through Solway's brain, he became convinced that his leftist past had somehow made him complicit in what happened on Sept. 11. He felt ashamed, guilty, useless—overpowering feelings that, he says, "jarred me to the very foundations."

After returning to Canada, Solway quit his job as a college teacher, put aside his poetry, and began work on manifestos against terrorism. His mortgage payments began to pile up. Lifelong literary friends began to drift away, estranged by the monomania of the erstwhile leftist. But Solway didn't care. "I wouldn't accept apostasy—even from a wife," he told me as his wife silently slipped back and forth between the kitchen and living room, serving us coffee. "I would not accept her living a lie, refusing to uncover the truth. If you can't do that, you're not my friend."

Inevitably, Solway's search for the truth led him to the Internet. From the right-wing sites he surfed, and his own extensive study of Islamic theology, Solway became convinced that the enemy facing Western civilization wasn't just al-Qaeda, but Islam itself. In our interview, he described the Koran as a "war manual," and the Prophet Mohammed as a "master of hatred."

What's worse, the Islamists have a stooge on the inside—none other than the president of the United States. Over the last several years, Solway tells me, he's been collecting a whole "closetful" of information about Barack Obama, all of it pointing to "world cataclysm."

"I fear Obama more than I fear Mahmoud Ahmadinejad," he says. "Obama is the one who's going to let Iran go nuclear. It's the same instinct that causes him to bow down to the Saudis, and shake hands with Hugo Chavez. His thinking is Far Left—very anti-Israeli. You can't listen to Jeremiah Wright for twenty years and not be an anti-Semite. And do we even know where he was born? He hasn't even released his school transcripts from Occidental College [in California]. Until proven otherwise, I believe the reason he won't release those transcripts is because they're marked with the fact that he's a foreign student.

"I still haven't seen a facsimile of his original birth certificate despite diligent searching for almost two years now and, in point of fact, no one else has," he tells me. "Again, there is only hearsay about its existence—from a Hawaiian official, Robert Gibbs, and Obama himself, and a short form certificate of live birth with no specific information, which actually doesn't count. Draw your own conclusions . . . We know next to nothing about this man's inscrutable past, his academic records are under seal, his financial statements from his time as a senator are lacking, and even his

Columbia thesis has gone missing . . . Deep down, we all know something's terribly wrong, but we're too afraid to risk ridicule and animadversion, or to be lumped in with conspiracy mongers and denounced as fruitcakes, so we steer our attention to other problems and issues involving this most disastrous of presidents, which is fine since there are so many of them. Myself, I don't know for sure whether Obama is a 'natural born American citizen' or not, but I have my strong suspicions, which have yet to be allayed. And I'm not afraid to write about or air my doubts."

These days, Solway spends his time in front of a computer, exchanging information about Obama with Birthers, and writing more essays about the Islamist threat. Once a poet whose name was known only to a few thousand literati, his articles now get tens of thousands of hits on websites such as FrontPage Magazine and Pajamas Media. While much of what he writes consists of stock anti-Islamist polemics, he also produces genuinely insightful flourishes that reveal his deep knowledge of literary culture, such as this gem from a FrontPage article, explaining why the Left is drawn to make common cause with Islamists: "The eloquent Imam, the jihadist [and] even the Palestinian gunman are only the latest incarnation of the [West's] anthropological romance with the 'pure primitive' who redeems us from our own evolved complexities and etiolated belief-systems. The new aborigine, as the contemporary embodiment of the Noble Savage invented by European exploration, thus acts as the counterfoil to our own repressed and guilt-ridden civilization. The enemy who commands our sympathies becomes the heroicizing projection of our own bad conscience. Because he possesses what we lack and desire, we are willing to live in a state of contradiction and hasten to pardon his atrocities. Thus feminists will wink at the monstrous usage of infibrilation."

As Solway ticks off the many corners of the world from which he gets fan mail, his tone is exhilarated, triumphant. His only regret, he tells me, is that he wasted all those years before waking up to the truth: "I've been a poet all my life. My first poem was published at the age of twelve. It's all I ever wanted to be. But that's changed. As Auden said, 'Poetry makes nothing happen.'"

On the spectrum of geopolitics, Truther Richard Gage and quasi-Birther David Solway lie at opposite ends. The former views the war on terrorism as a fraud. The latter views it as the defining struggle of our time. But in their psychology, the two activists appear to have been set down the road of radical politics by the same psychological impulse.

To understand these two men is to understand the strangely sudden, strangely radicalizing effects that middle age can impose upon the male psyche. This is a time when life can lose its luster. The children grow up, the hair falls out, careers plateau, physical powers ebb. Amidst the resulting ennui, the prospect of overturning the familiar patterns of life and starting over from scratch seems tempting. Some men do this by joining an ashram, moving to Tuscany, or reuniting with childhood sweethearts. Gage and Solway have done it through conspiracism. In their new role as radical truth-seekers, they have an opportunity to reinvent themselves in front of a new audience of strangers who have little knowledge of their past lives, and who evaluate them entirely on the basis of their newly created identity.

Like all forms of midlife crisis, this sudden lurch into conspiracism offers middle-aged men a sense of revitalization and adventure. In some ways, in fact, it offers an even more complete escape than the proverbial mistress and sports car. For a middle-aged man who's grown tired of life's familiar patterns, conspiracism provides more than just fresh surroundings: It offers an entirely new reality.

The Failed Historian

Many things that do amount to tampering with the effects of logic do not in our field necessarily present themselves as dishonesty to the man who practices such tampering. He may be so fundamentally convinced of the truths of what he is standing for that he would rather die than give new weight to contradicting facts or pieces of analysis. The first thing a man will do for his ideals is lie.

—History of Economic Analysis, *Joseph A. Schumpeter*

A good starting point for understanding the psychology of conspiracism's "failed historian" is Sigmund Freud. Not his theories, but his actual life: To the great embarrassment of many dedicated Freudians, it turns out that the founder of the psychoanalytic school of psychiatry spent years of his life pursuing the most durable and ambitious literary conspiracy theory of the twentieth century.

In 1898, Danish literary critic Georg Brandes published *William Shakespeare*, a book described as "perhaps the most authoritative work on Shakespeare, not principally intended for an English-speaking audience, which had been published in any country." Like many Shakespeare scholars of the age, Brandes was interested in the connections between Shakespeare's life and fiction. The creation of *Hamlet*, in particular, Brandes argued, grew out of Shakespeare's grief for his own father's passing in 1601.

As contemporary Shakespeare scholar James Shapiro has observed, Freud became fascinated by Brandes' theory at a critical point in his life—his own father had died in 1896—and incorporated its claims into *The Interpretation of Dreams*, in which Freud argued that *Hamlet* "is rooted in the same soil as Oedipus Rex."

"It can, of course, be only the poet's own psychology with which we are confronted in *Hamlet*," Freud concluded. "He was still mourning his loss, and [wrote the play] during a revival, as we may fairly assume, of his own childish feelings in respect of his father."

In chapter 5 of his great work, Freud not only put forward Prince Hamlet as a foundational case study in his Oedpial theory, but wound into it an ambitious explanation for the protagonist's hesitation in killing his uncle: "What is it, then, that inhibits him in accomplishing the task which his father's ghost has laid upon him? Here the explanation offers itself that it is the peculiar nature of this task. Hamlet is able to do anything but take vengeance upon the man who did away with his father and has taken his father's place with his mother—the man who shows him in realization the repressed desires of his own childhood . . . If anyone wishes to call Hamlet an hysterical subject I cannot but admit that this is the deduction to be drawn from my interpretation." Over the next twenty years, the play would become a central part of the psychoanalytic canon.

Then, in 1919, tragedy struck: Brandes repudiated his theory about *Hamlet*, citing the discovery of marginal notes, by one of Shakespeare's contemporaries, showing that the play actually had been written between early 1599 and early 1601—before Shakespeare *père* died in September 1601. In an instant, Freud's elaborate claims about *Hamlet* went up in smoke. More than that, the revelation implicitly cast Oedipal theory itself into doubt: If Freud's elaborate diagnosis of Prince Hamlet were this wildly off the mark, what did that say about the legions of flesh-and-blood patients who'd become convinced by Freud to trace their problems to similar intrafamilial causes?

Unless . . . and this was Freud's unconscious taking the reins— unless Shakespeare's life could somehow be altered in the eyes of history. Could it be that the man who wrote *Hamlet* somehow was other than the son of that Stratford-upon-Avon glover and borough ale taster?

As it happens, Freud seems to have dabbled casually in Shakespearean conspiracism since early days. But in the 1920s and 1930s—right up to his death in 1939—he became fixated on the emerging theory that Shakespeare's plays and poems had been written by Edward de Vere, the 17th Earl of Oxford—a spoiled, hysterical, and violent man who, as Freud later described him, "lost a beloved and admired father while he was still a boy and com-

pletely repudiated his mother, who contracted a new marriage very
soon after her husband's death." What a coincidence.

M any of the writers who've pronounced the Bard of Avon a fraud
("anti-Stratfordians" is how they sometimes refer to themselves) expanded their theories into elaborate political narratives.
Some nineteenth-century anti-Stratfordians, for instance, believed
that the works attributed to Shakespeare were in fact coded manifestos written by a group of closet protorepublicans led by Francis Bacon as a means to undermine Elizabethan tyranny. In the
most ambitious version of this fantasy, it is imagined that Shakespeare's plays actually created the template for the United States
Constitution—and that Bacon's plot against the monarchy, had
it succeeded, might have preempted the need for an American
Revolution. Nevertheless, even the most far-fetched claims about
the origins of Shakespeare's writings do not fall into the classic
Protocols-type conspiracy-theory template outlined in Chapter 2.

Even so, biographer Ernest Jones' reflection that Freud's theories about Shakespeare suggest a wish that "a certain part of reality
could be changed" applies to the many conspiracists who fall into
the category I call "failed historian." For this group, conspiracy
theories are a tool to eliminate the cognitive dissonance that arises
when the course of human events doesn't cooperate with the results
demanded by their ideology.

Often, this type of conspiracism arises on the militant fringes of
nationalist, religious, or identity-politics movements whose membership must explain away their failure to dominate their enemies,
gain power and influence, or fulfill some ordained purpose embedded in their scripture or dogma. Radical Islam—with its obsessive focus on the Jews' role in thwarting Allah's will—supplies an
example. So does Afrocentrism, a pseudohistorical movement that
confers an expanded dignity on troubled African American communities through the conceit that they are heir to a black civilization that once created the guiding forms of Western culture.

(Afrocentrism itself is not a conspiracy theory per se—even though it is often wrapped up with ancillary theories that accuse white historians of conspiring to suppress the Afrocentric truth. But on street corners and disreputable websites, it sometimes can be found side by side with the teachings of Louis Farrakhan and his Nation of Islam, which *are* genuinely anti-Semitic and conspiracist—not to mention bizarre, in that they declare the white race to have been the creation of a mad scientist named Yakub 6,600 years ago. Yet this conspiracist strain in American black nationalism is rarely discussed in polite American society—much as we avert our eyes from the copies of the *Protocols* openly on display at black bookstores. Thanks to lingering guilt regarding America's appalling treatment of blacks until relatively recently in the country's history, there is an implicit assumption among whites that such conspiracism is more understandable, and perhaps even less reprehensible, than other varieties.)

Even in the case of conspiracists whose theories seemingly have little to do with any particular national or religious cause, I will discover during my interviews that their initial radicalization came through a specific geopolitical issue connected with their ethnic identity. This includes Serbian-Canadian conspiracist Lubo Zizakovic, the former football player profiled in the first chapter. While he now talks about the Bilderbergers and 9/11, his initial radicalization came during the Balkan conflicts of the 1990s, when the United States and its NATO allies took sides against the Serbs:

The demonization of the Serb people started with falsified images of a Serb-run Bosnian refugee camp that appeared on the front page of every paper in the world and on every television station as a Serb-run concentration death camp. In August 1992, millions of people were shocked to see photographs of a supposed Bosnian Serb "death camp." Bush Sr, Clinton, and Blair used these images as justification for their involvement against the Serbs in Bosnia . . . The photos were produced by ITN, the

British TV news giant, from footage shot by an ITN film crew which spent a long day in Bosnia. The film was shot in a refugee center in the town of Trnopolje. Most of the photographs featured a tall, emaciated man with a deformed chest, stripped to the waist, apparently imprisoned behind barbed wire. Do you remember those pictures? They were a hoax. They were the start of the 'demonization' of the Serb people . . . [In 1999] came the so-called 'Racak Massacre.' Clinton and NATO used this staged event as [an] excuse to bomb Serbia into the stone age . . . Racak was a hoax, but then again, so were the Serb death camps and everything else that came from NATO press briefings . . . it made no sense that nineteen of the world's most powerful countries would gang up against such a small nation and bomb it for 78 days . . . Does the west care more for Kosovo Albanians that for Palestinians? Hardly. Let's not start on what is happening in Africa as well. The war on Serbia was not about Kosovo Albanians, but geopolitical goals. The pillaging of the resources of the former Yugoslavia was continuing. Insuring a Caspian and Black Sea pipeline through Yugoslavia to the Adriatic Sea and robbing Yugoslavia of its natural resources for the benefit of large corporations seems to always be the overriding goal . . . My rage grew fierce as I heard friends and coworkers regurgitate NATO propaganda. Over 100,000 dead and millions displaced by the Serbs . . . I [now] have a deep distrust when it comes to the [mainstream media's] reporting of international events.

The natural psychological alliance between conspiracism and radical identity politics is a phenomenon that George Orwell described in his landmark 1945 essay, "Notes on Nationalism." While Orwell generally did not use the term "conspiracy theory" to describe this marriage, he did directly hit upon the manner by which ardent nationalists—a term he defined loosely to encompass political fanatics and religious bigots of every description—inevitably lapse into fantasy when history does not unfold as their parochial visions demand:

> Every nationalist is haunted by the belief that the past can be altered. He spends part of his time in a fantasy world in which things happen as they should—in which, for example, the Spanish Armada was a success or the Russian Revolution was crushed in 1918—and he will transfer fragments of this world to the history books whenever possible . . . Events which it is felt ought not to have happened are left unmentioned and ultimately denied. In 1927 Chiang Kai Shek boiled hundreds of Communists alive, and yet within 10 years he had become one of the heroes of the Left. The re-alignment of world politics had brought him into the anti-Fascist camp, and so it was felt that the boiling of the Communists 'didn't count,' or perhaps had not happened . . . When one considers the elaborate forgeries that have been committed in order to show that Trotsky did not play a valuable part in the Russian civil war, it is difficult to feel that the people responsible are merely lying. More probably, they feel that their own version was what happened in the sight of God, and that one is justified in rearranging the records accordingly . . . Some nationalists are not far from schizophrenia, living quite happily amid dreams of power and conquest which have no connection with the physical world.

Orwell's analysis helps explain why conspiracism always finds its way into the mythology of totalitarian movements, such as in North Korea or Iran, whose bellicosity and brutal domestic policies can be justified only by recourse to the claim that they are guiding the nation on some infallible historical project. When history defeats this claim of infallibility, as it always does, every despot requires some version of the Ministry of Truth—so it can blame society's problems on the schemes of an invented army of infidels and counterrevolutionaries.

In *Nineteen Eighty-Four,* Winston Smith goes about this intellectual project self-consciously as part of his professional duties as a clerk in the Ministry of Truth's Records Department. But for the subjects of real-life totalitarian regimes, the process often arises subconsciously, as a crutch to make life endurable. "Among the Russian masses there was . . . a certain level of self-hypnosis about their Great Helmsman," journalist Robert Fulford wrote in a column summarizing Orlando Figes' 2007 book *The Whisperers: Private Life in Stalin's Russia.* "Figes introduces us to a man who grew up in a family of Soviet diplomats and believed all the Stalinist rhetoric about the necessity of imprisoning those who were 'enemies of the people'—even though his father, his older sister, six of his uncles and an aunt were all arrested in the purges of the 1930s. But in 1944, when his mother was jailed, he began to question his faith. He decided that the secret police must have been penetrated by the 'enemies of the people.'"

The psychological reflex that Orwell describes applies equally to sixties-era American leftists, who, as already noted, refused to believe that one of their own killed JFK; Japanese historians who have averted their eyes to the rape of Nanking (rightly described by Iris Chang as "the forgotten holocaust of World War II"); and Serbs—such as former Bosnian Serb leader Radovan Karadzic—who airily declare the Srebrenica massacre to be "a myth." Holocaust deniers are invariably failed historians. As Michael Shermer and Alex Grobman concluded in their authoritative 2000 book *Denying History: Who Says The Holocaust Never Happened And Why Do They Say It?,* these conspiracy theorists "find empowerment through the rehabilitation of those they admire and the denigration of those they perceive to be squelching their admiration. Many deniers seem to like the idea of a rigid, controlled, and powerful state. Some are fascinated with Nazism as a social/political organization and are impressed with the economic gains Germany made in the 1930s . . . The history of the Holocaust is a black eye for Nazism. Deny the veracity of the Holocaust, and Nazism begins to lose this stigma."

Over the last decade, many Muslims followed this same pattern in regard to the 9/11 terrorist attacks. Minnesota-based Muslim convert Kevin Barrett, for instance, tells his Truther audiences that Osama bin Laden could never have been behind 9/11 because the al-Qaeda leader embodies his religion's dedication to "peace and truth." As described in Chapter 9, Barrett, like many other Muslim conspiracy theorists, identifies Jews and Zionists as the true perpetrators of the 9/11 plot. In this way, their conspiracy theory does double duty for psychological purposes: It absolves Islam of a terrible crime, while furthering the preferred narrative of murderous Israeli aggression. For related psycho-political reasons, many Muslims (including Iranian president Mahmoud Ahmadinejad) also have joined the ranks of Holocaust deniers: Since the international movement to create a Jewish state gained strength and urgency following Hitler's extermination of six million Jews, it is imagined by militant anti-Semites that Israel's raison-d'être can somehow be undone by rewriting history to Hitler's advantage.

Many Westerners with no positive ethnic or religious attachments also fall into the failed historian category through their embrace of strident anti-Americanism. (As Orwell wrote in his essay, the nationalistic pathology "may work in a merely negative sense, against something or other and without the need for any positive object of loyalty.") According to this brand of thinking, which has come to dominate large swathes of the Western intelligentsia over the last half-century, the great engine of evil in the world is American hegemony—and so every epic tragedy the world suffers must somehow be laid at Washington's doorstep.

In this category, one finds antiwar and antinuclear activists of Cold War vintage, with political views steeped in the anti-American lore surrounding Hiroshima and Nagasaki, Vietnam, and the covert wars of Latin America. Their ideological heroes are Noam Chomsky and Howard Zinn, whose fixation on American "state terrorism" encourages the notion that Washington is capable of boundless evil.

English professors, cultural-studies specialists, and modern-languages types are well represented in this conspiracist niche. So, too, are experts in "globalization studies"—such as Anthony J. Hall of the University of Lethbridge in Alberta, one of Canada's most aggressive Truthers. One also tends to find a surprising number of poets (perhaps because their day jobs already require them to weave a self-invented reality from their own stream of consciousness). Rhyming conspiracists include British Columbia–based Truther Frank Moher, New York City's Jerry Mazza (who delivers poetry readings at 9/11 anniversary events in New York City), and black nationalist Amiri Baraka (born LeRoi Jones), whose poem *Somebody Blew Up America* got him ejected from his job as New Jersey's poet laureate:

> Who the Devil on the real side
> Who got rich from Armenian genocide . . .
> Who own the oil
> Who want more oil
> Who told you what you think that later you find out a lie . . .
> Who knew the bomb was gonna blow
> Who know why the terrorists
> Learned to fly in Florida, San Diego . . .
> Who killed Malcolm, Kennedy & his Brother
> Who killed Dr King, Who would want such a thing?
> Are they linked to the murder of Lincoln? . . .
> Who set the Reichstag Fire
> Who knew the World Trade Center was gonna get bombed
> Who told 4,000 Israeli workers at the Twin Towers
> To stay home that day
> Why did Sharon stay away?
> Who, Who, Who

Unfortunately, Baraka is hardly an outlier within the field of black identity politics, which (for understandable historical reasons) comprises America's most consistently fertile breeding ground for failed-historian conspiracism. Nation of Islam leader Louis Farrakhan, for instance, has suggested that the destruction of New Orleans' levee system in the aftermath of Hurricane Katrina was part of a plot to kill the city's black population; and delivers speeches in which he blames the world's problems on the "Jew Rothschild" ("Four things were set up in the year 1913: First, the Federal Reserve Bank, the IRS, the FBI, and the Anti-Defamation League of B'nai Brith. All were set up in the same year. Is that a coincidence, or is there a tie-in?")

Following the financial crisis of late 2008, the failed historian began showing up in the form of shell-shocked free-market purists (often in Tea Party garb), who could not accept that the greatest recession of our time had been sparked by the recklessness of homeowners, overleveraged banks, greedy mortgage brokers, and other private actors. As discussed in the previous chapter, they have conquered their cognitive dissonance with the theory that the crisis actually was part of a secret plot hatched by Barack Obama and other liberals to destroy capitalism. This theory has become so common in Tea Party circles that it now goes by a commonly recognized shorthand—the "Cloward-Piven Strategy," named after two 1960s-era left-wing Columbia University sociologists. (As with many of the conspiracy theories I have described in this book, there was a real grain of truth in this one: In their now-infamous 1966 article in *The Nation*, Richard Cloward and Frances Fox Piven truly did urge Americans to apply for welfare en masse so as to "produce bureaucratic disruption in welfare agencies and fiscal disruption in local and state governments"—with the ultimate goal being "to wipe out poverty by establishing a guaranteed annual income." This tactic was said to be necessary because "even activists seem reluctant to call for national programs to eliminate poverty by the outright redistribution of income.")

"The undeniable and shocking truth is that Barack Obama (perhaps purposefully, perhaps unknowingly) is actually following a carefully laid-out strategy for destroying the United States of America that was initially proposed and published by two social-ist faculty members at Columbia University (an institution that Barack Obama attended from 1981–83)," declared Joseph Farah's WorldNetDaily website in a September 2010 email blast. "Accord-ing to the strategy, the American way of life, as we know it, must be destroyed and discredited because the American people will not accept statism until the present system is destroyed and discred-ited. And how does one go about destroying and discrediting the system? If you need an example, look no further than the so-called economic stimulus schemes that the Obama Administration and Congress have implemented."

The Damaged Survivor

On April 2, 2008, World Autism Awareness Day, Larry King de-voted his nightly CNN program to "Jenny McCarthy's Autism Fight." Anyone who'd followed the debate over the devastating neurological condition instantly knew what to expect from Mc-Carthy that night: Since 2007, the former *Playboy* model had be-come the world's most influential spout of autism misinformation.

Sure enough, a few minutes into the broadcast, McCarthy be-gan telling King about the miraculous autism discoveries she had made on alternative health websites, which, she claimed, had al-lowed her own son to "recover" from the incurable condition. She also launched into familiar, discredited theories linking autism to vaccines:

> McCARTHY: "Parent after parent after parent says I vac-
> cinated my baby, they got a fever and then they stopped
> speaking and then became autistic."
> KING: "Is your link scientific or statistical?"
> McCARTHY: "Well, I believe that parents' anecdotal in-

formation is science-based information. And when the entire world is screaming the same thing—doctor, I came home. He had a fever. He stopped speaking and then he became autistic. I can't—I can see if it was just one parent saying this. But when so many—and I speak to thousands of moms every weekend and they're all standing up and saying the same thing. It's time to start listening to that. That is science-based information. Parents' [anecdotes] is science-based information."

A whole book could be written about the conspiracy theories that traffic on "alternative medicine" websites. These include the idea (as already discussed) that water fluoridation is a plot to destroy our minds; that the contrails emitted by passenger aircraft contain exotic chemicals—"chemtrails"—designed to alter human behavior; that wi-fi computer signals are eroding our children's brains; and that AIDS and other serious diseases were designed by the U.S. military for the purpose of culling the world's population. But of all of these, the most durable and widespread is the notion that vaccines cause autism. This is in large part thanks to the advocacy of celebrity laypersons such as McCarthy and their media enablers at *The Oprah Show* and, until recently, *Larry King Live*. Since 1998, when the theory was first put forward in a (since debunked) study published in *The Lancet* medical journal, millions of parents across the Western world have avoided vaccinating their children, leaving them exposed to deadly, and entirely preventable, diseases such as measles, pertussis, and Hib influenza. A disproportionate number of the parents opting out of vaccinations are from wealthy areas of the country, such as Marin County in California, where McCarthy's brand of quackery has gained a foothold among web-surfing soccer moms.

Vaccines typically are administered to small children in the first two years of life, at around the same time that the first behavioral symptoms of autism manifest themselves. Many doctors believe autism is a genetic disorder programmed into a child's brain before birth. But parents cannot *see* their child's genes. What they can see is the steel needle that penetrates their then-apparently-perfect bundle of joy, injecting a mysterious foreign substance that (according to strangers wearing white lab coats), prevents an as-yet hypothetical medical condition. When this experience is closely followed by a devastating diagnosis, a link is forged between the two experiences in the minds of many parents—a link that, as many will confess quite candidly, can never be shaken by science. "I know what happened to my son after he got his [measles, mumps and rubella] shot," the mother of an autistic child told science writer Arthur Allen. "I have no doubt. There's no way they'll convince me that all these kids were not damaged by vaccines."

The myth that vaccines cause autism permits emotionally vulnerable parents to blame politically accountable, human evildoers—the big pharmaceutical companies, and their apologists at the Food and Drug Administration—for a trauma that might otherwise be seen as a mere act of God. As religious martyrs and psychologists alike can attest, virtually any amount of suffering can be endured if the one enduring it feels it has a purpose. What I call "damaged-survivor" conspiracism emerges out of the mind's subconscious understanding of this fact: It is a quest to situate one's travails amid a meaningful struggle against some oppressive evil. The more oppressive the evil, the more meaningful the struggle.

Such myths provide another psychotherapeutic dividend, too: hope. The bogus vaccine-autism link is actually two conspiracy theories in one. Not only do McCarthy and her followers believe that the medical establishment is covering up evidence that its drugs are wrecking children's brains; they also promote the piggyback conspiracy theory that vitamins and other natural remedies can be used to "heal" the damage done by vaccines, but that this cure is falsely discredited by the very same medical-establishment evildoers. McCarthy, for instance, promotes something called "chelation therapy," which removes heavy metals from the body.

Other parents have turned to more exotic remedies. As Allen reports: "In the homes of autistic children, it is not unusual to find cabinets filled with 40 different vitamins and supplements, along with casein-free, gluten-free foods, antibiotics, and other drugs and potions. Each is designed to fix an aspect of the 'damage' that vaccines or other 'toxins' caused."

Many conspiracists I've met have themselves experienced a traumatic, life-threatening medical crisis that knocked them out of their normal mental orbit. Often, their stories follow the same pattern: Doctors tried to cure their condition with expensive drugs and painful surgical procedures—but failed. It was only once they'd turned to a "natural" cure—faith healing, homeopathy, Gerson Therapy, or some other kind of placebo-based remedy— that their condition was cured. In the aftermath of this experience, they become convinced that profit-obsessed pharmaceutical companies and the medical establishment more generally have been conspiring to prevent Americans from discovering the power of these natural cures. From their personal experience, they extrapolate to the notion that all of corporate America is engaged in active conspiracy against ordinary American citizens.

In fact, hostility toward conventional medicine is a popular theme in just about every modern conspiracist movement—including Scientology, UFO groups, and 9/11 Truth. Even right-wing conspiracy theorists, no enemies of the free market, tend to embrace herbal miracle-cures and other forms of quack medicine more commonly associated with the vegan Left.

During my interviews in the New York City area, I met a variety of Truthers who fell into the damaged-survivor category: emotionally traumatized parents, children, siblings, or spouses of 9/11 victims, including one genuinely pitiful middle-aged protestor who carries a sign featuring a picture of a handsome young man alongside the words "The NWO [New World Order] murdered my cousin Bradley Van Hoorn."

Other Truthers in this category include some of the "Jersey

Girls" whose activism helped spur the creation of the independent 9/11 Commission; Manny Badillo, a leading New York City-based Truther whose uncle and mentor, Joseph Sgroi, died on 9/11; and Bob McIlvane, a former Philadelphia schoolteacher who became a spokesmen for the Truth movement after losing a son in the North Tower.

Damaged survivors are particularly effective as recruiters for conspiracist movements because the spectacle of their grief short-circuits our intellectual faculties—much in the same way that graphic testimony from a crime victim can sway a jury to convict an innocent defendant. "When I saw Bob [McIlvane] cry at the commission hearings in New York in 2004, it broke my heart," Pennsylvania-based 911blogger.com founder Jon Gold told me when I asked him what drove his activism. "The anger I felt when I saw we were lied to was enormous. I couldn't imagine how much extra pain must have been felt by those who actually lost people. I believe they deserve better."

All of which to say: It is not just because Jenny McCarthy is attractive and famous that she is permitted to promote nonsense medical theories on national television. It is also because she has experienced suffering, a subject that usually can be counted on to arouse the interest of American television viewers, even as it blunts their critical faculties.

In November of 2008, around the time Barack Obama was winning the White House, former *Three's Company* star and Thighmaster pitchwoman Suzanne Somers awoke in a state of terror. She was covered in welts, and could barely breathe. By the time her husband had rushed her to the nearest emergency room, she was nearly dead.

When Somers recovered from this genuinely terrifying ordeal, doctors administered a CAT scan. The results were devastating. She'd survived an episode of breast cancer a few years before, and the disease apparently had returned with a vengeance, metastasizing throughout her innards. The tumors were literally too numerous to be counted. One doctor who saw the images told her flatly: "I've never seen so much cancer in my life."

Somers was stunned. She'd done everything right—eaten nothing but natural foods and natural dietary supplements, avoided stress, exercised regularly. Two years before, she'd published a *New York Times* number one best seller about how to live a long, healthy life. She'd been tested by doctors just three months previous, and come out clean. "How could I have cancer?" she thought to herself.

In fact, Suzanne Somers didn't have cancer. The images doctors saw on her CAT Scan apparently were the result of an exotic fever she'd contracted while working in her organic garden, possibly exacerbated by an alternative therapy to treat the effects of menopause.

One would imagine Somers being overjoyed by the news that she was cancer-free. But her dominant reaction was fury—not only at the doctors who'd misdiagnosed her, but at the Western medical establishment itself, which, she believes, is conspiring to destroy our health with chemotherapy and other "poisons." Days later, when Somers was discharged from the hospital, one of the first things she did was throw out the medications she'd been prescribed by hospital doctors. Eventually, the whole experience would find its way into her 2009 alternative-medicine book, *Knockout: Interviews With Doctors Who Are Curing Cancer*.

Like McCarthy and other radicalized critics of modern medicine, Somers has come to view the human body in essentially medieval terms. According to this view—of which there are endless variations, each with its own cult following and mail-order industry—the human body is powered by a natural energy field that becomes compromised when exposed to artificial Western foods, medicines, and medical therapies. Vitamins, obscure extracts, oils, balms, herbs, and meditation are presumptively good. Prescription drugs, radiological treatments, and surgical interventions are presumptively bad. It is a distinction upon which Somers herself is willing to stake her life: She tells readers that, if again faced with a cancer diagnosis, "my choice overwhelmingly would be to use only alternative treatments."

Knockout promotes a variety of dubious therapies—such as laetrile, an apricot extract that was proven ineffective decades ago; and "the Gonzalez protocol," a bizarre regimen involving twice-daily coffee enemas. If only the medical establishment and the FDA took these treatments seriously, Somers argues, researchers would receive the funds needed to prove their effectiveness. Instead, the health care industry and its cynical government allies conspire behind closed doors to protect the cash cow of conventional cancer therapies. "Pharma is not interested in anything that comes from nature. Anything from nature cannot be patented," Somers writes. "That is why so often many natural alternatives to serious diseases never see the light of day."

Before dismissing Somers as a Hollywood know-nothing, it's worth understanding her frame of mind, and how she came to it. The unfortunate fact is that a lot of her impressions about conventional, hospital-based health care practices ring true. The tests and treatments we receive for cancer and other serious ailments are painful and humiliating, just as she says. Often, they aren't even necessary, but are carried out simply to satisfy the preprinted checklists set out by hospital managers and insurance companies. Many doctors are brusque and patronizing. As anyone who's spent time with a cancer patient going through chemotherapy and radiation can attest, it's also true that there is—in Somers' words—a certain "hopelessness that accompanied so many of today's approaches to health. Even when they worked, there seemed to be an undesired reaction to the body. Somehow, you weren't the same person anymore; you became slowed down, aging faster, fragile." Chemotherapy—which Somers describes, not inaccurately, as "poison therapy"—can be especially traumatic.

Somers' mistake—the same one made by many alternative-medicine advocates—is to assume that something that *feels* artificial and degrading must somehow be harmful to our bodies; and, likewise, that something that *feels* natural and uplifting must somehow be beneficial. Obviously, every cancer patient in the world would prefer to be drinking vitamin cocktails at a California sweat lodge than lying under a CAT scanner. But that doesn't mean the former treatment will help us live longer than the latter: The human body is a complex machine, and sometimes the treatments that help us most in the long run are the most excruciating—and even inhumane—in the short run.

Most people have difficulty dealing with random, purposeless suffering—whether it's in the form of a great depression, a collapsing skyscraper or a chemo ward. As already discussed in this chapter, medical conspiracy theories of the Suzanne Somers/Jenny McCarthy variety ease our psychic torment in two ways. First, they provide a politically accountable villain. Second, they hold out the possibility of a healthy utopia once the villain's malign influence has been exposed.

Best of all, we're assured, all we need to find this utopia are the five senses: Central to the argument in *Knockout* and other alternative-health guidebooks is the idea that our own personal intuition about what is right for our bodies, not the scientific analysis provided by the medical establishment, should guide our health choices. Jenny McCarthy encapsulated this approach in 2010, when she airily dismissed a new *Pediatrics* study authoritatively debunking her theory that autism can be treated with special diets. "We [parents are] the ones seeing the real results. And until doctors start listening to our anecdotal evidence, which is, 'This is *working*,' it's going to take so many more years for these kids to get better. Every parent will tell you something different that helped their child."

Actually, doctors don't dismiss "anecdotal evidence": Every data point they collect in their double-blind research studies is, in a broad sense, an "anecdote" drawn from a particular patient, a particular family. Epidemiology is nothing more than the science of systematically collecting and categorizing this information, and using statistical methods to determine what causative factors, if any, are driving the studied variable. But of course, McCarthy and Somers don't actually mean that we should be studying *all* anecdotes, or even a randomly selected cross-section of them. They mean we should be studying *their* anecdotes, and those supplied by the handpicked experts and friends who support their theories.

The outsized influence of these two women is not a new problem: Social critics have wrung their hands over "celebrity culture" for as long as celebrities have existed. But in recent decades, it gradually has been exacerbated by entirely unrelated cultural phenomena: the rise of the self-help movement, the popularization of psychotherapy, and the attendant notion that our own subjective feelings about life are not only worthy of study, but in fact comprise the key to happiness, and even to truth itself. If this principle rings true on our therapist's couch, why shouldn't it ring true in our doctor's examining room? Both are in the "wellness" business, after all. According to this view, the medical theories of Jenny McCarthy are just as valid as any autism expert's; the cancer expertise of Suzanne Somers as authoritative as any oncologist's. *More so*, in fact, since these two women have *lived* the conditions they're writing about, whereas most conventionally credentialed health researchers are merely reporting the results of second-hand information.

The currency of a celebrity health expert lies not in her credentials, but in her endlessly repeated tale of pain and redemption. This explains why McCarthy, in particular, remains such a popular guest on television talk shows. Oprah Winfrey has made a fetish of what might be called "redemption through suffering"—a doctrine that puts the subjectively felt experience of victimhood at the center of the human condition; and which, like political correctness, makes certain forms of "resistance" narratives immune from intellectual rebuttal. Her guest list over the years has contained a steady parade of female heroines who have overcome some great trial—medical tragedy, racism, childhood sex abuse—and have emerged from it with an inspiring message for ordinary people. This emotional rags-to-riches formula not only supplies compelling human-interest fodder for Oprah's audience, it also satisfies our spiritual need to find meaning in our suffering (a need once satisfied by religion).

What makes all of this so maddening to public-health experts is that modern science supplies unprecedented tools for understanding what makes us sick and what doesn't. In the case of autism, for instance, the search for answers has led to massive metastudies involving hundreds of thousands of children in North America, Europe, and Asia. All of these studies have shown us that vaccine usage has no significant effect on autism rates—yet millions of parents believe otherwise, with the result that some of their children will contract diseases our grandparents once believed had become a thing of the past.

The Cosmic Voyager

David Icke was almost forty years old when he learned his true calling. Earlier in life, the Leicester-born Englishman had been a professional soccer goalie for Coventry City and Hereford United, a presenter on the BBC, and a national spokesman for the British Green Party. But everything changed on a psychic's couch in 1990. At the fateful moment, he remembers, he suddenly felt "something like a cobweb on my face," and the psychic began getting visions of a "Chinese-looking" figure—a messenger from another dimension, Icke later determined—who had come to tell him that "he is a healer who is here to heal the Earth, and he will be world famous." Then and there, Icke decided that he had been anointed a prophet.

Icke's message is that humans live in a virtual-reality universe— "very well symbolized by the *Matrix* movie trilogy." In 1991, he told a journalist that he was the "son of God"—but he insisted that the term was meant with no Christian connotation. "I used the term [to describe my relationship with] the Infinite Consciousness that is everything," he wrote in his 2010 book, *Human Race, Get Off Your Knees: The Lion Sleeps No More.* "We are like droplets of water in an ocean of . . . awareness. We are 'individual' at one level of perception, but still part of the infinite whole. More than that, we *are* the infinite whole, just as a droplet is the ocean and the ocean is the droplet."

Icke has written sixteen books, and most of them are full of meandering New Age rhapsodies such as this. But unlike ordinary gurus, Icke has wrapped his spiritual message into an ambitious conspiracy theory—one that weaves together the Illuminati, Jews (or "Rothschild Zionists," as Icke prefers to call them), the Mossad and CIA (which be believes engineered 9/11), and the London School of Economics. The conspiracy is so enormous, he argues, that it transcends the human race: At the top of the pyramid sits an alien race of lizard-people who control the world by projecting their extradimensional identities onto handpicked world leaders such as Queen Elizabeth II and George W. Bush. "'Modern man' was manipulated genetically by the Reptilian 'gods' to be their slaves, and Homo sapiens were given the brain capacity and physical frame that could best serve the Reptilian[s] as administrators," he writes in *The Lion Sleeps No More.* "[The Reptilian brain] acts like an enormous microchip, and locks us into their control system."

Fortunately, hope is at hand: According to Icke, "Truth Vibrations" now are being emitted into the "Metaphysical Universe" from distant solar systems—which will help all of us "break down the energetic barriers and blocks and lift the veil on the illusions and secrets about self and the world." Icke's mission now, as he sees it, is to get all of us to "tune in" to these vibrations so we can rise up together against the lizard overlords.

Epitomized by men such as Icke and Ken Jenkins, the Northern California–based New Age film producer profiled in Chapter 3, the Cosmic Voyager is the hippy of conspiracist typology. In

broad terms, he resembles what University of York cult expert Colin Campbell called a "seeker"—a spiritual omnivore perpetually
spiraling out toward the margins of Western cultural and political
life.

The Cosmic Voyager often will follow eccentric food regimens,
dabble in Eastern religious doctrines, and exhibit a pronounced
suspicion of conventional medicine. His conspiracism flows naturally from the instinctive sense that the world around us is not
what it seems; and that we are all bound together by some kind of
unseen natural life force that is being suppressed or degraded by
the guardians of our materialistic society. For the Cosmic Voyager,
conspiracism is a sort of spaceship ticket to another world—or even
another dimension. Since his mythology is vague and labile, he acts
as a sort of conspiratorial Zelig, popping up at everything from
Truther conventions to quack autism websites.

Central to the Cosmic Voyager's worldview is the fictional reconstruction of human history—often according to some foundational myth about an ancient, Edenic society whose inhabitants
frolicked about blissfully, until some cataclysm or shadowy cabal
dispersed them. In this spirit, Cosmic Voyagers usually become
obsessed with Stonehenge, Mayan eschatology, the lost tribes of
Israel, Dan Brown-esque Christian pseudohistory, Atlantis, the
pyramids of Egypt, Easter Island, and other markers of a supposed
master civilization. (Campbell dubbed this hodgepodge "the cultic
milieu"—a world "of the occult and the magical, or spiritualism
and psychic phenomena, of mysticism and new thought, of alien
intelligences and lost civilizations, of faith healing and natural
care.") Like devout Christians awaiting the Messiah's return, or
Shiite Muslims awaiting the return of the twelfth Imam, Cosmic
Voyagers imagine that this ur-civilization is not lost in the mists of
time, but rather will reawaken and assert itself somehow, either to
teach us its ancient wisdom, or (as in the film *2012*) render apocalyptic judgment.

In many cases, the Cosmic Voyager will hybridize with other

forms of conspiracy theories to form exotic ideological combinations. Ignatius Donnelly, the prototypical "crank" profiled in the next section, for instance, sometimes would veer into the Cosmic Voyager category when he rhapsodized about the lost civilization of Atlantis. Another notable specimen is failed-historian/cosmic voyager Ernst Zundel, a Holocaust denier who claimed—as one conspiracist website summarized it—"that Hitler and his last battalion had boarded submarines at the end of the war, escaped to Argentina, and then established a base for flying saucers in the hole leading to the inside of the Earth at the South Pole." Zundel—a by-turns paranoid and affable fellow who happened to live across the street from me during the late 1990s, in the Toronto neighbourhood of Cabbagetown—also suggested "that the Nazis had originated as a separate race that had come from the inner-earth."

Some radicalized feminists likewise have fused the Cosmic Voyager's alternative-minded utopianism with conspiracist man-hatred. Central to this vision is the idea that early Paleolithic civilizations were "Goddess cultures," in which men and women coexisted in egalitarian bliss, inspired by the kinder, gentler "gynocentric" fertility goddesses that predated (in the words of self-described "radical lesbian feminist" and influential Goddess-cult proponent Mary Daly) the "phallocracy, penocracy, jockocracy, cockocracy, call it whatever—*patriarchy*." This hybridized form of conspiracism became further hybridized in the 1980s, when the Goddess cult was grafted on to crackpot interpretations of early Christian history, leading (most famously) to the *Da Vinci Code* notion that the Vatican has been engaged in a centuries-long cockocratic conspiracy to suppress the "sacred feminine" core of Jesus' message (but more on that in the next chapter).

Many Cosmic Voyager conspiracists, such as Icke, are UFO obsessives, and interweave their belief in alien civilizations with their suspicion of our own (human) government in intricate ways. A central theme in many of these conspiracy theories is that America's political leaders are in contact with space visitors, but that this fact has been hidden from the rest of us.

Lurid as these science-fiction fantasies may be, they dovetail with the Cosmic Voyager's more general, overarching belief that the world we see is merely a fragment of some much deeper reality. Just as a conventional New Order conspiracy theorist sees Barack Obama and George W. Bush as puppets for some shadowy petro-industrial cabal, a UFO conspiracist sees mankind itself as a mere pawn in a giant galactic space opera.

The Clinical Conspiracist

Only a small minority of the Truthers I encountered seemed out-and-out insane. This should not be surprising: The 9/11 Truth movement is a *socially constructed* conspiracist phenomenon—cobbled together on the Internet from the contributions of thousands of different people. Genuinely insane paranoiacs usually cannot take part in this sort of collaborative effort because they are incapable of extended social interaction in any medium. And so, their paranoid fantasies tend to be highly personalized narratives of their own individual construction—typically involving spouses, relatives, landlords, and work colleagues.

When clinically insane individuals do take a prominent role in conspiracist movements, it typically is in the early stages, when they can work their own idiosyncratic notions into the movement's foundational mythology. A famous example in this category is L. Ron Hubbard, who wove the "religion" of Scientology out of his own paranoid obsessions regarding psychiatrists, "suppressive persons," and 75-million-year-old intergalactic ghosts. Another is Delia Bacon, the emotionally unglued (yet strangely influential) Connecticut Congregationalist who spent much of her life preaching the notion that William Shakespeare's plays and poems actually had been written by Francis Bacon (no relation) and his friends—

before she died in a lunatic asylum at the age of forty-eight. The Truther movement has included several similarly unhinged specimens—including British Truther David Shayler, a former MI5 officer-turned-peace activist who now believes that "no planes were involved in 9/11." (He insists they were holograms.) In 2007, he came forward with the claim that he is "the messiah," and possesses "the secret of eternal life."

In some cases, the preoccupations of insane individuals have filtered into the wider conspiracist community, and have become part of its baseline lore. This includes the idea that government agents are continually monitoring our communications, and even, somehow, our private thoughts, with secret implants or with microchips inserted into our bloodstream—a fear sometimes observed in schizophrenics. And as noted previously, some conspiracy theorists support the notion that the government creates "doubles" (and even triples) of alleged murderers such as Lee Harvey Oswald and Mohammed Atta—a suspicion somewhat analogous to Capgras syndrome, whereby the afflicted imagine that family members have been replaced by *doppelgängers*. Echoes of the same phenomena can be found in the fringe Truther theory, championed by the aforementioned Alexander Dewdney and others, that the 9/11 hijacking "victims" who called their relatives in the minutes before their deaths were CIA actors.

The telltale indicator of genuine clinical insanity lies with the structure of the conspiracist narrative. Sane conspiracists subconsciously erect a rigid mental firewall that insulates their real day-to-day lives from the life-and-death implications of their fantasies: The resulting doublethink allows them to sleep at night and maintain productive, functional lives without succumbing to the dread fear that their government will punish their truth-seeking activism with murder. (Indeed, one of the great ironies of the Truth movement is that its activists typically hold their meetings in large, unsecured locations such as college auditoriums—even as they insist that government agents will stop at nothing to protect their conspiracy for world domination from discovery.) Truly disturbed conspiracy theorists, on the other hand, can't sustain that firewall. They weave themselves into the fantasy, usually as both hero and target.

The best example I have come across is veteran conspiracy theorist Michael Ruppert, whose 2004 book, *Crossing the Rubicon: The Decline of the American Empire at the End of the Age of Oil*, likely ranks as the most influential Truther tome ever published. (Ruppert says it has sold more than one hundred thousand copies.) From a commercial perspective, his psychological state sits in a perfect sweet spot: He is psychologically balanced enough to write lucidly and command a following with his books, but also sufficiently delusional to imagine himself at the center of fantastic, Hollywood-style cloak-and-dagger narratives.

Ruppert's descent into paranoia began in 1976, with a woman. At the time, Ruppert was a rookie LAPD narcotics detective with stellar performance evaluations and a bright future. Then, during an evening out at Brennan's Bar in Marina del Ray, he met "Teddy," and fell in love. After the two became engaged, the relationship soured, and Teddy headed east, to New Orleans. Unable to make phone contact, Ruppert hopped on a plane in romantic pursuit— and entered what he describes as a "Dantean" demimonde of James Bond intrigue, one he seems to inhabit to this day. "Arriving in New Orleans, I found her living in an apartment across the river from the Gretna. Equipped with a scrambler phone and night vision devices, and working from sealed communiqués delivered by naval and air force personnel from nearby Belle Chasse Naval Air Station, she was involved in something truly ugly. She was arranging for large quantities of weapons to be loaded onto ships leaving for Iran. The ships were owned by a company that is today a subsidiary of Halliburton—Brown and Root. She was working with Mafia associates of New Orleans Mafia boss Carlos Marcello to coordinate the movement of service boats that were bringing large quantities of heroin into the city. The boats arrived regularly at Marcello-controlled docks, unmolested by the New Orleans police she introduced me to. Through her I also met hard-hat drivers, military men, Brown and Root employees, former Green Berets, and CIA personnel . . . Disgusted and heartbroken at witnessing my fiancée and my government smuggling drugs, I ended the relationship."

It's hard to say whether any of this is true—or whether the entire episode wasn't an extended psychotic delusion: After interviewing the man for two hours at his small, tidy Culver City, California, home, I'm still not sure. But it's beyond question that the trauma of this romantic breakup turned this once up-and-coming law enforcement officer into a full-time paranoiac. Within two years of meeting "Teddy," Ruppert checked himself into a psychiatric hospital, complaining about death threats. Soon thereafter, he left the LAPD, and began peddling different versions of his story—including the contention that the CIA tried to recruit him to protect its L.A.-area drug operations—to whatever credulous journalists would listen.

As noted previously, he jumped early and hard onto the Truther bandwagon following 9/11, touring college campuses on the West Coast as early as November 2001. In that early period, he developed key tenets of the movement's mythology—such as the notion that the attacks were the brainchild of Dick Cheney, and that the planes were flown by remote control. He even claimed to have developed a source—a small-time criminal and con artist named Delmart Vreeland, a man that JFK conspiracy buffs might describe as the Rose Cheramie of 9/11 conspiracy mythology—who could prove foreknowledge of the 9/11 attacks.

Like Estulin and other megalomaniacal paranoiacs, Ruppert describes his life as a cycle of near-death experiences and epic triumphs. He's been targeted by secret-service assassins several times, he says—most recently in Switzerland in 2003. While in "exile" in Hugo Chavez's Venezuela a few years back, he claims to have been poisoned with a local drug called Burandenga ("picture a date-rape drug times fifty," he tells me). He describes black helicopters circling overhead when he meets with other "insiders," and claims that the government attacked the offices of his (now defunct) website, *From the Wilderness*, using "microwave weapons." He also casually compares himself to Lenin, and claims that his investigations led to the resignation of Donald Rumsfeld.

The Crank

"Angry" is an adjective often used to describe the current state of American politics. But nothing in today's Washington could possibly compare with a speech delivered to Congress in 1868 by Ignatius Donnelly, Republican congressman for Minnesota's Second Congressional District. Rising before his peers to rebut charges of impropriety made against him by Illinois congressman Elihu Washburne, Donnelly fulminated thusly:

> If anywhere on God's earth, down in the mire of filth and nastiness, [Washburne] can pluck up anything that touches my honor, let it come. I shall meet it on its merits. I have gone through the entire catalogue; I have analyzed the contents of the gentleman's foul stomach. I have dipped my hand into its gall; I have examined the half-digested fragments that I have found floating in the gastric juices; but if it is possible for the peristaltic actions of the gentleman from Illinois to bring up anything more loathsome, more disgusting than he has vomited over me [already], in God's name, let it come . . . If there be in our midst one low, sordid, vulgar soul; one barren, mediocre intelligence; one heart callous to every kindly sentiment and every generous impulse, one tongue leprous with slander; one mouth which like unto a den of foul beast giving forth deadly odors; if there be one character which, while blotched and spotted all over, yet raves and rants and blackguards like a prostitute; if there be here one bold, bad, empty bellowing demagogue, it is the gentleman from Illinois.

Donnelly, who already had developed a reputation in Washington as a loose cannon, flamed out of national politics shortly thereafter. Yet the meltdown proved a blessing in disguise, for it allowed him to follow the calling for which he was ideally suited: crankdom.

Even during his career as a politician, Donnelly spent much of his time in the Library of Congress, devouring the contents stack by stack. After returning to his home in rural Minnesota, he became a bookworm full time, developing a particular interest in life under the ocean. Out of this obsession came his 490-page epic, *Atlantis*: *The Antediluvian World*, in which Donnelly instructed readers

> That Atlantis was the region where man first rose from a state of
> barbarism to civilization; that it became, in the course of ages,
> a populous and mighty nation, from whose overflowings the
> shores of the Gulf of Mexico, the Mississippi River, the Amazon, the Pacific coast of South America, the Mediterranean, the
> west coast of Europe and Africa, the Baltic, the Black Sea, and
> the Caspian were populated by civilized nations; that It was
> the true antediluvian world, the Garden of Eden; that the gods
> and goddesses of the ancient Greeks, the Phoenicians, the Hindus, and the Scandinavians were simply the kings, queens and
> heroes of Atlantis; and the acts attributed to them in mythology, a confused recollection of real historical events; . . . that
> Atlantis perished in a terrible convulsion of nature, in which
> the whole island was submerged in the ocean, with nearly all its
> inhabitants; that a few persons escaped in ships and on rafts,
> and carried to the nations east and west tidings of the appalling
> catastrophe.

The book became a best seller, going through dozens of editions. (It remains in print to this day as a staple of New Age reading lists.) But Donnelly was just getting started. From his home in

Minnesota, the "Prince of Cranks" (as he later was dubbed) followed up *Atlantis* with *Ragnarok: Age of Fire and Gravel*, which argued that Atlantis was destroyed by a passing comet, and that the contours of our earth were formed by a massive barrage of extraterrestrial gravel. Then came *Caesar's Column*—the dystopic protoscience-fiction novel discussed in Chapter 1–which warned humanity about the catastrophic revolution that would come if America did not reform its political system. A few years later, he produced an arcane anti-Stratfordian manifesto called *The Great Cryptogram*, in which Donnelly tried to prove—by counting and multiplying the number of different kinds of words in Shakespeare's plays—that Francis Bacon had encoded a secret cipher proving his authorship of the Bard's entire *oeuvre*. By the time Donnelly died on New Year's Day, 1901, in fact, he had put his stamp on just about every strain of conspiracism and crankdom that would emerge in the eleven decades following his death.

And yet, as you read through Donnelly's life story—as told in Martin Ridge's 1962 biography, *Portrait of a Politician*—it's hard not to root for the man. He's not exactly a likeable character (as Elihu Washburne might have attested). But he did have the quality then known as pluck—what today we would call chutzpah. "Donnelly genuinely believed he was a genius, and that, by applying his mental powers to any problem, no matter how tangled or intractable, and regardless of the established body of relevant scholarship or scientific tradition, he could solve it with a fresh look," is how J. M. Tyree put it in a 2005 essay. "Congressman, master orator, pseudo-scientist, student of comparative mythology, crackpot geologist, futurist, amateur literary sleuth, bogus cryptologist, Donnelly did it all with a charmingly boundless energy and a voracious intellectual appetite."

In his fearless commitment to truth-seeking (as he imagined it), Donnelly personified one of America's defining intellectual traditions. America, it is important to remember, has always been a land of cranks. Just as capitalism and the industrial revolution set every yeoman free to build a better musket or mousetrap in his barn or basement, the American Enlightenment set loose a million eccentrics to sweep away the dogmas inherited from Europe, with each championing his own cobbled-together religious movement, political party, or civic group.

As a conspiracist, the crank's defining feature is an acute, inveterately restless, furiously contrarian intelligence. Many cranks have an Asperger's-like obsession with arithmetic, flowcharts, maps, and lengthy data lists. Like Donnelly, they are unable to take any expert's word on even the most technical subject. The crank can be satisfied only once he has personally established the truth of his theories using nothing but primary sources and the rules of logic.

What drives cranks on an emotional level isn't the substance of their theories: Many of the Truther cranks I've interviewed—including David Ray Griffin, Barrie Zwicker, and Paul Zarembka, all discussed in this book—treated the issue of 9/11 Truth in large part as a debating exercise, and seemed curiously detached from the profoundly disturbing implications that flow from their claims. What cranks truly crave is the exhilarating sense of independence, control, and superiority that come from declaring oneself a self-sufficient intellectual force. Conspiracism is a natural outlet for this craving since conspiracy theories always exist in opposition to some received truth that enjoys the blessing of experts, and because the associated claims are regarded as daring and controversial.

Cranks typically are intellectual workaholics—"independent researcher" is how they often refer to these activities—furiously endeavoring to master all of the specialized knowledge required to prove their theories from first principles. Over the years, their homes become transformed into archives, overrun with great stacks of research materials. Within conspiracy movements, they comprise the role of "back office," churning out the tracts that less dedicated and energetic conspiracy theorists use as their source material. Cranks rarely are bigoted or hateful in their attitudes—but their penchant for fringe crusades sometimes draws them into movements that answer to these descriptives. (A textbook example is writer Joseph Sobran [1946–2010], who gained renown as a stylist and conservative thinker at the *National Review* under William F. Buckley Jr., but who slid into crankdom during the 1990s. In his final years, he became so thoroughly detached from reality that he saw nothing wrong with appearing at Holocaust-denier conferences alongside full-fledged anti-Semites.)

Social interactions with cranks usually are memorable. One of the oddest interviews I conducted for this book was with Barrie Zwicker, an amiable crank who became Canada's leading 9/11 Truther in the aftermath of a long career as a mainstream journalist. When I spoke with him at his cluttered Toronto home, he announced that he would be interviewing me (about my *nonbelief* in Trutherdom) in parallel with my own questions. As we talked, he hit buttons on a chess clock to regulate our usage of time—making sure we each questioned the other for exactly the same number of minutes. For reasons that seem obvious to me from such experiences, there are no crank women, only crank men.

Typically, the crank is a math teacher, computer scientist, chess player, or investigative journalist—careers in which the mind is trained to tease complex patterns out of empirical data. Like Donnelly, many come to their crankdom in middle age, or at the end of their working lives, as they are casting about for some project to occupy their hyperactive brains. In some cases, cranks are high-functioning intellectuals frustrated by a menial profession (the most notorious example being the voluble taxi driver with a crank theory about every news item that comes across his radio).

Marshall McLuhan—the communications theorist who told us "the medium is the message"—was a classic crank: He spent much of his leisure time scanning the personals columns in Toronto newspapers, seeking out coded messages about the time and place for "black masses" where, he believed, the Masons and other secret societies would meet to hatch their conspiracies. McLuhan's obsession with the Masons, politely ignored by most of the scholars who've analyzed his life and work, is described in Philip Marchand's biography, *The Medium and the Messenger*. According to Marchand, McLuhan believed that the American Civil War had really been a feud between Masonry's northern and southern branches; and—closer to home—that Masons "controlled book reviews in important periodicals."

McLuhan's obsession with book reviewers is telling, since many mainstream intellectuals get pushed into crankdom by the conviction that they are being unfairly ignored or disparaged by their peers. In the current age, liberal arts professors who have spent their careers laboring in fusty academic obscurity, in particular, find they are able to become instant YouTube superstars merely by adding some sensational twist on an established conspiracy movement—all without having to go through the lengthy, frustrating process of legitimate peer review.

"If you look at a lot of the leading characters in the [9/11 Truth] movement, they tend to be people who are smart but never really got to the top [in their field]," says James Bennett, one of the cocreators of the well-traveled anti-Truther blog *Screw Loose Change*. "Look at [former Brigham Young University physicist] Steven Jones. He had his brush with fame [in the mid-80s] with cold fusion. But it didn't pan out. And it became a miniscandal in the scientific community. He *almost* accomplished something. But now he's in the Truth movement. He's lauded by thousands. He gives speeches. People talk about him in the same breath as Gandhi and Jesus."

Even when the crank is ignored or shunned, he derives satisfaction from the sense that he possesses secret truths about the world that ordinary people are too cowardly to accept. "Throughout the fringe movements that I've seen—whether it's the 9/11 Truth movement, or New Age theories, or Holocaust revisionism—the people tend to have something in common: They think they're smarter than the average person," says Phil Molé, a Chicago-based freelance writer and veteran debunker who investigated the 9/11 Truth movement for a 2006 article in *Skeptic* magazine. "And often they *are* smarter than the average person. They usually have some professional success under their belt. They've earned a degree. They think they're entitled to interpret things the way they see it—that they can declare everyone else to be wrong. The fact they happen to be smart doesn't deter them from conspiracy theories. Just the opposite: It *enables* them. It shields them in their own mind from criticism. They think that the reason these other people are criticizing them is, 'They just don't get it. They're not as smart as I am. They don't know the things I know.'

"In the 9/11 Truth movement, you see a lot of that. These are people who pride themselves on being well informed. They read lots of stuff—a lot of it is just regurgitated from other 9/11 Truth sites, but they do read *something*. They can tell you exactly where such and such a plane was on such and such a day, or what was going on in Afghanistan at such and such a time. It's all isolated scraps of information, of course. But they pride themselves on having all these scattered facts in their brains. So they tell themselves, 'Where do other people get off telling me that I'm wrong?'"

Truther-wise, the leading crank is the dean of 9/11 Truth authors, David Ray Griffin. To this day, Griffin is known as one of the world's foremost experts in the field of Process Theology, a complex metaphysical discipline that defines God in relation to the exercise of free will. After retiring from the Claremont School of Theology in California, he filled his days by taking up conspiracism full time. His work ethic is legendary: When I visited him at his seaside California home in 2009, he told me that he sometimes spends fourteen-hour days on his research. (During our interview, he spoke to me for three hours straight—and seemed prepared to speak for hours more had I not gotten up to leave.) Since 2004, he has written no fewer than eleven books, in which he methodically examines virtually every minute of the 9/11 timeline—much as Donnelly examined every word of *King Lear* and *Othello*. The table of contents for his 2008 book *9/11 Contradictions: An Open Letter to Congress and the Press*, for instance, includes these chapters:

1. How long did George Bush remain in the classroom?
2. When did Dick Cheney enter the underground bunker?
3. Was Cheney observed confirming a stand-down order?
4. Did Cheney observe the land-all-planes order?
5. When did Cheney issue shoot down authorization?
6. Where was General Richard Myers?
7. Where was Donald Rumsfeld?
8. Did Ted Olson receive calls from Barbara Olson?
9. When was the military alerted about Flight 11?
10. When was the military alerted about Flight 175?
11. When was the military alerted about Flight 77?
12. When was the military alerted about Flight 93?
13. Could the military have shot down Flight 93?

SUNY Buffalo economics professor Paul Zarembka takes an even more granular approach to his Truther research, dwelling at length on such arcane subjects as the price of individual airline stocks in the run-up to 9/11, and the tail numbers of the hijacked 9/11 aircraft, both of which he discusses at numbing length in his 2008 book *The Hidden History of 9/11*. To quote at random: "AA 11 is listed with tail number N334AA. Returning to BTS data, it had arrived into Boston from S.F. at 5:52 a.m. on 9–10 (as AA 198), judging from airborne time. While BTS data do not report arrival into Dulles (any time in September 2001) of an aircraft with tail number N644AA, airgames.bravehost.com ascertained that the FAA tail number N644AA is replaced in American Airlines reporting procedures by N5BPAA . . ."

Another (unusually young) 9/11 crank is Craig Ranke—a manic, elfin, endearingly odd thirtysomething software salesman who proudly introduced himself to me at a New York City Truth forum as the founder of an outfit called the 9/11 "Citizen Investigation Team." At the time we met, he'd spent the last three years of his life investigating little else besides the flight path of American Airlines Flight 77, in hopes of proving that no plane ever hit the Pentagon. As with other cranks I've met, Ranke is certain that his narrow area of interest is the sardine-can key that will roll up the whole of the conspiracy.

It is an impulse that Donnelly and his fellow anti-Stratfordian cranks would have understood well. As I listened to Ranke recite his elaborate adventures crisscrossing the flight corridors of northern Virginia, it was difficult not to be reminded of Orville Ward Owen, a successful Detroit doctor who became so obsessed with Shakespearean conspiracism in the 1890s that he built a machine to "decode" Bacon's secret messages—a device consisting of two garbage-can sized spools, onto which was mounted a thousand-foot-long canvas sheet containing all Bacon's known works (including, of course, those attributed to William Shakespeare). Owen and his assistants would take a seat directly in front of the tautly mounted catalog of Bacon's mind, and then spin the spools rapidly, making the canvas sheet whip around like the magnetic ribbon in an audio cassette. While staring intently at the sheet, they captured and recorded the various repeating words and phrases that jumped out of Bacon's life work—and from this, cobbled together a six-volume opus called *Sir Francis Bacon's Cipher Story*, which not only confirmed Owen's theory that Bacon had written Shakespeare's works—as well as those of Christopher Marlowe and a half-dozen other famous writers—but that Bacon was Queen Elizabeth's son.

Sadly for Owen, the theory didn't fly. Even in this, the late golden age of Baconian conspiracism, Owen's "Cipher Wheel" was widely mocked. On his deathbed, in 1924, he warned a confidante to steer clear of Baconianism, "for you will only reap disappointment. When I discovered the Word Cipher, I had the largest practice of any physician in Detroit . . . Instead, [I] lost my fortune, ruined my health, and today am a bedridden almost penniless invalid."

The Evangelical Doomsayer

In 2002, *Megadeth* founder and front man Dave Mustaine—regarded by many aficionados as the greatest heavy metal guitarist of all time—thought his music career was over. "I had fallen asleep on my [left] arm," he later told an interviewer. "The circulation was cut off to the nerve on the inside of my left bicep. When the nerve lost circulation, it shrunk like a crunched up straw . . . The doctors said that I wasn't going to play again. They said I would get 80 percent use of my arm back, but not 100 percent, and I was told that I was certainly never going to play the way I played before again."

But the doctors were wrong. After months of physical therapy, Mustaine taught himself to play the guitar again. In 2004, he reformed *Megadeth*, and the band has been a going concern ever since.

Mustaine returned to music a new man. At one point during his recovery, he climbed a hill and beheld a faraway cross. "Looking up at [it], I said six simple words: 'What have I got to lose?'" he later recalled. "Afterwards, my whole life has changed. It's been hard, but I wouldn't change it for anything. [I'd] rather go my whole life believing that there is a God and find out there isn't than live my whole life thinking there isn't a God and then find out, when I die, that there is."

Some rockers who find Jesus migrate to the Christian-rock genre—which combines a conventional guitar-driven music style with pious lyrics that offer praise to God. Mustaine didn't go down that path. But he did begin to infuse his *Megadeth* compositions with apocalyptic imagery drawn from the modern American Evangelical tradition. The result was the 2009 album *Endgame*, whose title he described this way: "As a Christian, I believe [the elites' 'end game'] is one-world government, one world currency . . . It's part of the master plan. It's what I believe. I [signed on] to that when I became Christian. I know that there's going to be a cataclysmic ramping up of all of these things that we're seeing right now. And it gets worse and it gets worse and we're watching our country disintegrate right now . . . That's what *Endgame* is all about. It's about educating our fans."

The album cover of *Endgame* (which is also the name of a 2007 film written by Mustaine's friend, radio host Alex Jones) is a conspiracist masterpiece, combining an assortment of New World Order motifs in a single, vivid scene. Dominating the image is a legion of bald prisoners, their heads branded with government markings, marching to their doom down a narrow metal chute, which is formed by walls made up of FEMA coffins. "[We wanted it to be] like these Hebrews being marched through the Red Sea," Mustaine explained. "And all the people that are in the Homeland Security jumpsuits with the bar code on their head—you know it doesn't say in the Bible if the bar code is going to be going this way or if it's going to be going that way, so we did some cool imagery . . . We made it look like a mohawk, but then when you zoom in on it, it's actually their bar code."

The album's title track begins with a mock public-address announcement, declaring, "Attention! Attention! All citizens are ordered to report to their District detention centers! Do not return to your homes; do not contact anyone! Do not use any cellular or GPS devices! Surrender all weapons at once! Attention! This way to the camps!" And then come these lyrics:

> *I woke up in a black FEMA box*
> *Darkness was all around me, in my coffin*
> *My dreams are all nightmares anymore*
> *And this is what I dream every night*
> *The Leader of the New World Order, the President of the*
>   *United States*
> *Has declared anyone now residing inside the US of A*
> *Without the [radio-frequency identification] chip, you're just*
>   *an illegal alien*
> *An enemy combatant of America, welcome to the New World*
>   *Order*

This is the end of the road; this is the end of the line
This is the end of your life; this is the . . .

A society in a society, inside the fence life as you know it stops
They got their rules of conduct and we got ours
Be quick or be dead, you crumble up and die, the clock is
Ticking so slowly and so much can happen in an hour

I learned my lessons the hard way, every scar I earned
I had to bleed, inside the day yard
A system of controlled movement, like a giant ant farm
Any time is long time, now you're not in charge of your time
    anymore

The Ex-President signed a secret bill that can
Land a legal US Citizen in jail and the
Patriot act stripped away our constitutional rights
They say a concentration camp just popped up, yeah, right!

Refuse the chip? Ha! Get persecuted and beat by the
Tyranny of mind control, for the mark of the beast
All rights removed, you're punished, captured, and enslaved
Believe me when I say, "This is the Endgame!"

Like Joseph Farah, the Birther and WorldNetDaily editor profiled in the previous chapter, Mustaine epitomizes the conspiracist
type I call the Evangelical Doomsayer. Conspiracism is attractive
to the Doomsayer because it organizes all of the world's menacing threats into one monolithic force—allowing him to reconcile
the bewildering complexities of our secular world with the good-
versus-evil narrative contained in the book of Revelation and other
religious texts.

The prototypical Doomsayer is an Evangelical Christian who vigilantly scans the news for signs that the world is moving toward some final, apocalyptic confrontation between good and evil. Early American history is littered with Doomsayer cults founded on this practice. But over the course of the twentieth century, as described in Chapter 1, the Doomsaying tradition fused with secular New World Order conspiracy theories that predict America's subjugation by a godless evil empire based in Moscow, London, Turtle Bay, or Tora Bora.

In many cases, the Evangelical Doomsayers I've met are not actually Evangelists, or even Christian: So saturated is American culture with the imagery of Christian eschatology that it has been widely co-opted by esoteric religious movements and cults such as Jonestown, the Nation of Islam, Garveyites, Rastafarians, Heaven's Gate, and the Branch Davidians. As scholar James Alan Patterson has reported, the common denominator in all of these is not any particular conception of God or theology, but a fascination with "visions pertaining to endtime, imminent cataclysm, judgment, and redemption."

Once you strip away their jargon, radicalized Marxists also can be classified as Evangelical Doomsayers. Clipped to its spiritual essentials, their view of society is one in which injustice upon injustice will be heaped upon the toiling classes until some final cataclysmic revolution against the capitalist oppressor will deliver a classless New Jerusalem, in which man himself will be transformed into a viceless, iron-willed slave to the revolution. A similar analysis applies to Marxism's *tier-mondiste* offshoot, "decolonization," which Frantz Fanon rhapsodically described in *The Wretched of the Earth* as "quite simply the substitution of one 'species' of mankind by another . . . the creation of new men."

The Firebrand

Every radical political movement needs a street leader—someone with the self-confidence required to bark commands into a megaphone, and the charisma required to elicit compliance. For the New York City–area Truther movement, that man is Luke Rudkowski, a blond, baby-faced twenty-four-year-old Polish American construction worker who lives with his parents in Brooklyn's working-class Bensonhurst neighborhood. At rallies, Rudkowski always dresses the part of Truther statesman—in a funeral director's suit that he bought for two dollars at the Salvation Army. At Truther "street actions" on 9/11 anniversaries, he tends to affect a solemn, weary look—as if his knowledge about the New World Order weighs heavily on his shoulders.

It was April 2007 when Rudkowski made a name for himself in activist circles. At the time, he already was dabbling with the 9/11 Truth movement—but he was frustrated by its emphasis on low-key tactics. Rudkowski believed it would take something more than blog postings and church-basement lectures to rouse America from its ignorance. One day, by chance, he noticed a headline in one of his father's Polish-language newspapers: Former national security advisor Zbigniew Brzezinski—Trilateral Commission cofounder, Council on Foreign Relations member, Bilderberger— was speaking on the Upper East Side. In an instant, Rudkowski realized what he had to do.

A few hours later, Rudkowski was in the crowd at the 92nd Street Y, activated camcorder in hand. After patiently waiting during Brzezinski's presentation about the war on terrorism, he rose to his feet during the Q&A, and delivered this statement, captured for all to see on a widely circulated YouTube video:

> Earlier on this year, you gave a speech to the Senate Foreign Relations Committee where you alluded to the fact that the Bush Administration may stage a terrorist attack to justify a military action against Iran. And then in your book, you also acknowledged the fact that a memo was uncovered where Bush and Blair discussed painting a U2 spy plane in U.N. colors so Saddam would shoot it down. Although you have argued that

deceptions to the American people may be necessary in order to deal with these enemies, how are we to know how many other terrorist incidents have been state-sponsored false-flag incidents including the largest one—the attacks of 9/11? How do we know, how do the American people know that 9/11 wasn't staged, wasn't engineered by you, David Rockefeller, the Trilateral Commission, the CFR, and Bilderberg Group, sir?

As Rudkowski can be heard saying all this on the video, the crowd remains silent—until he gets to the end, when the radical gist of Rudkowski's accusation dawns on everyone all at once, and the room erupts in boos. Rudkowski perseveres, but is reduced to shouting staccato barbs through the repeated pleas to "sit down and shut up":

It's a question. Answer my question. You sponsored al-Qaeda, sir. You are a criminal. You sponsored al-Qaeda. In 1979, you gave them money. That's true. You are CFR. scum. You are CFR. and New World Order scum. You and David Rockefeller will never have a New World Order. National sovereignty will prevail. Answer my question. Answer my question . . .

At this point, event organizers approach Rudkowski and ask him to turn off his video camera. Instead, he starts screaming, "9/11 was an inside job! Mr. Brzezinski is responsible!" and, "Wake up, people!" Then he dashes for the exit, camera rolling, guards in pursuit. Only after putting a few blocks between himself and the Y does Rudkowski stop to catch his breath, turn the camera around, and triumphantly declare into the lens: "Yeah, Brzezinski—you got yours!" The YouTube clip ends with Rudkowski on the subway back to Brooklyn, removing his suit jacket and white shirt to reveal a T-shirt emblazoned with the slogan, "F**k the Federal Reserve."

The next day, Rudkowski put his video from the Brzezinski confrontation on YouTube. Almost immediately, the link went viral. Accolades poured in from Truthers around the world, who were thrilled to see their theories get an airing—if only for a few seconds—at a respectable Manhattan speaking event. Admirers contacted Rudkowski, asking if they could be part of his next guerilla theater stunt.

Coalescing under the banner, "We Are Change," Rudkowski and his followers began ambushing other alleged New World Order insiders at public events—including Rudy Giuliani, who then was making a run for the GOP presidential nomination. They also slipped into a subway car carrying New York City mayor Michael Bloomberg, and managed to hector him for a full sixteen minutes. Rudkowski got up during a pretaping of Stephen Colbert's *The Colbert Report* and began speechifying about the Bilderberg Group—an episode that didn't make it to the air, but, like everything else We Are Change does, was posted with much fanfare on YouTube. In their most ambitious stunt, group members secretly configured a public-address sound system in a Barnes & Noble bookstore the day before a scheduled appearance by Bill Clinton. While the former president signed books, the system was activated, causing a loud disembodied voice to announce that "9/11 was an inside job."

In time, Rudkowski became a regular on Russian television news station RT (which often features conspiracy theorists), as well as Alex Jones' popular Texas-based radio show. Some even have begun speaking of Rudkowski as Jones' protégé—high praise in the world of right-wing conspiracism. And he has begun branching out from the Truth movement to other causes. In one widely circulated video from the 2009 G–20 Conference in Pittsburgh, for instance, Rudkowski, megaphone in hand, can be seen shouting slogans as he leads a pack of protestors being routed by an advancing line of police: "We are American citizens! This is not China. This is not Nazi Germany! We have freedom of assembly under the First Amendment to the Constitution of the United States of America, and we shall uphold our rights as American citizens because we

love this country, and we love national sovereignty! . . . U-S-A!
U-S-A! U-S-A!"

Eventually, the Pittsburgh police arrested Rudkowski for dis-
orderly conduct and threw him in jail for a night—an event that
he played for pity on his web postings. Increasingly, Rudkowski
presented himself to his followers as a sort of Truther martyr, destined to suffer until the New World Order had been overthrown.
One Facebook status update for September 2009, for instance,
read: "When a man goes in front of a wave of oppression, he is beat
down, but it is his persistence and willingness to stand there, that
motivates and inspires others to stand with him and in that creating a relentless force that cannot be beaten down nor stopped . . ."
This was followed by: "I want to thank everyone for the love and
support, I do this for you and all humanity," and "Another long
night[with] a lot to do . . . 4 a.m. now, been up since 7 a.m. yes-
terday. But I am thankful for the energy I get from your support
because without [it], I wouldn't be as strong as I am." The follow-
up comments from his admirers included, "You're a hero for the
republic," "I fear if 9/11 truth is uncovered, the elite will stage
something bigger to 'shut you up,'" and "It takes courage to go
against the grain, Luke. Keep up the good work!"

Conspiracists of the firebrand type are the easiest ones to spot,
because they always are the noisiest. For the firebrand, conspiracism supplies an ideological pretext to strike shocking, militant political postures, and thereby satisfy his hunger for public attention.
Most specimens of the type are in their late teens or early twenties,
a time when the developing mind is most vulnerable to angry, to-
talizing ideologies.

In another age, the firebrand manifested himself as a communist or anarchist. But since those creeds now seem merely quaint—
not shocking—he instinctively has migrated to more exotic beliefs.

CHAPTER SIX

The Church of Conspiracism

Homer conceived the power of the gods in such a way that whatever happened on the plain before Troy was only a reflection of the various conspiracies in Olympus. The conspiracy theory of society is just a version of this theism, of a belief in gods whose whims and wills rule everything. It comes from abandoning God and then asking: "Who is in his place?"

—*Karl Popper*

The writing and telling of history is bedeviled by two human neuroses: horror at the desperation and shapelessness and seeming lack of pattern in events, and regret for a lost golden age, a moment of happiness when all was well. Put these together and you have an urge to create elaborate patterns to make sense of things and to create a situation where the golden age is just waiting to spring to life again.

—*Diarmaid MacCulloch,* Christianity: The First Three Thousand Years

Enter Satan

In the late 1920s, a British anthropologist named Edward Evan Evans-Pritchard deposited himself in the lightly wooded savannah of Southern Sudan, and took up residence with the traditional farmers and hunter-gatherers of the Azande tribe. The Zande people were divided into a number of separate tribal kingdoms, each with its own dynastic aristocracy, separated from one another by stretches of unpopulated bushland. But as Evans-Pritchard discovered, they all shared very specific beliefs about the supernatural, the details of which became the centerpiece of his 1937 classic, *Witchcraft, Oracles, And Magic Among the Azande.*

In the Zande mythology, people do not die of "natural" causes: Almost always, blame can be traced back to a witch in the community, or a conspiracy of multiple witches, who have cursed the unlucky victim. Witchcraft, they imagine, is not an abstraction, but an actual substance found in the body (attached to the edge of the liver), which grows with age (thus making the elderly especially vulnerable to sorcery allegations), and passes from generation to generation. At night, this witchcraft substance leaves the body of its host, floats through the air in a haze of bright light, and implants itself in its target—sometimes without the witch even being aware. Once implanted, the vampiric miasma slowly eats away at the soul of the unlucky recipient, until the soul has been entirely consumed and the victim dies.

As Evans-Pritchard continued to study the Azande, he noticed that witchcraft and its related mythology were used to explain not just death, but virtually every aspect of life. "Its influence is plainly stamped on law and morals, etiquette and religion; it is prominent in technology and language," he wrote in his 1937 book. "If blight seizes the ground-nut crop, it is witchcraft; if the bush is vainly scoured for game, it is witchcraft; if women laboriously bale water out of a pool and are rewarded by but a few small fish it is witchcraft; if termites do not rise when their swarming is due and a cold useless night is spent in waiting for their flight, it is witchcraft; if a wife is sulky and unresponsive to her husband, it is witchcraft."

The Zande worldview may sound fatalistic. But it is not. For their mythology also incorporates an array of countermeasures that victims can execute to block, and even reverse, the effect of witchcraft and magic spells.

Many Zande tribespeople, Evans-Pritchard found, made a regular visit to local oracles, who would inform them if they were under attack from nearby witches—and would even supply them with their names. In the most popular oracular approach, a smidgen of red powder extracted from a poisonous forest insect was thrust down the throat of a fowl, who would then enter violent convulsions. The accusation of witchcraft put to the oracle would be decided on the basis of whether the fowl died or not.

Once the Zande tribesperson found out who was bewitching him, he could confront the witch, and ask him to desist. Or he could threaten vengeance magic. Or he could simply move out of the area for a short while, since it is imagined that the witchcraft, being physical in its transmission, can travel only short distances. Whatever path the putative victim chose, the important point was that he could do *something*. He was not without recourse in the face of uncooperative nuts, animals, termites, and women.

The beliefs of the Azande are unique in their particulars. But they exhibit a universal aspect of human nature: our need for control. When we can't control something directly, we invent gods and witches who can; gods and witches who themselves can be controlled through chants, ceremonies, amulets, and magic.

In primitive societies, religion typically is a polytheistic affair involving a menagerie of bickering deities. Homer, for instance, described the Trojan War as the result of a jealous argument among the goddesses Athena, Hera, and Aphrodite. In the *Aeneid*, similarly, Virgil cast the founding of Rome as originating in a petty grudge held by the goddess Juno against the defeated Trojans. But this began to change—at least, in regards to what we now call the Western tradition—with the narrative of the Hebrew Bible, whose basic elements began taking form approximately three thousand years ago.

In the emerging theology of the Israelite religion, there was only one true God, the all-powerful Yahweh. In Deuteronomy (among other places in the Bible), he pronounced polytheism to be a sin: "You shall have no other gods before me. You shall not make for yourself an idol, whether in the form of anything that is in heaven above, or that is on the earth beneath, or that is in the water under the earth. You shall not bow down to them or worship them; for

I the Lord your God am a jealous God . . ." Through Judaism, Christianity, and Islam—the Abrahamic faiths—this once-novel vision of a world controlled by a single divine entity eventually would become the overarching theme of religious life in Europe, the Middle East, North Africa, Central Asia, and the New World.

But even from early days, monotheistic adherents were presented with an agonizing philosophical problem: the presence of evil. Under polytheism, tragedies could be explained by the careless cruelty of warring deities (of which Homer's *Odyssey*, for instance, was one long catalog). But under monotheism, that dodge was difficult. If Yahweh was omnipotent and benign, why did he permit natural disasters, mass murders, war, and other forms of slaughter? In short, why did he let bad things to happen to good people?

It is a question presented (but not satisfyingly answered) in the book of Job, when one of God's angels afflicts the long-suffering protagonist with boils, destroys all his possessions, and kills his ten children—all for no other reason than to see how the ostensibly pious man would handle it. Job's agonized plea to God expresses the timeless confusion and agony of a man who has done everything right in life, yet sees his virtue repaid with suffering:

> My body is clothed with worms and scabs,
> my skin is broken and festering.
> My days are swifter than a weaver's shuttle,
> and they come to an end without hope . . .
> When I think my bed will comfort me
> and my couch will ease my complaint,
> even then you frighten me with dreams
> and terrify me with visions,
> so that I prefer strangling and death,
> rather than this body of mine.
> I despise my life; I would not live forever.
> Let me alone; my days have no meaning.
> What is man that you make so much of him,

that you give him so much attention,
that you examine him every morning
and test him every moment?

The godly helper who sets Job's agonies in motion is none other than Satan. But he is not playing his later role of "horrid king, besmeared with blood of human sacrifice, and parents' tears" (as Milton described him). In the book of Job, as throughout the Hebrew Bible, Satan functions as the divine court's chief prosecutor—a vital, if necessarily sinister, member of God's angelic entourage. (His name derives from the Hebrew *ha-satan*, meaning "the accuser.") His primary mission is to test Job's spiritual mettle, not make him suffer for suffering's sake. It is only much later, in Revelation, that Satan assumes his form as a dragon-like creature bent on destroying God's kingdom.

As T. J. Wray and Gregory Mobley argue in their 2005 book, *The Birth of Satan: Tracing the Devil's Biblical Roots*, this satanic transformation arose from a profound psychic need to divide the single God of the Hebrew Bible into two components—an omnipotent King of Kings to receive human prayers, and a demon to take the blame when those prayers weren't answered. By bending the rules of monotheism to permit the existence of a lesser, malevolent superhuman entity, Christians could ponder a less existentially numbing answer to the prophet Amos' chilling question, "Does disaster befall a city, unless the *LORD* has done it?"

The seeds of Satan's transformation were sown amid the Babylonian exile, at a time when the idea of monotheism was taking its definitive place in the canon of the Hebrew Bible, and Jewish scholars were casting about to explain how Yahweh could have permitted them to be thrown out of the Kingdom of Judah by Nebuchadnezzar II. The Babylonian exile also coincided with the religious dualism conceived by the ancient Persian prophet Zarathustra, originator of Zoroastrianism, who viewed existence as a struggle between light and darkness. In the Zoroastrian faith, a god of light (Ahura Mazda) battles for supremacy against a "fiend-ish spirit" known as Ahriman—a battle involving a Christ-like sav-ior figure (Saoshyant) that culminates in a decidedly Revelation-like eschatological climax.

"This type of storytelling sought to reveal the reason for the frustrated hopes of a people who could not reconcile their mis-fortunes with their theology," conclude Wray and Mobley in *The Birth of Satan*. "If the descendants of Abraham and Sarah were partners to a covenant with the Architect of the Universe, then why had their cultural and political properties been condemned by a parade of Near Eastern tyrants? The response of the Jewish apocalypticists was to construct a new theory to explain this co-nundrum. They built the theory from pieces of Jewish folklore, puzzling Biblical passages, and the myths of surrounding cultures. The theory revealed a cosmic conspiracy at work, led by a super-natural criminal mastermind (Satan) who controlled a vast, nefari-ous network of demonic forces dedicated to frustrating the divine purpose at every turn."

It's a dark vision of the world. Yet it came with a happy ending. As Norman Cohn noted in his definitive 1957 study of medieval millenarian cults, *The Pursuit of the Millennium*, it is no coinci-dence that the Bible's earliest apocalyptic fantasies—the dream se-quences contained in the book of Daniel—were written during the agonies and upheavals of the Maccabean revolt. Daniel's revolu-tionary eschatology allowed Jews to believe that their suffering was not in vain: The plagues rained down upon the Jews were merely building up to a climactic cosmic counterreaction, with the Saints of God rising up at the last possible moment to defeat Satan and establish a timeless earthly utopia.

Centuries later, the same theme would be picked up by Chris-tians—in far more lurid fashion—in Revelation, which some schol-ars interpret as an allegorical commentary on the Roman persecu-tion of Christians dating from the first century AD. Eventually, it would also find its way into the eschatology of Islamists, who imagine that jihad and martyrdom will propel the world toward a one-state paradise, cleansed of conspiring infidels, under the reign of Sharia.

This analysis shows why conspiracism and millenarianism often go together: Both of them put the fact of human suffering at the center of the human condition. Conspiracism is a strategy for explaining the origin of that suffering. Millenarianism is a strategy for forging meaning from it: Once our tears and blood fill up some cosmic chalice, the scales of history will tip, and New Jerusalem will open its gates.

The Devil's Legacy

Aside from Christian Doomsayers, for whom conspiracism and scripture often are one and the same, very few of the conspiracy theorists I've met are conventionally observant members of mainstream Christian denominations. Consistent with their generalized skepticism toward any conventional institution that commands the obeisance of the masses, most nonevangelical conspiracy theorists tend to embrace the dissident fringes of American religious life. Richard Gage, for instance, has been an active supporter of the Unity movement, which emphasizes New Age concepts such as life force and spiritual healing. Steven Jones, a celebrity Truther who pioneered the myth that the World Trade Center buildings were brought down with thermite, is a Mormon who has authored an article called "Behold My Hands," in which he presents a mishmash of Mayan-era evidence aimed at proving that Jesus Christ once visited America. Robert Bowman, a former military man who directed the Pentagon's early Star Wars antimissile research in the 1970s, declares himself the "Bishop Protector of the Society of Blessed XXIII," a pro-gay, pro-feminist, pacifist, "pre-Constantinian" fringe offshoot of Catholicism.

But such heterodoxy is immaterial: The mythology of Satan

and the End Times is hard-wired so deep into the circuitry of Judeo-Christian civilization that its influence has become universal—even in regard to avowedly secular ideologies. Marx may have declared religion to be "the opiate of the people." But as noted previously, his theory of class struggle—whereby history's final act would play out in a Manichean struggle between a virtuous proletariat and its evil capitalist overlords—would have been recognizable to the ancient prophets. (It is telling that the first writer to use the term "communism," French utopian socialist Étienne Cabet, took his inspiration from Christianity.) In the minds of many secularists, government long ago replaced God as our omnipotent protector. And when that secular god fails in some epic way—when a president is killed in broad daylight, or the heart of Manhattan is pulverized—his worshippers tend to hunt for Lucifers and Christ-killers.

Wrapped up in their Manichean narratives is the implicit notion that ordinary citizens must choose sides in the coming conflict—and that, when the Day of Judgment comes tomorrow—our fates will be dictated by the choices we make today. By publicly embracing a dissident ideology such as 9/11 Truth, the conspiracist isn't just making his views known about a particular issue. On a deeper spiritual level, he is marking himself as a righteous one who stands apart from the rottenness around him. The "9/11 Truth" T-shirts, banners, and bumper stickers sold at Truther events serve as modern versions of the dab of lamb's blood that Jews put on their doorposts to ward off the Angel of Death coming to slay the Egyptians' firstborn.

Like religious converts who suddenly see the light of Christ, a surprisingly large number of Truthers told me that they "just knew" that 9/11 was an inside job the second they saw the towers collapse—even though they admit that they couldn't initially identify any outward signs of foul play. In many cases, Truthers even have unwittingly co-opted the language of proselytization and born-again religious conversion. In his biographical blurb, for instance, San Francisco–area 9/11 Truth leader Ken Jenkins declares that he "completed his awakening to 9/11 truth by Nov. 2001." His email signature file contains the vaguely Messianic line (adapted from an unrelated 2008 speech delivered by Barack Obama) "We are the ones we have been waiting for. 9/11 Truth is the cause we have been waiting for."

Given conspiracism's common psychological role as a form of *ersatz* religiosity, it's no coincidence that several of the late twentieth century's most commercially successful conspiracy theorists grafted a rejection of mainstream Christianity right into their plots. The resulting tracts—from which Dan Brown's *Da Vinci Code* took its multimillion-dollar inspiration—provide all the usual *Protocols*-inspired narratives about creepy men in smoke-filled rooms, plus a second tantalizing treat: the promise of receiving Jesus' true, *hidden* message once those patriarchs are defeated.

Of the many pseudohistorical books that have followed this formula over the years, the most influential has been *Holy Blood, Holy Grail*, by Michael Baigent, Richard Leigh, and Henry Lincoln. It became a sensation not once, but twice—the first time on its publication in 1982, and then again two decades later, around the time that the authors sued Brown for allegedly plagiarizing their theory.

According to the authors' ambitious re-creation of history, Jesus Christ's bloodline did not end on the cross. Instead, it traveled to France with his wife, Mary Magdalene, and eventually combined with Frankish royalty to produce the Merovingian dynasty. The authors also describe the existence of an ultraelite, ultrapowerful, ultrasecret society—the Priory of Sion—which will soon spring the truth of Jesus' surviving bloodline on the world, thereby leading to a sort of divine Merovingian restoration that brings much of Europe into a "pan-European confederation assembled into a modern empire and ruled by a dynasty descended from Jesus."

Yet these rulers will be no medieval-style theocrats. The true

Christian faith—as *Da Vinci Code* readers know—supposedly is nothing like the patriarchal, artificial faith encoded in the New Testament by the grandees of the fourth century church. Instead, it is a humane, feminized creed, vaguely infused with the teachings of Mrs. Christ and the ancient, gentle doctrines of the pagan Mother Goddesses.

As *Holy Blood, Holy Grail* weaves its way from the Languedoc, to Solomon's Temple, to Paris and the other centers of European power, it sucks up every stray bit of conspiracist esoterica imaginable—from the Knights Templar (the collective Zelig of old-school conspiracy theorists) and the Holy Grail, to "the mysterious Rosicrucians" to *The Protocols of the Elders of Zion*, all larded up with Sunday-morning anagrams, testimonials from mail-in conspiracists befriended by the authors, and the writers' own library-stall melodramas.

Like every popular conspiracy theory, this one has a greedy, murderous archvillain that will stop at nothing to protect its illegitimate power. (It's the Vatican, of course.) The book also comes with a lost utopia, the one that might already have come to pass if the truth of Jesus' Merovingian bloodline had not been suppressed at the time the Crusaders took Jerusalem in 1099: "Once installed on the throne of the kingdom of Jerusalem . . . the [Merovingian] king of Jerusalem would then have taken precedence over all monarchs of Europe, and the patriarch of Jerusalem would have supplanted the Pope. Displacing Rome, Jerusalem would then have become the true capital of Christendom, and perhaps of much more than Christendom. For if Jesus were acknowledged as a mortal prophet, as a priest-king and legitimate ruler of the line of David, he might well have become acceptable to both Muslims and Jews. As king of Jerusalem, his lineal descendant would then have been in a position to implement one of the primary tenets of Templar policy—the reconciliation of Christianity with Judaism and Islam." (It turns out the Priory of Sion had another chance to restore the Merovingian dynasty seven centuries later, the authors argue. But their hopes were dashed by—you guessed it—the French Revolution. *Plus ça change.*)

This provides a context for those who wonder how *The Da Vinci Code* could become such a blockbuster despite its far-fetched plot and wooden prose: By putting cloak-and-dagger plots and dissident religiosity between the same two covers, Dan Brown—like the authors on whom he relied—hit upon the (with apologies) Holy Grail of conspiracism. From a Christian reader's perspective, the most alluring part is that finding an earthly utopia doesn't even require switching religions or joining an ashram.

Lives of the Prophets

Conspiracy-theory expert Chip Berlet calls them "Gnostic heroes": prophets who have dedicated their lives to spreading their secret knowledge in an effort to save the world from a coming apocalypse. Ken Jenkins is an archetypal Gnostic hero. So is Richard Gage, Michael Ruppert, Ignatius Donnelly and many of the other figures described in this book.

Even rank-and-file conspiracists see their belief system as something that elevates them from the mass of humanity that has not yet "awoken" to the Truth. Dan Tyler, a sixty-year-old Truther from Nashville, Tennessee, told me, "I don't know why it is that some of us can 'see' where others are blind, that some of us will question while others demur, that some of us will persevere despite the ridicule and damage we suffer for our unorthodox opinions. I don't know why it is, but I think the answer is important, for it goes to the very nature of truth. Is truth merely a consensus? Or is truth something else, something holy and sacred?"

Like religious fundamentalists and cult members, Truther activists tend to observe a rigid distinction between believers and infidels—between those with the courage to embrace the Truth and those who prefer to wallow in ignorance. As with Marxists who accuse nonbelievers of inhabiting a "false consciousness," many Truthers see non-Truther "sheeple" as not merely misinformed, but mentally deficient in some very basic way.

Yet enlightenment comes with a price. Regarding the actual moment when the truth dawned upon them, Truthers typically describe a complex mix of pride, psychic agony, and spiritual delirium—a phenomenon that can be observed in many conspiracist movements. In her study of UFO conspiracy theorists, for instance, American political scientist Jodi Dean found that "for most [self-reported UFO] abductees, the struggle over the real is interminable, ceaseless, an entangled process of tracing and retracing signs and events . . . At the same time, certain pleasures accompany abductees' break with conventional reality. Not only do they find themselves in the thick of conspiracies of global political significance, not only are they now important historical figures . . . but they are no longer duped by 'the system.'"

During my interviews, a surprising number of Truthers spun the same cinematic metaphor when describing this choice—the scene in the 1999 film *The Matrix* in which the heroes offer hallucinating slaves a simple pharmacological choice with existential consequences: "You take the blue pill, the story ends, you wake up in your bed and believe whatever you want to believe. You take the red pill, you stay in Wonderland, and I show you how deep the rabbit hole goes." Truthers commonly use the term "awake" to describe their embrace of conspiracist mythology—implying that their previous life comprised an artificial dream state not unlike the suspended animation imposed on Keanu Reeves' Neo.

But for some, the red pill proves too powerful a narcotic—and they lapse melodramatically into another Church-inspired role: the martyr.

The *Protocols* supplies an early prototype—Victor E. Marsden, the mysterious journalist who produced the most widely distributed English-language version of the WWI-era fraud. In a preface to Marsden's translation, which still circulates widely on the Internet, an admirer writes of the man's heroic efforts to escape Soviet Russia and communicate the truth to the English-speaking world: "It may be said with truth that this work was carried out at the cost of Mr. Marsden's own life's blood. He told the writer of this Preface that he could not stand more than an hour at a time of his work on it in the British Museum, as the diabolical spirit of the matter which he was obliged to turn into English made him positively ill. [In 1920], he was taken suddenly ill, and died after a very brief illness. May this work be his crowning monument!"

Many modern conspiracy theorists I've met similarly describe sickness or debilitating emotional agony that they blame on sudden exposure to the magnitude of evil threatening the world. "For three years I worked on this book, and the facts threaded through the fiction made me physically ill," writes Steve Alten in the "personal message" contained at the beginning of his Truther novel *The Shell Game.* "Three months after the original manuscript was finished, I was diagnosed with Parkinson's Disease. I was only 47, with no family history of the disease."

Likewise, Daniel Estulin, whose conspiracy theories about the Bilderberg Group were described in Chapter 1, writes of the "unimaginable hardships" he has endured "to expose the Bilderbergers' master plan for Global Government and One World Order." As he prepares for yet another stakeout at one of the group's annual conferences—this one in Stresa, Italy, in 2004—he lapses into the language of Revelation, with a lachrymose dose of self-congratulation: "Incoherent images danced in my head. Total Enslavement, Man-made famines that swept millions to their grave. Suffering, more suffering. Unspeakable human sacrifice. Why? Is it really possible that someone might want to inflict so much pain on the world for personal gain? As I struggled to hold back tears, I kept reminding myself that my quest for the truth was a vindication of decency at the expense of greed and power."

Michael Ruppert, too, has become something of a self-styled martyr since his days leading the 9/11 Truth movement in the early years after 9/11. Though he was briefly married in the mid–1990s, he lives alone now, in a tidy house that he shares with no one besides a dog. "No woman—no human being alive—could walk through what I was doing, could travel that path," he told me by way of explanation as we spoke in his living room. "Lots of poverty. Stress like you cannot believe. My whole life was taken away from me when I was twenty-seven. My attitude was 'I'll just put my personal life on hold till I straighten out this CIA and drug shit'—and here I am, thirty years later. I don't think I'm being boastful that when I say that of all the activists out there, I've had as much or more impact, but that came at a horrible price."

The Cultic Milieu

My argument in this chapter has been that conspiracy theories provide believers with many of the same psychological comforts as religion. Like many faiths, conspiracism supplies adherents with a Manichean moral structure, a satanic explanation for evil, and the promise of utopia. But since they do not require believers to express faith in an actual deity, they are well suited for our secular age.

Conspiracism is different from conventional religious faiths in at least one other respect, however: It is inherently unstable.

Because the conspiracy theorist is driven by a need to smash the façade of conventional reality and existing power structures, he is forever seeking to probe deeper than his peers, to uncover truths that they are not quite bold enough to confront. This is why conspiracist networks, like radical revolutionary movements, are prone to continual schism, with members on all sides accusing one another of being secretly in league with the evildoers.

Jew-hating conspiracy theorists, for instance, are forever outing one another as closet Jews. During infighting at the Holocaust-denying *Journal of Historical Review* in the mid–1990s, claims were traded about which side was in the pay of the

Anti-Defamation League. More recently, anti-Semitic Truther Eric Hufschmid has claimed that Ernst Zundel is a "Zionist agent." Meanwhile, Hufschmid's anti-Semitic naysayers claim he is "a member of the Jewish criminal network that he claims to expose." (One website set up in 2009 is actually called "Eric Hufschmid works for the Jews.")

A similar pattern plays out among Shakespeare conspiracists, who in the early twentieth century began abandoning Francis Bacon as the true Great Bard, and instead focused on Edward de Vere, 17th Earl of Oxford. These Oxfordians, in turn, schismed in the 1930s over the so-called Prince Tudor theory, which had it that Oxford and Queen Elizabeth were in fact the parents of the (illegitimate) Earl of Southampton—following which came a yet more elaborate theory ("Prince Tudor, Part II"), according to which Oxford was both Elizabeth's lover *and* son. (As James Shapiro explains in *Contested Will*, the Prince Tudor theories help clarify Oxfordians' status as—what I call—failed historians: "If Oxford had been given his due in his own day, and his son Southampton had ascended to the throne upon their mother's death in 1603, perhaps Britain might have avoided an irreversible breakdown in hierarchy and order that led to a wrenching Civil War, and subsequently to the rise of modernity, imperialism, and capitalism"—all of these creeds being the bugbear of Positivists, and in particular, of the Oxfordians' authoritarian, medievalist guru, J. T. Looney.)

The wider Truth movement exhibits the same dynamic. Though less than a decade old, it already has split into anti-Israeli and anti-anti-Israeli factions; into an older, left-wing, anti-American wing and a younger, right-wing, libertarian wing; between those who insist that Truther activism should focus on the internal demolition of the Twin Towers, and those who entertain more exotic theories involving space weapons and cruise missiles. The most common tactic in these schismatic battles is the cloak-and-dagger accusation that the other side has been compromised by "COINTELPRO"—an acronym for Counter Intelligence Program, which refers to a covert Cold War–era FBI program aimed at covertly infiltrating and discrediting dissident political organizations.

At the same time, these conspiracists also tend to be perennially on the search for entirely unrelated theories that nourish their gut sense that mainstream society is counterfeit and morally bankrupt. And so a conspiracist whose initial obsession revolved around Jews may eventually migrate toward conspiracy theories involving water fluoridation and vaccines. Or a JFK conspiracy theorist may become convinced the government is hiding evidence of UFO landings. Often these "migratory" conspiracists will combine their new and old obsessions in bizarre and unique ways—blurring the lines of the typology I supplied in the previous chapter.

At Truther events, I make a special point of browsing the DVDs being sold by the vendors who inevitably set up shop in the back of the room. Truther classics such as *Loose Change* and *9/11*: *Blueprint For Truth* were always brisk sellers. But so, too, are *Vaccine Nation* (which promotes the myth that vaccines cause autism), *Vatican Assassins* (contending the assassination of JFK was "ordered by the Jesuit General and executed by Pope Paul VI"), and *Children of the Matrix*: *How an Interdimensional Race Has Controlled the World for Thousands of Years . . . And Still Does* (whose title, I think, is self-explanatory). Another popular genre is the pseudohistory that British author Damian Thompson calls "hyperdiffusionism"—which postulates that all of the West's greatest cultural achievements and archeological artifacts originate from some mysterious ancient civilization (Atlantis is a popular choice, largely thanks to the nineteenth-century writings of Ignatius Donnelly) whose forebears roamed the earth in ancient times.

For many conspiracists I encountered, the hopscotch from one theory to the next becomes a sort of addiction—with the promise of total enlightenment always being just another mouse click or DVD away. On a web forum created for ex-Truthers by the James Randi Educational Foundation, for instance, one contributor described his pinballing through the various species of conspiracism and New Age hocus-pocus this way:

It [started] with Google/Google videos of 9/11. During the af-
ternoons I just couldn't stop watching that. And from [Loose
Change] I went to Alex Jones' [radio show] and I was curious
about his claims, so I listened to him. And I just took in everything he said. From Info wars to skull and bones to Owl
worshiping. I took it all in. I got to the Bilderberg group, then
black helicopters interacting with lights near crop circles, then
abductions and UFO videos to New Age interpretations of
them, then [eschatological theories of] 2012. I became a Raelian at one point, seeing design in nature (these aliens supposedly created every tree and bird and animal thanks to their
creativity), and from the Elohim (the aliens of the Raelian cult)
I went to Greys [humanoid aliens visiting earth] and . . . the
reptilians. Of course, the reptilians were behind every triangu-
lar architecture and ancient symbolics found ANYWHERE,
including Mars, and probably were the Illuminati, thinking of
taking over the world with a New World Order, using Fugifilm
zeppelins with some occult technology to look into our houses
and spread mind controlling poison through contrails. Obviously, 9/11 was just one step in their plan . . . I was, what? 16,
17? [My mother] would shake her head with [laughter] when I
told her that I knew a lot more than her. Now, I understand her.

It's a sad story, but at least it has a happy ending. Most Truthers
who set off down the rabbit hole never come back.

| PART III |

Accessories to Trutherdom

In Part I of this book, I described the history of conspiracism, and its changing face from the French Revolution to the post-9/11 era. In Part II, in which the focus narrowed from the sociological to the psychological, I analyzed the motives and belief systems of individual conspiracy theorists. My goal throughout was to show how conspiracism threatens the intellectual foundations of rationalism by eroding the baseline presumption that we all inhabit the same reality.

In the next three chapters, I will analyze why rationalism has given way to conspiracism so readily—even in the face of a trio of intellectual trends once expected to render superstitious and hateful ideologies obsolete: the rise of information technology, widespread access to higher education, and the enshrinement of tolerance and diversity as state-sanctioned secular creeds.

CHAPTER SEVEN

Democratizing Paranoia: How the Web Revolutionized Conspiracism

The Legacy of Flight 800

On July 17, 1996, Trans World Airlines Flight 800 took off from JKF airport in New York en route to Leonardo da Vinci Airport in Rome, climbed toward an altitude of about 15,000 feet, and then exploded near the Long Island town of East Moriches. All 230 people on board were killed.

Many Americans immediately assumed the tragedy was a terrorist attack. Several eyewitnesses said they saw a streak of light heading upward in the seconds before the aircraft exploded. But after a lengthy investigation, the FBI announced they'd found no evidence of a criminal act. The National Transportation Safety Board eventually concluded that Flight 800 probably exploded due to an explosion within a fuel tank set off by faulty wiring.

But the controversy surrounding TWA Flight 800 refused to die. To this day, conspiracy theorists insist the NTSB organized a cover-up to protect the U.S. Navy, which supposedly downed the plane with a missile. In 1997, a retired police officer even broke into a hangar housing the reconstructed wreckage of Flight 800 to steal seat-fabric samples that he believed would help disprove the official theory. The next year, the prestigious *New York Review of Books* published an article by a Harvard English professor suggesting that

Flight 800 had been brought down by electromagnetic interference from a passing military aircraft. Others theorized that the incident was connected to the upcoming trial of Ramzi Yousef, who was then awaiting trial for his role in the 1993 World Trade Center bombing—and that the FBI had been tipped off in advance.

The swirl of suspicion and confusion initially surrounding the tragedy was understandable. The destruction of the aircraft seemed to resemble a number of earlier terrorist attacks, including the Lockerbie bombing of 1988. Just a month previous, terrorists had blown up the Khobar Towers housing complex in Saudi Arabia, killing nineteen U.S. servicemen. The year before, Timothy McVeigh had blown up the Oklahoma City federal building. The Atlanta Olympics—a ripe terrorist target—were just two days away. Terrorism was on America's mind.

But there was another exacerbating factor, as well, one that would herald a new era for all species of conspiracists: the release of the Netscape Navigator web browser in late 1994, and the explosive growth of the World Wide Web that would immediately follow. For the first time, conspiracists were able to get their theories into the public sphere instantly. As Eastern Illinois University scholar Shane Miller concluded in a published analysis of the Flight 800–themed websites that came online in late 1996 and the years following, "this was the first major conspiracy of the internet age."

Over the last decade and a half, the Internet has utterly transformed conspiracism—no less than it's transformed pornography, music distribution, journalism, and social networking. Prior to the mid–1990s, conspiracy theorists pursued their investigations in isolated obscurity, typing out manifestoes on basement card tables, or amid the nonfiction stacks at their local library. The stigma associated with their craft, in conjunction with the communications limitations predating the World Wide Web, meant that each conspiracist was essentially a unique movement unto himself, his ideas mutating and evolving without social input from others—like an obscure species of land animal confined to a remote island.

Just about every author in the field of JFK conspiracism, for instance, has the president dying in a somewhat different way, at the hands of a customized menagerie of secret agents, gangsters, and Cubans (a state of conspiracist confusion captured nicely by a *faux* headline in the *Onion*, datelined in 1963: "Kennedy slain by CIA, Mafia, Castro, LBJ, Teamsters, Freemasons: President shot 129 times from 43 different angles").

Flight 800 marked the moment that the solitary aspect of the conspiracist métier ended. Amid the plethora of newly blooming blogs and discussion fora, the construction of conspiracy theories became a collective exercise—what modern computer scientists would call an "open source" project. Rather than authors offering their own scattered, mutually incompatible, proprietary ideas, they began operating within a collaborative network, much like the editors and contributors who produce Linux and Wikipedia. All of the tiny little islands of paranoia suddenly were linked up by virtual causeways.

One result is that elaborate conspiracy theories now can be cobbled together literally overnight through the efforts of hundreds of scattered dilettante conspiracists. Another result is that conspiracists all around the world now tend to focus on the same few dozen talking points that figure prominently on the top websites.

Within only a few weeks of investigating the Truth movement, for instance, I found I already was hearing the same handful of 9/11 "anomalies" recited to me over and over from emerging Truther factions—Larry Silverstein's use of the words "pull it," the molten WTC metal that could only have been melted with thermite, the neat collapse of WTC 7, the failure of NORAD to intercept the hijacked jets. In the case of JFK, and even the French Revolution, conspiracists still can't agree on who gets the blame—despite the passage of generations. Yet with the 9/11 Truth movement, it took only months for conspiracists to collectively declare *J'accuse* at the trio of Dick Cheney, Donald Rumsfeld, and Paul Wolfowitz.

The Internet has produced a radical democratization of the

conspiracist marketplace of ideas. No longer does one have to spend years researching and writing a book to attract attention: One can simply set up a blog, or chime in on someone else's, with some refinement of the existing collective lore. In fact, today's conspiracists don't even have to *read* books—they can pick up all their talking points from Truther websites, or, better yet, from Truther propaganda videos. *Memoirs Illustrating the History of Jacobinism*, Augustin Barruel's 1798-99 classic conspiracist opus about the French Revolution, ran for thousands of pages, and took weeks to read. The Warren Commission report ran to twenty-six volumes. Watching the latest edition of *Loose Change*, on the other hand, takes about an hour and a half.

The prototypical JFK conspiracist was Harold Weisberg, a lifelong Warren Commission critic who wrote eight books, and accumulated sixty filing cabinets full of JFK documents (many procured through his own laborious Freedom of Information Act requests) at his Frederick, Maryland, farmhouse over the course of thirty-five years. By contrast Weisberg's 9/11-era equivalent—mega-Truther David Ray Griffin—wrote even more books in the space of just five years, all of them based in large part on material he found while surfing the Internet.

This dumbing-down effect explains the downward shift in the age profile of conspiracists: While influential JFK conspiracy theorists tended to be bookish middle-aged eccentrics, many of the Internet's noisiest Truthers are barely old enough to shave: Conspiracism is something they fit in between video gaming and Facebook.

Muckraking 2.0

The birth of the Internet was not the first time a media revolution had remade the world of conspiracism. In 1906, U.S. President Theodore Roosevelt delivered a speech denouncing a new kind of journalist—"the man with the Muck-rake, the man who could look no way but downward with the muck-rake in his hands; who was offered a celestial crown for his muck-rake, but who would neither look up nor regard the crown he was offered, but continued to rake to himself the filth of the floor."

Roosevelt was thought to be singling out the yellow journalism produced by William Randolph Hearst's media empire. But Hearst wasn't the only offender: By the early twentieth century, "muckraking" was a well-established practice everywhere across the American journalistic landscape.

The negative connotation associated with the term is undeserved: The muckrakers' mission—to expose corruption in business and government, and document the wretchedness of society's have-nots—aroused popular support for the reforms ushered in by the Progressive Era, and set the stage for the modern forms of investigative and human-interest journalism we know today.

Early muckraking investigations detailed payoffs at city hall, inhumane working conditions in factories and mines, and the predatory practices of great industrialists. The common theme throughout was power and its abuses. As legendary twentieth-century journalist Robert Cantwell put it, the muckrakers "traced the intricate relationship of the police, the underworld, the local political bosses, the secret connections between the new corporations . . . and the legislatures and the courts. In doing this, they drew a new cast of characters for the drama of American society: bosses, professional politicians, reformers, racketeers, captains of industry."

Readers of this new brand of journalism came to view their country as a dark, dog-eat-dog place, full of secret conspiracies. "Reality now was rough and sordid," Richard Hofstadter wrote in *The Age of Reform*. "It was hidden, neglected, and off-stage. It was conceived essentially as that stream of external and material events which was most likely to be unpleasant. Reality was the bribe, the rebate, the bought franchise, the sale of adulterated food. It was

what one found in [Upton Sinclair's] *The Jungle*, [Frank Norris']
The Octopus, [Henry Demarest Lloyd's] *Wealth Against Commonwealth*, or [Lincoln Steffens'] *The Shame of the Cities* . . . Reality
was a series of unspeakable plots."

As we've seen, populist fearmongering against big government
and greedy corporations was a dominant political theme in the
United States long before the rise of the muckrakers. But the new
forms of journalism, coupled with a trend toward realism in literature, invigorated populism by providing a vivid human element.
Till the early twentieth century, America's bogeymen generally
were ill defined in the public imagination. In many cases, they
were simply crude caricatures—fat men in top hats who appeared
in editorial cartoons and satirical pamphlets. Beginning with the
rise of the muckrakers, newspapers, radio stations, and eventually
television would show Americans the true face of America's power
structure. To quote Hofstadter again, this time writing in *The Paranoid Style in American Politics* (1964): "The villains of the modern
Right are much more vivid than those of their paranoid predeces-
sors . . . For the vaguely delineated villains of the anti-Masons, for
the obscure and disguised Jesuit agents, the little-known papal delegates of the anti-Catholics, for the shadowy international bankers of the monetary conspiracies, we may now substitute eminent
public figures like Presidents Roosevelt, Truman, and Eisenhower,
Secretaries of State like Marshall, Acheson, and Dulles, Justices of
the Supreme Court like Frankfurter and Warren, and the whole
battery of lesser but still famous and vivid alleged conspirators
headed by Alger Hiss."

Even in the 1950s, Hofstadter seemed to understand the threat
to rationalism posed by the mass media. Indeed, much of what he
wrote in his era directly foreshadowed the overall shrillness and
paranoia that would come to infuse cable television and the Internet—technologies that wouldn't arrive in American homes till
after his death in 1970. "The growth of the mass media of communication and their use in politics have brought politics closer to

the people than ever before and have made politics a form of entertainment . . . an arena into which private emotions and personal problems can be readily projected. Mass communications have made it possible to keep the mass man in an almost constant state of mobilization": These are words that could have been written about the media climate surrounding the 2010 midterm elections. Yet they were published by Hofstadter (in his essay "The Pseudo-Conservative Revolt") during Dwight D. Eisenhower's first term.

During my law school years in the mid–1990s, I spent a lot of time on east coast highways, driving back and forth between the Yale campus in New Haven, Connecticut, my family home in Montreal, and my various summer jobs at law firms in Washington, D.C., New York City, and Pittsburgh. During my late-night drives, I would flip through the AM dial trying to keep myself entertained.

My favorite station was WFAN, a popular all-sports outfit broadcasting throughout the northeastern states from its studios in Astoria, New York. The Fan, as it's widely known, covers all major American sports. But the overwhelming focus is on the Giants, Jets, Yankees, Mets, Knicks, and Rangers—with a significant dose of Islanders, Nets, Devils, and college sports when circumstances warrant. Listening to the Fan was like hanging out with a bipolar friend: When a New York team won, the mood of WFAN's callers was euphoric. If they lost, the callers' collective mood ranged from depressed to apoplectic.

Coming from Montreal, where hockey is a secular religion, I was used to obsessive sports-fan culture. But the New York City variant has a different tone. For the regulars who called in to WFAN, a loss could never be chalked up to something so banal as the other team just playing better. There was always a scapegoat—the coach, the ref, league officials, an underperforming deadbeat star. The loathing heaped on these figures was like something out of a Stalin-era communist shaming ritual. While rooting for the home team is seen as an all-American activity, there was something unhinged about these radio rants. Looking beyond the slick burbling of the hosts, and the canned studio effects, I sensed a sort of seething, tribalized fury at the unjustness of a world in which Patrick Ewing was incapable of bringing the Knicks an NBA championship.

As I surfed the dial, I found that the motifs of resentment and outrage were constant and inescapable. Dr. Laura Schlessinger—who seemed always to be on the air back in the mid–1990s, no matter what time of day it was—held forth dogmatically about the evils of sexual promiscuity, the gay lobby, permissive parents, and doormat girlfriends. The Evangelical stations offered the "Good News" of Jesus' message, but in the same breath denounced the depravity of modern America, and urged godly listeners to prepare for a coming apocalyptic confrontation with the forces of the Antichrist. In the wee hours, one could hear whole shows given over to secular conspiracy theories—UFOs, bizarre medical experiments, flying cars.

Then there was the king of the dial, Rush Limbaugh, a former disc jockey from Sacramento who'd become a force of radio nature in the late 1980s. Like the preachers, his tone was superficially chipper—but his message was serious. "Liberalism is a scourge," he declared to an interviewer in 1993, summarizing his worldview. "It destroys the human spirit. It destroys prosperity. It assigns sameness to everybody." I found myself hypnotized by his style—which channeled all of the populist rage I'd heard on WFAN into the equally tribalized world of American politics.

As Brian Anderson argued in his 2005 book, *South Park Conservatives: The Revolt Against Liberal Media Bias*, the populist AM talk-radio movement that Limbaugh godfathered changed the face of American politics. Among other accomplishments, it sank Hillarycare, propelled the Republicans to domination of both houses of Congress in 1994, and (most significantly) convinced tens of millions of Americans that the news they read and saw in the mainstream media was tainted by liberal bias. Better yet, Limbaugh spread his message with a confident, entertaining, self-satirizing brio that differed sharply from conventional network news broadcasts. The fact that it was a mass phenomenon—a world away from the somewhat haughty, rarified world of NPR—was itself a selling point for the Limbaugh brand: Many of his listeners felt they were enlisting in a newly formed ideological legion, not unlike the modern Tea Party, that would make its collective voice heard in Washington. In 1996, that legion would go on to become the core audience of a brand new, unapologetically opinionated television network called FOX News.

What launched Limbaugh's career wasn't a backlash against any particular development in American politics or culture. (He started his nationally broadcast show in 1988, at a time when the Republicans still controlled the White House, and Bill Clinton was still the governor of Arkansas.) It was something more mundane: the reform of broadcast regulations that had been muzzling American radio hosts since 1949.

The old policy was the Federal Communications Commission's Fairness Doctrine, a rule that required broadcasters to give equal time to both sides of an issue. In theory, the rule meant that if a radio host promoted, say, gun control, his station was required to provide time for the NRA to deliver a rebuttal. In practice, most station owners simply avoided political talk entirely. But in 1987, Dennis Patrick, named as FCC chairman by Ronald Reagan, repealed the doctrine, setting off an immediate boom in political programming.

When Limbaugh began broadcasting nationally in 1988, Americans still thought of political talk as a stuffy business conducted by Beltway insiders and bow-tied pundits, the sort of thing one endured before football on Sundays. But Limbaugh was an entertainer who salted his rhetoric with satire. "Greetings, conservatives across the fruited plain," went an introductory riff. "This is Rush Limbaugh, the most dangerous man in America, with the largest hypothalamus in North America, serving humanity simply by opening my mouth, destined for my own wing in the Museum of Broadcasting, executing everything I do flawlessly with zero mistakes, doing this show with half my brain tied behind my back just to make it fair because I have a talent on loan from . . . God. Rush Limbaugh. A man. A legend. A way of life."

Prior to the 1980s, the primary forum for movement conservatism had been think-tank newsletters and wonky magazines like *National Review*. But these weren't outlets for the common man: *National Review*'s circulation peaked in 1994 at 270,000, about one-fiftieth the number of listeners that Limbaugh attracts every week. With the rise of conservative talk radio and then FOX, William Buckley, George Will, and other members of conservative's old, patrician guard suddenly found themselves on the sidelines.

But even after deregulation, the basic structure of the mass media still presented a problem for true conspiracy theorists: Radio stations and cable channels, no less than newspapers and magazines, generally remained in the control of large, profit-seeking, risk-averse corporations. And all of them—including Limbaugh's show—remained staffed by a hierarchy of gatekeeping producers and editors.

Historically, these factors never have served to exclude conspiracism from the mass media entirely (as a late-night trip through the AM radio dial will attest). But they generally have restricted it to themes that were politically popular, or at least tolerated, by society at large—such as anti-Masonry in the nineteenth century, racism and anti-Semitism in the decades before WWII, and anti-communism in the 1950s. In all other contexts, conspiracists were forced to the disreputable margins of the media marketplace: pornographic magazines, leaflet handouts, church-basement lectures, late-night radio, and community-access television.

The Internet destroyed all of these communications barriers overnight, which is why it immediately became the dominant hub for virtually every conspiracist subculture in existence—including jihadism. (The only exception is Scientology, which continues to be promoted primarily through the movement's well-funded bricks-and-mortar urban drop-in centers—and this only because its controlling body operates as a moneymaking business, and therefore aggressively enforces copyright on the movement's texts.) Communication on the web is cheap, global, immediate, and uncensored. And so it is perfectly suited for unfunded, geographically disparate activists seeking to promote a dissident message.

Just as importantly, the Internet fuels the conspiracist's fervor by providing him with a sense of community. In the modern age, conspiracism has blurred into social networking in many contexts: Activists are constantly leaving comments on one another's blogs and Facebook pages, emailing tips and links back and forth, and even interviewing one another on Internet radio shows. While some of this networking consists of the exchange of substantive information, it also represents an exercise in mutual self-congratulation and emotional support.

As this positive social feedback becomes addictive, the conspiracist's network of enablers grows—often to such a point that it crowds out the conspiracy theorist's nonbelieving friends. The process resembles the formation of an electronic cocoon that envelops a conspiracist with codependents. Surrounded by an enabling group of the like-minded, he gradually embraces the delusion that his movement has gained critical mass, and that his blog postings and email petitions are being read in the corridors of power.

The modern web-based conspiracist has a conflicted attitude toward the mainstream media. On the one hand, he is a futurist who triumphantly dismisses the printing press and the evening news as a relic of a bygone pre-Internet age. And so he takes a reflexive, shoot-the-messenger approach to any mainstream criticism of his movement. Whenever a mainstream newspaper or magazine cuts jobs or goes bankrupt, conspiracist websites inevitably erupt in spasms of *schadenfreude*—citing the news as proof that the old top-down, elitist model of journalism is giving way to an epic communications revolution that they themselves claim to be leading.

To quote Truther Kevin Barrett: "It is necessary that folklorists and others in the human sciences think about the way the many-to-many medium of digitally-enhanced folk communication is overthrowing the old one-to-many media of elite-generated social control that have dominated more and more of this planet over the past 5,000 years. To study the 9/11 truth movement is to study what may turn out to be the cutting edge of the most significant social-structural change in the history of humanity."

Yet notwithstanding such utopian notions, most conspiracists understand that the hated "MSM" is still an influential player in the marketplace of ideas. And so it is maddening that CNN and the *New York Times* persist in ignoring their "discoveries" about 9/11 and other false-flag plots. At Truther events where I was publicly outed as a journalistic observer by someone at the microphone (a common occurrence after I'd published a few *National Post* columns about my interest in conspiracy theories), I noticed a mix of contradictory reactions. On one hand, I was applauded for my "courage" in breaking an MSM taboo, and exposing myself to the Truth firsthand. On the other hand, I also was treated as a flesh-and-blood target on which Truthers could unleash cultish, pent-up hostility against my industry. Often, angry activists would lecture me about what other journalists had written about their profession—as if I bore some fraternal responsibility for the crimes of my MSM colleagues.

Through the Internet's Looking Glass

In 2005, Harvard Law School professor Cass Sunstein and two other researchers performed an experiment involving sixty Colorado adults. Sunstein divided the participants into two sets of small groups—one conservative, one liberal—based on their responses to a screening questionnaire, and then asked them to discuss three contentious questions: (1) "Should states allow same-sex couples to enter into civil unions?" (2) "Should employers engage in 'affirmative action' by giving a preference to members of traditionally disadvantaged groups?" (3) "Should the United States sign an international treaty to combat global warming?"

Not surprisingly, the self-identified conservatives were more likely than self-identified liberals to answer no to all of these questions, both before and after their discussions. But Sunstein noted another interesting pattern: In virtually all of the groups, members ended up embracing more polarized positions following fifteen minutes of conversation with their ideological bedfellows—a phenomenon he describes in his research as "group polarization."

These results help demonstrate why modern electronic communication tools have done little to break down ideological divides—and, in many cases, have helped exacerbate them.

When the Internet became a truly mass medium in the late 1990s, there was a widespread belief that it heralded a golden age not only in communication, but in human relations: With so much information available for free from all around the world, futurists gushed, human beings would come to understand one another as never before. Like the ham-radio enthusiasts of yesteryear, we would spend our days conversing with people from other continents and opposite points on the ideological spectrum, building bridges of knowledge and understanding.

The result has been just the opposite: The Internet actually has exacerbated the human instinct toward parochialism, tribalism, and conspiracism.

Most web surfers, it turns out, have little interest in meeting pen pals in faraway places. Instead, people tend to use the web for work, school, shopping, entertainment, celebrity gossip, cute videos, photo-sharing, and chatting with people they already know. (It's notable, for instance, that MySpace, which facilitates social networking between strangers, has for years been losing market share to Facebook, which is designed to create virtual networks out of real-life flesh-and-blood friendships.) When using the Internet to access news, most of us tend to consult a small set of sites that cater to our preexisting ideological niche. Politically active leftists, for instance, tend to get their news from sites such as Huffington Post, Daily Kos, Democratic Underground, *The Guardian*, and CounterPunch; while those on the Right go to Instapundit, National Review Online, Free Republic, and FOX News. Among bloggers and cable TV talking heads, the need to get noticed amid the din of competing voices has had a centrifugal effect, pushing commentary to the outer fringes on both sides of the Left-Right spectrum. According to a principle known as Godwin's Law, attributed to famed Internet lawyer Mike Godwin, every argument on the Internet always ends up with one side being compared to Adolf Hitler. Thanks to Glenn Beck, Godwin's Law may be observed on your TV screen as well.

Many true conspiracy theorists I've met don't even bother with web surfing anymore—they rely for their news on the menu of stories that are delivered automatically to their email accounts through RSS feeds, daily email newsletters, and Facebook groups. From the very instant they first boot up their computer in the morning, their inboxes comprise an unbroken catalog of outrage stories ideologically tailored to their preexisting obsessions.

The image of the world that emerges from this catalog bears little resemblance to the world most of us know. It is a dark, conspiratorial place where (to take the right-wing sites as an example) Christianity is under siege, political correctness has gone amok, militant gay activists have taken over every school board, and the White House flies the green flag of Islam. A sampling of WorldNet-Daily news alerts from late 2009 and early 2010, for instance, presented readers with this itemized description of the state of America: "Lesbian awarded custody of Christian's only child," "Fistgate: Obama chief 'knew' of 'disgusting' sex subjects," "Christian fathers put in jail for shunning explicit sex ed," "Obama's Christmas tree has Chairman Mao, transvestite," "Girl Scouts hiding secret sex agenda?" and "Banished! City forbids Bible studies in homes."

Overtorqued as WorldNetDaily's stories may be, they qualify as blue-chip journalism compared to much of what gets passed around on peer-to-peer email networks. In late 2008, for instance, a message declaring that Barack Obama was a secret Muslim made its way into millions of inboxes. Another popular claim was that the U.S. government was going to create a 9/11 memorial that was crescent-shaped, in tribute to the Islamic faith of the terrorists—a myth that effectively tapped into conservatives' (not entirely baseless) belief that the nation's media and government were bending over backwards to avoid offending Muslims. Such tall tales typically remain popular on the Internet for months or even years at a stretch—the Internet-era equivalent of medieval folk legends. In all cases, it would take the credulous recipient just a few seconds to check these rumors against a reputable website such as Snopes or Wikipedia. But if the rumor accords with his or her preexisting conspiracist fears, he often will simply assume it is true and forward it to his friends.

In some cases, Internet rumor-mongering—or even just the fear thereof—has served to reverse government decisions and policies. In October 2010, for instance, Barack Obama canceled a scheduled trip to the Sikh Golden Temple in Amritsar, India, because Sikh tradition would have required the president to wear a head covering before entering the temple; and the resulting photo-op would have encouraged rumors that Obama is Muslim. (Americans often confuse the Islamic and Sikh faiths. Four days after 9/11, in fact, a murderer gunned down a Sikh gas station attendant in Mesa, Arizona, believing him to be Muslim.)

In Texas, an Internet-based conspiracist campaign helped preempt one of the largest infrastructure projects in U.S. history—the Trans-Texas Corridor (TTC), a four-thousand-mile road-and-rail transportation network that would parallel Interstate 35 and US 59, both of which have become congested in recent years thanks to the increased flow of goods to and from Mexico. The tipping point came after a business coalition called North America's SuperCorridor Coalition (NASCO) put out a stylized map showing how the TTC would anchor a spine of road-and-rail arteries extending from southern Mexico to Montreal, Winnipeg, Edmonton, and Vancouver. The most strident critics of the TTC—including WorldNetDaily writer Jerome Corsi, who included a chapter on the subject in his 2007 conspiracist book *The Late Great USA: The Coming Merger With Mexico and Canada*—seized on the image as proof that the plan actually was part of a larger plot (hatched by the Council on Foreign Relations) to destroy America's national sovereignty by creating an EU-style "North American Union"—complete with a new currency (the "Amero") and a secret "shadow government" created under the auspices of the American-Canadian-Mexican Security and Prosperity Partnership. These conspiracy theories became so popular in the latter years of the Bush presidency—almost entirely on the strength of web-circulated propaganda—that legislatures in eighteen states actually introduced resolutions condemning the mythical "NAFTA Superhighway" of which the TTC supposedly was a part; and Lou Dobbs denounced it on CNN. In the end, the TTC plan became so politically toxic that it fizzled.

Mainstream journalists have been known to turn their noses up at the Internet's rumor mill. But the paranoid character of the blogosphere has, without a doubt, rubbed off on them. During the Bush administration, *New York Times* op-ed columnists Frank Rich and Paul Krugman became celebrities by portraying George W. Bush and Dick Cheney as outright liars seeking to turn the United States into a warmongering theocracy. On the Right, FOX News host Glenn Beck—whom a Gallup poll identified in December 2009 as the fourth-most-admired man in America (between Nelson Mandela and Pope Benedict XVI)—has described President Barack Obama as "a guy who has a deep-seated hatred for white people or the white culture," likened Democratic health care plans to the content of *Mein Kampf,* and warned that the

United States is headed toward "totalitarianism beyond your wildest imagination." (For a time, Beck even spread the notion that FEMA is building concentration camps in the United States to jail "dissidents.") Seized by the same spirit, Rush Limbaugh has suggested to his listeners that Barack Obama might cancel the 2012 elections, and that environmentalists might have blown up BP's Deepwater Horizon offshore drilling rig in the Gulf of Mexico as a plot to derail offshore oil exploration. ("The Constitution has just been ripped to shreds, so why is anything safe?" he asked listeners.) In this overheated media environment, with extremists from both sides cheering one another on in their self-selected echo chambers, the stigma against conspiracism enforced by the professional journalist guild of the postwar era is eroding.

Thanks to the way information is accessed on the Internet, even the most prosaic inquiries can lead users down the path of conspiracism. Columbia University Shakespeare expert James Shapiro was appalled to learn, in 2009, that "Nine of the top 10 hits in a recent Google search for 'Shakespeare' and 'authorship' directed the curious to sites that called into question Shakespeare's authorship." Anxious parents who enter "vaccines" and "autism" into Google's search engine will find prominent links to sites that promote the debunked link between vaccine "neurotoxins" and autism. Enter "9/11" into Google, and you will find links to Truther conspiracy sites. Google "WTC 7," and the very first site is a Truth site—which means it will pop up automatically using Google's "I'm feeling lucky" option.

The problem is that Google, the most popular search engine, generally ranks sites according to their popularity—not their reliability. So a flashy, well-traveled site peddling discredited conspiracies will be featured more prominently in Google's search results than, say, a government website full of accurate information about the same subject. In many cases, the most authoritative information doesn't turn up in a Google search at all—because it is buried in "deep web" repositories such as subscription-only scientific journals, journalistic archives, court records, and government databases.

Once ensnared, Internet conspiracists often exhibit the same obsessive behavior patterns as people addicted to Internet gambling services, pornography, and video games: The material they crave is cheap (or free), unlimited, and accessible within the privacy of their own home. Like other kinds of addicts, they describe an initial period of addiction in which they remained glued to their computer screens for weeks on end. One former Truther, for instance, described this descent into addiction following a tip from a Rastafarian Truther who worked at his local "head shop": "Feeling very Matrix-ish, I watched *Zeitgeist* [a 2007 Truther film] and thought it made sense. I was poor and unsuccessful and here was why. The Federal Reserve, Bilderbergers, NWO, CENTCOM, Henry Kissinger, and Karl Rove were all keeping me down. Now that I was on Google Video, I had a whole library of CT movies to watch for free . . . I literally spent two weeks watching what I thought was a worldwide conspiracy being unveiled before my very eyes."

Internet conspiracism propagates itself using a cross-fertilization model: Facebook pages, email lists and blogs associated with a given conspiracist camp invariably become sympathetic sounding boards for related conspiracy theories. In the Summer of 2005, for instance, 9/11 Truth sites became inundated with theorists claiming that the London transit bombings were an inside job. And when the H1N1 virus hit in the fall of 2009, the established network of autism/antivaccine conspiracy theorists immediately incorporated the new vaccine drive into their propaganda.

Often, conspiracist propaganda appears just days, or even hours, after the underlying event—even before the "official" narrative has been fully developed in the mainstream media. On the afternoon of November 5, 2009, as I was writing this chapter, Nidal Malik Hasan walked into the Soldier Readiness Center at Ford Hood military base outside Killeen, Texas, jumped onto a desk, and began firing shots from a semiautomatic pistol. By the time his rampage was over, thirteen people were dead, and thirty others were wounded. The circumstances of the killings—perpetrated by a military psychiatrist with a documented record of erratic behaviour and religious radicalism, and observed directly by dozens of surviving witnesses—hardly lent themselves to conspiracy theories. Yet shortly thereafter, a conspiracist narrative began taking shape on FederalJack.com, a self-described "user driven news source dedicated to exposing information and multimedia relating to the New World Order takeover of the United States and the rest of the free world":

> Ok, let's get this out of the way. Fort Hood—tragic. Now let's look at some reality. *One* guy shooting a hand gun killed *how* many people—and on a military base? Are you serious? And the one shooter is now in a coma? And, as of now at least, there's no surveillance camera footage? And he's a Muslim who also happens to be a serviceman with a mental disorder involving gunplay who did it with privately owned weapons? This thing could not have been scripted or casted better if Hollywood had produced it. Let's see: Private gun ownership demonized—check. Muslims demonized—check. Military personnel demonized—check. Base-dwelling troops at home terrorized by a fellow American—check. Yet another chance to distract the public—check . . . Thirteen killed and 30 wounded by one man with two pistols. Nearly a 50% kill rate. Ever fired a handgun? Ever tried aiming and firing two at a time? Under pressure? Ever reload a handgun under pressure? There were people shooting at him. That's a little pressure. We're talking about yet *another* superhuman performance by a 'lone gunman' who is conveniently not conscious to tell the tale . . . 'But the government would never do such a thing to its own troops!' Uh, excuse me. It's putting thousands of them through a meat grinder in a pointless, unwinnable charade of a war as we speak—in two countries, while gearing up for two more (Iran and Paki-

stan). Do you think the dead and wounded from overseas are any less dead and wounded [than the] victims from Fort Hood?

Links to the FederalJack site began popping up all over the established Truther groups I was monitoring, and the narrative was quickly assimilated into their mythology. For the web addicts who get their news from such sites, the official theory never had a chance.

In the real world, all of us learn—usually quite early in life—that some sources of information are more trustworthy than others; that some people are experts, and others are not, that some people lie, and other people tell the truth. When people try to convince us to buy something from them, or sleep with them, or take their advice, we scrutinize their faces, their clothes, their mannerisms, their backgrounds, for indicators of expertise and sincerity. But on the Internet, where disreputable sources can hide behind the anonymizing silkscreen of a professional-seeming website, all these age-old human safeguards are short-circuited—making it an ideal medium for conspiracists who, in person, often seem eccentric. In many cases, fringe conspiracy theorists even have managed to create professional-seeming "journals" that lend scholarly prestige to their fantasies, such as the "peer-reviewed" *Journal of 9/11 Studies*. Many of the Truthers I correspond with now back up their theories with citations from such publications, expecting that they be treated with the same seriousness as *Nature* or *Proceedings of the National Academy of Science*.

Like everything else discussed in this chapter, this toxic distortion of the marketplace of ideas has arisen from a supposed *virtue* of the Internet: its utility as a medium for "crowdsourcing"—defined by (what else?) Wikipedia as "the act of taking tasks traditionally performed by an employee or contractor, and outsourcing them to a group of people or community, through an 'open call' to a large group of people (a crowd) asking for contributions."

In many contexts, crowdsourcing can be an accurate and highly cost-effective means of collecting information. In James Surowiecki's influential 2004 book *The Wisdom of Crowds*: *Why the Many Are Smarter Than The Few*, he tells the story, borrowed from Francis Galton, about how the averaged estimates of random English fairgoers more accurately assessed the weight of a particular ox than estimates provided by individual cattle experts. Facebook members use the crowdsourcing principle when they put out a status-update inviting friends to suggest a good restaurant in a particular city, or a good doctor for their family. And then there's Wikipedia, a crowdsourced encyclopedia that in the space of just a few years has become perhaps the single most influential information resource on the entire planet.

But the only reason Wikipedia works is that its entries—particularly those relating to controversial subjects—ultimately are controlled by a corps of dedicated editors working in a traditional top-down hierarchy. When those editors step into the background, the site becomes just another free-for-all dominated by spammers and propagandists.

In the context of conspiracy theorists, the problem arises from the fact that the people with the most bizarre and extreme views tend also to be the most enthusiastic and prolific contributors to crowdsourced media—since those who hold conventional attitudes usually see little point in expressing the obvious.

This becomes clear if you peruse the "customer reviews" that pop up on the product-information screen for books sold on Amazon and other electronic bookstores. Here, a naïve reader seeking to gauge the veracity of a conspiracist tract usually will find an almost unbroken string of rave reviews—not a surprise, since the only people willing to plow through such books, let alone bother to post online about them, tend to be conspiracy theorists to begin with. In the spring of 2010, for instance, WorldNetDaily reporters Aaron Klein and Brenda Elliott published *The Manchurian President*: *Barack Obama's Ties to Communists, Socialists and Other Anti-*

American Extremists, a standard-issue catalog of Birtheresque guilt-by-association conspiracy theories panned by those few respectable media outlets that deigned to acknowledge the book's existence. Yet in the review section of Amazon, the authors are portrayed as nothing short of Woodward and Bernstein. As of mid-May 2010, more than half of reviewers gave the book a perfect five-star rating. Similarly, when I looked up Daniel Estulin's *The True Story of the Bilderberg Group*, on Amazon, the main page featured just a single negative review among the dozen or so on offer—and even that lone naysayer was upset principally by the fact that Estulin hadn't probed deeply enough into the Rothschild family and their "hidden agenda of the New World Order."

Because of the fleeting way in which many people consume the mass media, conspiracist causes can gain strength even when mainstream journalists seek to tackle the underlying subject in a professional and objective way.

In late 2009, I appeared on the CBC television documentary program *The Fifth Estate*, in an hour-long episode dedicated to the 9/11 Truth movement. The show gave plenty of airtime to various conspiracy theorists, but also provided an opportunity for me and other critics to debunk their claims and put their movement in historical context. The next day, a teacher at my daughters' school told me she'd seen the show, and found it interesting.

"All that stuff about the World Trade Center is pretty mind-blowing, huh?" she said off-handedly as I removed my youngest daughter's coat and boots. "Maybe there's something to it. What do you think?"

"Not really," I said. "Didn't that come through in the show?"

"I guess I missed that," she said, half-apologetically. "To be honest, I wasn't really listening that closely. I was on my cell phone."

Later that day, other friends and colleagues mentioned they'd seen the CBC show. When I asked them to describe their impressions, they also seemed to have only a vague idea about what actually had been discussed. Some confessed they'd been eating or

BlackBerrying while watching, or flipping from one channel to the next. In any case, the big deal, as they saw it, wasn't what I'd said, but simply that I'd been *on TV*—an accomplishment in its own right.

The teacher's words, "maybe there's something to it," worried me in particular. While the producers had intended the show as a profile of a conspiracy movement, she clearly saw it as part of a legitimate debate between two rival camps. Like me, the Truthers appeared on camera dressed in suits. Like me, they seemed confident about their position. More importantly, someone had made the decision to put them on television. And so their message must somehow be legitimate.

The idea that we should take seriously the viewpoint of anyone who appears on television, or who earns a high ranking on a Google search, or a stellar hit count for his YouTube video, is part of a phenomenon that might be called "informational relativism"—to complement the moral relativism that's been a feature of our cultural landscape since the 1960s. Genuine expertise now means little. Instead, we rely on what Internet pioneer Andrew Keen decried (in his 2007 book of the same name) as "the cult of the amateur."

"The 9/11 Truth movement is a perfect example of the disappearance of truth—or even a general agreement of what truth is," he told me in an interview. "If you throw enough garbage at the wall, some of it is going to stick. It reflects how media-illiterate people are. Even if you put a clear lie out there, it will be picked up and spread by the mob, virally."

Like the medical patients who now imagine they are qualified to diagnose their maladies just by plugging a list of symptoms into Google, modern conspiracy theorists imagine themselves better qualified to analyze the collapse of the World Trade Center, the medical effect of vaccines, or the machinations of the Federal Reserve Bank than accredited structural engineers, immunologists, and economists. Many 9/11 Truthers I spoke with told me they were certain that the World Trade Center buildings were destroyed by explosives because the collapse looked somewhat like demolition jobs they'd seen in movies or on the news. In their propaganda videos, this point is "proven" by setting footage of WTC 7's collapse alongside implosion footage from professionally collapsed structures in other parts of the world. The fact that no legitimate expert on the demolition of large buildings has ever embraced their view is not seen as problematic: The conspiracist imagines his own native intelligence and instinctive suspicion to be a sufficient arbiter of truth.

Unlike the true expert, whose spurious leaps of logic might be spotted through the process of peer review, the conspiracist-minded amateur doesn't care about appearing ridiculous in the eyes of informed observers. In fact, he imagines that their ridicule proves his status as a freethinker, uncorrupted by the suffocating dogmas imposed by the credentialed intellectual establishment. He is completely satisfied merely to attract attention from other amateurs, which he accomplishes by providing a narrative that is more lurid and titillating than the informed technical fare served up by people who have earned degrees in the field.

The Revolution Will Be Televised

There is no medium of communications better suited to political propaganda than film. Literature and the spoken word can be used to bombard a person with facts. But only cinema can transport him wholesale into an invented world. Through the artful use of music, lighting, and shocking visual images, a propagandist can entirely control the emotional mood of his audience. Unlike an essayist, the propaganda filmmaker can short-circuit the rules of logic—or, preferably, ignore them entirely.

This can be done in a matter of seconds, a classic example being the 1964 *Daisy* TV ad for Lyndon Johnson: A small child counts off the plucked petals of a flower as the camera zooms in on her face. Then comes another countdown—this one from an ominous male narrator. The screen is filled with a mushroom cloud, and the voice-over switches to Johnson: "These are the stakes! To make a world in which all of God's children can live, or to go into the dark. We must either love each other, or we must die." The target of the ad—Barry Goldwater, who had mused about using nuclear weapons in Vietnam—was never mentioned. It wasn't necessary, or even desirable. The purpose of the ad wasn't to make an argument, but to create emotional linkages—between a child's sweet face, LBJ's resolute voice, and the terrifying sense that the world, with all its cute little girls, will descend into apocalypse without him leading it.

On both sides of the Cold War, propaganda bore the indirect imprint of Nazi directors, who had pioneered the use of film as an instrument of brainwashing. As Philip Taylor wrote in *Munitions of the Mind: A History of Propaganda from the Ancient World to the Present Day* (quoting British American film historian Roger Mavell): "'Nazi newsreels were not informative, they were impressionist, emotive, all-conquering—a blitz in themselves of sound and image.' Their message was clear: German military superiority was plain for all to see and the ease with which victory was achieved was testimony to the superiority of the German race and the will of the Führer."

The best-known specimen of this genre is Leni Riefenstahl's *Triumph of the Will*, which chronicled the 1934 Nazi Party Congress in Nuremberg. Like all the most effective propaganda of our own era, the film pressed its message by leveraging the inborn human impulse to make broad moral judgments about complex issues, even whole races of people, based on fleeting, emotionally charged human images. Not a minute goes by in which Riefenstahl does not remove the viewer from the mass spectacle of the Party Congress to focus on a single person, whether Hitler himself lecturing sternly from a stage, or one of the proud, confident, clean-cut youth members in rapt attention. It is in their faces that her story is told: The planes, the flags, the architecture, and the spectacle are all presented as mere manifestations of their iron will and commitment to national glory. Riefenstahl's images, scored with themes from Wagner's *Götterdämmerung* and similar compositions, were so powerful that they effectively created our modern understanding of the prewar Nazi movement as a clockwork-precise machine, burying the reality of Hitler's amateurish, disorganized personality cult. And the same cinematic formula would be copied by other totalitarian movements—especially Stalin's Soviet propaganda apparatus, which filmed May Day parades and other set pieces in a recognizably Riefenstahlian manner.

George Orwell, the twentieth century's most insightful student of propaganda and its toxic effect on Western societies, understood that film could equally be used to vilify others to the point of murderous hatred. His lengthy description of "The Two Minutes' Hate" is one of the most memorable passages in *Nineteen Eighty-Four*, and worth quoting at length:

> As usual, the face of Emmanuel Goldstein, the Enemy of the People, had flashed on to the screen. There were hisses here and there among the audience. The little sandy-haired woman gave a squeak of mingled fear and disgust. Goldstein was the renegade and backslider who once, long ago (how long ago, nobody quite remembered), had been one of the leading figures of the Party, almost on a level with Big Brother himself, and then had engaged in counter-revolutionary activities, had been condemned to death, and had mysteriously escaped and disappeared. The programmes of the Two Minutes Hate varied from day to day, but there was none in which Goldstein was not the principal figure. He was the primal traitor, the earliest defiler of the Party's purity . . . It was a lean Jewish face, with a great fuzzy aureole of white hair and a small goatee beard— a clever face, and yet somehow inherently despicable, with a

kind of senile silliness in the long thin nose, near the end of which a pair of spectacles was perched. It resembled the face of a sheep, and the voice, too, had a sheep-like quality. Goldstein was delivering his usual venomous attack upon the doctrines of the Party . . . And all the while, lest one should be in any doubt as to the reality which Goldstein's specious claptrap covered, behind his head on the telescreen there marched the endless columns of the Eurasian army—row after row of solid-looking men with expressionless Asiatic faces, who swam up to the surface of the screen and vanished, to be replaced by others exactly similar. The dull rhythmic tramp of the soldiers' boots formed the background to Goldstein's bleating voice . . . In its second minute, the Hate rose to a frenzy. People were leaping up and down in their places and shouting at the tops of their voices in an effort to drown the maddening bleating voice that came from the screen . . . A hideous ecstasy of fear and vindictiveness, a desire to kill, to torture, to smash faces in with a sledgehammer, seemed to flow through the whole group of people like an electric current, turning one even against one's will into a grimacing, screaming lunatic.

Six decades after *Nineteen Eighty-Four* was published, video propaganda continues to lure viewers into extremist ideologies—but not in the way Orwell predicted. During the World War II and Cold War eras, video propaganda was the domain of governments and established studios—since only they had the money needed to rent studios, hire actors and film crews, and run media distribution networks. Riefenstahl, for instance, had a crew of 120 people, and an unlimited budget, for *Triumph of the Will*. During World War II, the U.S. War Department alone spent in excess of $50 million on film production. On the Soviet side, film propaganda was supervised by the well-founded Directorate of Propaganda and Agitation of the Central Committee—the origin of the term "agit-prop." In his 1958 *Blue Book of the John Birch Society*, Robert Welch devoted a scant two paragraphs to television, dismissing it as a tool for promoting his cause: "I know the fantastic cost of television programs. So let me point out that I do not think any early extensive use of television by us would be [wise] . . . Its separate impacts are glancing blows of little depth, compared, let us say, to that of a great book which can be read again and again."

In purely quantitative terms, moreover, there simply wasn't that much stock footage available for the era's conspiracists to cobble into their productions. Had JFK's assassination taken place in 2011, the event would have been recorded by dozens—possibly hundreds—of amateurs using camcorders and cell phones. Within hours, much of that footage would be uploaded to YouTube, Facebook, and other sites, where it would be dissected by conspiracists for "anomalies." In the case of the actual Kennedy assassination, the event was recorded by precisely one individual—dress manufacturer Abraham Zapruder. And even his 8mm footage was of limited use to conspiracists, since Zapruder had signed over the rights to *Life* magazine. It wasn't until 1975—twelve years after JFK was killed—that assassination researchers were able to show the Zapruder film on network television.

Beginning in the 1990s, the amount of amateur-available video surged radically thanks to the Internet and the widespread availability of digital imaging technology and video-editing software. Costs plummeted. In fact, many of the most widely distributed films now on YouTube were made for quite literally nothing— since they consist only of material shot by other people, and then edited using shareware software. One particularly popular video genre on conspiracist websites, for instance, is what might be called the Smoking Gun Mash-up—which consists of decontextulaized video snippets in which some public figure, or group of figures, is made to seem as if they are repeatedly admitting to some shocking crime or secret. One popular ten-minute video, entitled *Obama Admits He is a Muslim*—which had been viewed about two million times by the time I saw it in the spring of 2010—consists of dozens of such snippets from Obama speeches and interviews—many of them shorter than even a single sentence.

In many cases, conspiracists can even cast themselves as the stars of their own propaganda videos. As discussed, obsessive 9/11 street demonstrators such as Luke Rudkowski, for instance, habitually post YouTube videos in which they "confront" public figures with the Truth, a practice that generally involves harassing them with bullhorns at public events, or reciting manifestos during the Q&A sessions following speeches at colleges.

But some things haven't changed. Like Riefenstahl, or Orwell's imaginary Big Brother, today's Internet propagandists overwhelm viewers' intellectual defense mechanisms with the endless piling on of disconnected snippets of footage that build toward a single, overarching, spine-tingling capital-T Truth. Internet-circulated jihadi propaganda movies, for instance, usually consist of endless carnage scenes featuring dead and dying Muslims slain by American bombs or Israeli tank shells, interspersed with claims that Islam is being besieged on all sides by genocidal infidels. Where possible, the camera lingers on the dead child's face, the shrieking parents, the mangled corpses. The underlying circumstances of the killings are either ignored or fantastically misrepresented. Many terrorists have admitted that these videos were the most powerful factor in their indoctrination.

Compared to other forms of conspiracist video propaganda, 9/11 Truth material typically is more sophisticated—since both the creators and consumers tend to be technically minded college-educated Internet addicts. Instead of focusing on blood and gore, typical Truther films, such as the popular *Loose Change* series, intersperse shocking footage of the World Trade Center's destruction with stock footage of Bush administration officials looking menacing or smug. Meanwhile, an authoritative-sounding narrator recites a lengthy stream of unconnected facts that seem to tie the act and the administration together.

The narrator typically will linger, for instance, on the various corporate, political, and family connections binding the World Trade Center buildings to the White House—such as the fact that George W. Bush's brother Marvin had once been on the board of directors for a company (Securacom) that provided security for the World Trade Center. None of these facts would have much meaning to a normal person who read them in a book, or heard them in a conversation. But strung together on video, they can be made to seem significant, even frightening.

This is especially true in the case of viewers with altered states of mind. Mikey Metz, a graduate of SUNY Albany who runs a blog called *Confessions of an ex-Truther* ("The ranting and raving of someone who wasted a year of his life being sucked into the lies of the 9/11 Truth Movement") describes his years in the movement as a perpetual haze of marijuana addiction. "There were a lot of nights when someone would go off on revolutionary rants, and we would be all rah-rah and get excited," he told me. "At the time, I smoked a lot of pot with those guys. If you're doing it every day and watching propaganda, you're not going to be exercising your critical faculties. Over time, you get very paranoid. If you watch a propaganda film when you're high, you're susceptible." (Metz ended up abandoning the Truth movement just weeks after going clean.)

While conspiracy theorists often are stereotyped as excitable lunatics, creators of the most popular modern propaganda videos take the opposite approach: Narrators speak in a clipped, confident, understated just-the-facts-ma'am monotone, thereby suggesting that the material is dispassionate scientific analysis. (There is a notable exception, however: Medical-conspiracy-theory films aimed explicitly at parents—such as the vaccine-autism genre— usually feature an emotional tone and a heart-tugging soundtrack.) The best narrators—such as Daniel Sunjata, the professional actor who narrates the latest installment of *Loose Change*—wear the viewer down with their catalog of human evil. To augment the hypnotic effect, these films also typically feature metronomic soft-techno soundtracks. (A Jungian therapist who'd seen *Loose Change* told me the soundtrack reminded her of the baroque music she used, toward the same effect, in her therapy sessions.)

The narrative of such propaganda films typically follows the same pattern: The first third of the movie or so is devoted to cataloguing the historical sins of the targeted cabal—be it the U.S. government, the United Nations, the pharmaceutical industry, or what not—using stock publicly available video footage. Once the viewers' mind is adequately softened, the film hits its crucial pivot point, and the narrator commences extrapolating the protagonists' villainy into the realm of fantasy. The 2009 film *Camp FEMA: American Lockdown*, for instance, commences with a lengthy (and largely accurate) description of the internment of Japanese Americans during World War II, followed by footage from the aftermath of Hurricane Katrina. Only after a half hour or so do the producers get around to their main point: That the Federal Emergency Management Agency is plotting to imprison millions of Americans who oppose Washington's plan for a New World Order.

Similarly, in a video titled *Carbon Eugenics*, circulated in late 2009, a conspiracist named James Corbett took the viewer through a largely accurate discussion of Francis Galton and his nineteenth-century notions of eugenics. In the space of a minute, he deftly pivots from this theme to the notion that modern-day greenhouse-gas-reduction policies comprise a Galtonian scheme for a new Holocaust: "In the logic of the eugenicists, the meaning of human life is itself transformed. Instead of something valuable, something precious, something to be desired and nurtured, fought for and celebrated, humanity is re-imagined as a cancer, something inherently evil, the mere existence of which is a burden on the world. This, unsurprisingly, encapsulates the modern environmental movement's position almost perfectly: human life is no longer something to be treasured, but something to be measured in carbon and then reduced. In the manmade global warming myth, humans are merely an obstacle to the proper functioning of nature. In the eugenicist fantasy, the earth is saved when people die. In both ideologies (if they really are separate) the ultimate genocide becomes thinkable."

History Belongs to the YouTube Victors

In September of 2009, after I'd marched around with a group of "We Are Change" Truthers on the anniversary of 9/11, I asked some of them what they thought about the day's activities. There had been a few hundred of us parading up and down Midtown Manhattan with our banners and leaflets. Yet none of the onlookers had seemed particularly interested. "Aren't you discouraged?" I asked.

Just the opposite, they told me: The day had been a massive success.

The whole event, they explained, had been filmed from start to finish, and a lot of the footage was already on the Internet. One "We Are Change" organizer, Matt Lepacek, had even shown up with a backpack of network-connected computer gear, and apparently had been simulcasting every second of it. The marchers I spoke with were particularly excited about a segment in which a Truther gave an excited speech to a bored-looking police officer. "That thing is going to be all over YouTube!" one exclaimed to me. "A million people are going to see it!"

That seemed to be an exaggeration. But the number was beside the point. What mattered to these people was that a million people *could* be watching—that their activities were part of the historical archive, and so would mark their role as prophets and pioneers when the revolution finally came.

Early in my research of the 9/11 Truth movement, I interviewed Philip Zelikow, the American diplomat and historian who served as executive director of the 9/11 Commission. At first, our conversation focused on the history of the Sept. 11 attacks, and the various strategies that Truthers had used to distort the facts. But as we talked, Zelikow increasingly homed in on the aspect of the movement he found most bizarre and exasperating—the Truthers' obsession with video.

"Whenever these folks try to accost me, they always film it," he told me. "It happened in Chicago when I was trying to check in at a hotel—and someone accosted me. Or they'll stand up at a speech I'm giving, and someone will stand up and scare everyone by blowing a loud whistle, and then post it to YouTube. It's happened many times.

"By doing this, it makes their movement *real*," Zelikow adds. "They're basically trying to set themselves up as chroniclers of an alternative history, in which they are the key truth-tellers and their story is chronicling the story of how that truth unfolded. It's the same with all cult-like groups [in the modern era]—even al-Qaeda."

CHAPTER EIGHT

Tin-Foil Mortarboards: Conspiracism's Ivy League Enablers

I have heard it confidently stated . . . that the American troops had been brought to Europe not to fight the Germans but to crush an English revolution. One has to belong to the intelligentsia to believe things like that: no ordinary man could be such a fool.

—*George Orwell, 1945*

Jacques Derrida's Hall of Mirrors

Though his name will forever be associated with "deconstruction" and other avant-garde literary doctrines, Paul de Man was an anachronism—a throwback to an age when gentleman scholars with scant formal credentials could be catapulted into the loftiest reaches of the Ivy League on the strength of charm, native intelligence, and personal connections.

After fleeing postwar Belgium in his late twenties, de Man began life in American letters at the bottom rung—serving customers at a Grand Central Station bookshop. But he managed to make friends at *Partisan Review,* and a letter of introduction from Mary McCarthy landed him a teaching position at Bard College. That in turn led to postings at Harvard's Society of Fellows (where he overlapped in the 1950s with an up-and-coming linguist named Avram Noam Chomsky), Cornell and, finally, Yale. There, he bestrode the comparative literature program until his death in 1983, preaching austere sermons to graduate students about the "limitations of textual authority." Conventional literary criticism, he argued, is a sham—a naïve and romantic project aimed at extracting intrinsic meaning from written words that, by their nature, are mere chicken scratches on paper.

As the fad for such ideas crested in the 1970s and 1980s, and scholars made increasingly radical claims about their capacity to reimagine language, de Man became a sort of secular prophet. At his university memorial service, recalls David Mikics, a Yale PhD who later went on to teach English at the University of Houston, onlookers were "struck by the fervent devotion, almost religious in tone, shown to the dead de Man by his disciples. They would carry his work on, in his memory; he had shown the way for all future reading." Jacques Derrida himself, the father of the deconstructionist creed, and de Man's close friend, spoke at the event, praising "the ever so gentle force of his thought."

It is only in this context that one can understand the traumatic impact of what happened three years after his death, when a researcher discovered that de Man had written collaborationist articles during his years as a journalist in Nazi-occupied Belgium. In the most notorious essay, "The Jews and Contemporary Literature," de Man described the Jews as a "foreign force," and expressed relief that European cultural forms had not been *enjuivées.* It was published next to a crude anti-Semitic caricature of two elderly Jews, with a caption reading: "May Jehovah confound the Gentiles!" "By keeping, in spite of Semitic interference in all aspects of European life, an intact originality and character, [our civilization] has shown that its basic character is healthy," the article concluded—this, at a time when Belgium recently had passed laws excluding Jews from a variety of professions, including de Man's own, journalism. To those who took deconstructionism as their religion, these revelations constituted the secular equivalent of a sex-abuse scandal implicating the Vatican's most powerful cardinal.

Derrida, in particular, became obsessed with the issue—and published a lengthy essay about it in 1988. But astonishingly, this giant of textual analysis insisted on pretending that de Man's words signified the exact opposite of their plain meaning, and that the "scandal" over his alleged collaboration was nothing but a conspiracy hatched by malevolent journalists, whose campaign resembled nothing so much as the Nazis' own "exterminating gesture" against the Jews. Applying his deconstructionist art to "The Jews and Contemporary Literature," Derrida performed a series of logical back-flips in arguing that de Man had in fact offered an "indictment" of anti-Semitism, not to mention an "uncompromising critique" of the Nazis. At the climax of this fantasy, de Man is claimed to be actually *praising* the Jews: "The manner in which he describes the 'Jewish spirit' remains unquestionably positive."

Given deconstructionism's unworkably bleak character ("existentialism at its height, without the existentialist's belief in human heroism," as Mikics concisely describes it), its fall from academic fashion was inevitable. But the descent was given a solid push by the de Man revelations. As one Boston University professor told a *Newsweek* journalist, the creed suddenly seemed like "a vast amnesty project for the politics of collaboration during World War II."

Perhaps more than de Man's words themselves, Derrida's defense of them highlighted the true problem with deconstructionism: Pregnant within the view that words have no stable meaning outside their existence as symbols—*Il n'y a pas de hors-texte*—is the suggestion that they can mean *anything*, even their apparent opposite, depending on the perspective of the person communicating or interpreting them. In the political arena, in particular, deconstructionists often have fallen back on Michel Foucault's maxim that all knowledge—including historical knowledge—is merely a pretext for justifying existing power relationships. There was no "truth," Foucault declared—only a "regime *of* truth" that shifted day by day.

"The world begins to seem a realm of illusion, where we have tricked ourselves into supposing that we are real," wrote Mikics in his 2009 book-length meditation on the subject, *Who Was Jacques Derrida? An Intellectual Biography.* "The whole history of ideas seemed to him to be a debate, carried on between the lines of great philosophical texts, between the masterful coherence of metaphysics and its deconstructionist opponent, skepticism."

Out of this view came the idea that destroying the conventional, bourgeois construct of objective truth was not merely a tool of literary analysis, but a sacred intellectual duty to the world's oppressed. The deconstructionist approach "revealed the volatile core of instability and indeterminacy lurking underneath every philosophical assertion, every scientific method, every work of literature," literary critic Judith Shulevitz wrote in her reminiscence about studying at Yale under de Man. "Nothing we'd learned (we learned) meant what it claimed to mean. All texts were allegories of their own blindness . . . All this gave me an unusually palpable sense of purpose. I was a mole burrowing under the foundations of the tottering edifice of Knowledge."

Contrary to caricature, Derrida did not inhabit a universe of pure subjectivity: In many cases, he argued, facts *did* matter. (Holocaust denial, for instance, was something he found quite troubling.) But the great thinker never found any coherent way to harmonize that concern with his insistence that truth is just a yarn that we spin at each other. In any event, as Derrida himself unwittingly demonstrated in the de Man affair, deconstructionism was the ideal smokescreen for scholars and activists peddling counterfactual interpretations of the world. Even after 9/11, just a few years before his own death, the ur-deconstructionist was still at it, babbling vapidly about the phrase "September 11": "The telegram of this metonymy—a name, a number—points out the unqualifiable by recognizing that we do not recognize or even cognize that we do not know how to qualify, that we do not know what we are talking about." On the broader question of political violence, he served up to the same interviewer the usual left-wing digressions into state terrorism and Western imperialism, but also a turgid disquisition about the very unknowability of terrorism: "Semantic instability, irreducible trouble spots on the borders between concepts, indecision in the very concept of the border: All this must not only be analyzed as a speculative disorder, a conceptual chaos or zone of passing turbulence in public or political language." By the popularization of such bafflegab to legions of impressionable modern-languages students, the great French scholar became the conspiracy theorist's polite Ivy League cousin—a famous name, and a set of impressive-sounding terms of philosophical art, to be trotted out whenever the blurring of black into white requires a scholarly footnote.

In this regard, deconstructionism dovetailed with a separate intellectual trend that had been underway since the 1960s: modern identity politics, which involved the reconstruction (and in some cases, the wholesale invention) of history according to the viewpoint of women, blacks, gays, and other minorities—a project that replaced the historian's once-unquestioned goal of objective truth with an explicitly political, Marxist-leaning agenda aimed at empowerment and solidarity-building.

While all good historical scholarship relies, to some degree, on challenging received wisdom about the past, many radicalized New Left historians took this approach to an extreme, romanticizing any historical narrative, however counterfactual or even conspiracist, that challenged dominant attitudes. Scholarship became a species of "resistance"—even to this day, the term appears everywhere in radicalized scholarship and activism—suggesting an analogy to warfare and its maidservant, propaganda. Many faculty-lounge guerillas took their cue from Franz Fanon's 1961 opus, *The Wretched of the Earth*, which sanctioned any tactic (even wanton murder, as Jean-Paul Sartre emphasized in his famously nihilistic preface) in the service of anti-colonialism. Committed intellectuals, Fanon declared, must create "combat literature" to inspire the coming revolution. The question of objective "truth," as most people would understand the term, was, of course, secondary. As Peter Novick put it in his extraordinary 1988 book, *That Noble Dream: The Objectivity Question And The American Historical Profession*: "Most leftist historians agreed with Barrington Moore's observation that 'in any society the dominant groups are the ones with the most to hide about the way society works,' and that to the extent that radicals took a jaundiced view of dominant ideology they were more likely to penetrate to the truth, to resemble Mannheim's 'free floating intelligentsia.'"

Some scholars went farther and argued that no single set of truths about the world could be said even to *exist* for all peoples—since blacks, women, "queers," and other oppressed groups all have inherently different cognitive approaches. Following on Paulo Freire's *Pedagogy of the Oppressed*, some academics turned the podium around, and made students the stars of the classroom: Since challenging oppression was the main goal of education, why should the theoretical ramblings of an educator be privileged over the more "authentic" life lessons related by female, black, and gay students?

In certain fields, entire areas of academic research and inquiry were declared off-limits. In my native Canada, for instance, it has become impossible to have any sort of intelligent debate about the relationship between the continent's white European settlers, and the aboriginals whose ancestors first migrated from Asia at the end of the last glacial period. The historical truth about first contact between seafaring European explorers and North America's animist hunter-gatherers—that it was a meeting between two peoples at vastly different stages of technological development—was progressively phased out in favor of a narrative that suggests a meeting of two equal "nations." (Thus the rebranding of small, scattered aboriginal tribes as "First Nations" in the politically correct Canadian lexicon.) In the same vein, academic curricula were revised according to the fiction that our Western intellectual tradition had been built on the sayings and customs of wise old Indian chiefs.

In one trendy book, for instance, *Aboriginal Education*: *Fulfilling the Promise*, Brenda Tsioniaon LaFrance argued that science students should study "units of the Haudenosaunee teachings of the Four Winds, Thunder, Lightning and Sun, along with overall notions of conservation and ideas stemming from Western science." The study of math should focus on "a survey of aboriginal number systems [as well as] the limits of counting." In 2008, Canadian philosopher John Ralston Saul went further, arguing in his book *A Fair Country*: *Telling Truths About Canada* that Canada is "a Métis civilization" that owes all it has (except for the nasty racist bits) to "Aboriginal inspiration." The question of how, exactly, groups of occasionally warring, preliterate aboriginal hunter-gatherer societies can claim credit for the creation of a modern, democratic, capitalist, industrial powerhouse built entirely in a European image never gets resolved. But most readers probably didn't notice: For decades, the unspoken agreement in Canadian academia has been that scholars can peddle any sort of historical nonsense they like about aboriginals—so long as it functions to enhance their dignity. In 1997, no less an authority than the Supreme Court of Canada even declared that aboriginal "oral traditions" stood on a par with written documents as a form of legally admissible evidence.

Such doctrines typically have come packaged with a reductionist, militantly anti-Western view of history that draws a straight line from slavery and imperialism to such modern, "neoimperial" phenomena as globalization, free trade, counter-terrorism, humanitarian military intervention, and nation-building. Even the language we speak to one another became a weapon in the culture war against dead white males: Armed with deconstructionism and related theories, scholars began teasing out the hidden racist, sexist, and heterosexist messages encoded in everything from the *Iliad* to the Archie Comics to the SAT. University administrators created Black Studies and Women's Studies departments, laboratories in which society's bigotries could be diagnosed, and perhaps even cured. In the process, Novick notes, much historical scholarship was transformed into a form of abstruse cheerleading along a set of motifs preapproved by radicalized activists: "overcoming historical neglect; stressing the contributions of the group; an emphasis on oppression, with its troublesome complement, victimization and damage; a search for foreparents in protest and resistance; finally, a celebration of an at least semiautonomous separate cultural realm, with distinctive values and institutions." It was in these "realms"—detached from the bourgeois conventions of objective truth-seeking, and insulated from mainstream criticism by a cult of political correctness—that deconstructionism and identity politics combined to produce a climate in which university professors felt entitled to spout historical fantasies (Afrocentrism being the most prominent example) and full-blown conspiracism so long as they were cast as doctrines of empowerment.

Consider, for instance, the manner in which men were portrayed by self-described "radical lesbian feminist" and "ecofeminist" Mary Daly, who taught courses in theology and "patriarchy" at Boston College from 1967 to 1999 (at which point she was fired for refusing to admit men into her classes). According to Daly, the human race was divided between "necrophilic" men and "biophilic" (life-loving) women. Christianity and other organized religions also were anathema to the pagan Daly—since she regarded them as interchangeably patriarchal. She even refused to identify herself as a "human being," since this category was infected by the neurotoxin of maleness: "I hate the 'human species'—look at it!" she told an interviewer in 1999. "I hate what it is doing to this earth: the invasion of everything. The last two frontiers are the genetic wilderness and the space wilderness; they've colonized everything else. It's a totally invasive mentality—rapist. That is *alien*, and insofar as I've internalized any of that, I'm sorry. I'm contaminated by it. We all are."

Like an early Zionist, Daly sought to create a geographical "homeland"—one reserved for "women who identify as women." In her book *Quintessence*, she rhapsodized that such an all-female, "gynocentric" society wouldn't need men: reproduction would be accomplished through parthenogenesis. When magazine interviewer Susan Bridle asked Daly what she thought about a related proposal put forward by another radical lesbian feminist, Sally Miller Gearhart, that "the proportion of men must be reduced to and maintained at approximately 10% of the human race," Daly responded: "I think it's not a bad idea at all. If life is to survive on this planet, there must be a decontamination of the Earth. I think this will be accompanied by an evolutionary process that will result in a drastic reduction of the population of males. People are afraid to say that kind of stuff anymore."

The "stuff" Daly referred to here was, of course, eugenics—the "improvement" of humankind through the selective extermination of "undesirable" elements within the population. As the quotation in the paragraph above illustrates, Daly often spoke of men the way the Nazis spoke of Jews. Should any modern scholar make similar remarks about breeding out, say, blacks, or Jews, or gays, they would instantly become an object of disgrace. Yet Daly continued to be a cult hero among radical feminists until her death in 2010: According to Bridle, she is "one of the most revered visionaries of the contemporary women's liberation movement" and "the grande dame of feminist theology"—not to mention "a demolition derbyist of patriarchal 'mindbindings.'"

On a basic level, Daly's hyperpolitically correct conspiracism can be viewed simply as radical populism stood on its head: Like the militant fringe of the Tea Party movement, Daly believed American society is locked in an ideological war between effeminate, left-wing, pagan ecopacifists and traditionally minded, star-spangled Christian culture warriors. The only point of disagreement is which utopia we should be rooting for—the "necrophilic" America of yesteryear, or the "biophilic" cloud city of the future.

But in one very profound way, Daly's left-wing campus conspiracism is actually more radical than the sensational YouTube fare served up even by the most delusional New World Order types. That's because, for all their paranoia, men such as Alex Jones, Michael Ruppert, David Ray Griffin, Richard Gage, and Joseph Farah truly do believe that the facts of history matter—that there is a central, objective, historical truth out there, and that their own investigations are crucial for finding out what it is. Daly, on the other hand, freely admitted that her historical reveries about a utopian "pre-patriarchal" stage of human history were based on romantic invention. But as she told Bridle, this shouldn't bother anyone:

> What is the risk? I mean, we live in hell. This is called hell. H-E-L-L—patriarchy. . . . Is it romantic to try to remember something better than that? There's a reality gap here. How can I make it clearer? We're living in hell and [a critic is] talking about a danger of romanticism in imagining something that is a hope for something better in the future? I think that the question comes from not looking deeply enough at the horror of phallocracy. . . . If you experience the horror of what is happening to women all the time, it is almost unbearable, right? All the time! . . . Then, when you are acutely aware of that and desire to exorcise it, the exorcism welcomes, requires, some kind of dream.

All this, I believe, helps explain why there is such a paucity of academic research in the field of conspiracy theories. The tone of the available papers suggests why: Most researchers seem hesitant to suggest that *any* view of the world—no matter how preposterous—is unambiguously wrong. The guiding notion, echoing the plot of Thomas Pynchon's influential blockbuster, *Gravity's Rainbow*, was that the institutionalized conspiracy woven into the fabric of corporate capitalism is more sinister than any narrative concocted by the likes of the Truth movement.

In some cases, I found, full-blown conspiracy theories have even made their way into seemingly mainstream university programs. In late 2010, for instance, the University of Lethbridge, in the Canadian province of Alberta, announced that it was award-ing a $7,714 scholarship to conspiracy theorist Joshua Blakeney so that he could pursue his 9/11 Truth research under the direc-tion of Globalization Studies professor Anthony Hall, a fellow Truther.

In 2006, the peer-reviewed *Administrative Theory & Praxis*, a prestigious quarterly devoted to "critical, normative, and theoretical dialogue in public administration," and supported by the School of Public Affairs at Arizona State University, published an article by tenured Florida State University professor Lance deHaven-Smith, lamenting that "citizens of the United States continue to be victim-ized by suspicious incidents that benefit top public officials, and yet Americans have no way of knowing whether the incidents are unavoidable events or, instead, crimes initiated or facilitated by the officials themselves." DeHaven-Smith's bill of particulars includes "the defense failures on September 11, 2001 (9/11); the anthrax at-tacks on U.S. Senators a month later; and the series of terror alerts issued on the basis of flimsy evidence."

As it turned out, deHaven-Smith was just getting started. In 2008, he coauthored an academic paper detailing the machina-tions of a "criminal, militaristic/fiscal cabal" operating at the high-est echelons of the U.S government—a group of super-secret James Bond–like agents that he calls "SCAD-Net." (The acronym stands for State Crimes against Democracy, a term deHaven-Smith pro-poses as an alternative for "conspiracy theory," which he complains is "associated with paranoia and hare-brained speculation.") While the paper begins with the usual array of rarified academic jargon and dense footnotes, it quickly morphs into a freeform conspiracist meditation on Skull and Bones, Malcolm X, and dozens of other conspiracist obsessions. In particular, we learn, JFK's death was "probably" the work of J. Edgar Hoover, [CIA official] Richard Helms, Lyndon Johnson, [US Air Force Chief of Staff] Curtis Le-May, and ("almost certainly") Richard Nixon. The Warren Commission was a "cover-up." SCAD-Net also likely murdered Robert Kennedy, stole the 2000 presidency for Bush-Cheney, and perpetrated the 9/11 attacks. And more plots are on the way: One chapter is entitled "SCAD-Net is likely to strike again in 2012–2013, probably with a 'dirty' bomb at a sporting event." Two years later, in 2010, deHaven-Smith again found a respectable scholarly home for his SCAD-Net conspiracism, this time in *American Behavioral Scientist*, which devoted its entire February 2010 issue to the subject—much of it consisting of full-blown 9/11 conspiracism.

According to one of my correspondents, who was present when deHaven-Smith and his coauthors presented their 2008 paper at Virginia Commonwealth University, no one in the crowd seemed distressed that their conference had become a forum for conspiracist fantasies. This did not altogether surprise me: Modern academics tend to romanticize the conspiracy theorist (at least in his nonracist manifestation), imagining him to be a source of "countercultural opposition," "narratives of resistance," or (as Foucault called them) "subjugated knowledge." Many, like deHaven-Smith, refuse even to use the term "conspiracy theory." Writing in the *Journal of Black Studies*, for instance, Denison University scholar Anita Waters argued instead for the term "ethnosociology," and urged that we "reserve opinion" about their truth. By way of example, she cited AIDS conspiracy theories, which might be seen as "a logical outcome of the process by which 'urban African Americans are struggling to conceptualize the threatening ecological and social decay' that surrounds them."

In his introduction to the 2002 book *Conspiracy Nation: The Politics of Paranoia in Postwar America*, University of Manchester professor Peter Knight assures his readers that "the essays in this collection refuse instantly to dismiss [conspiracism] as the product of narrow-minded crackpot paranoia or the intellectual slumming of those who should know better." Rutgers University media-studies professor Jack Bratich, another prominent commentator on conspiracism, criticizes the "expertism" of those who would dismiss AIDS conspiracy theories out of hand, and instead seeks a "nuanced approach" that "looks for their origins in social, cultural and economic conditions." Skip Willman of the University of South Dakota (formerly of the Georgia Institute of Technology) applauds conspiracy theories as "an oppositional political culture in the shadow of the marketplace and its attendant consumerism." And then there's Eithne Quinn, one of a long line of university academics to build her career on the literary analysis of rap-music lyrics. In her essay "All Eyez On Me: The Paranoid Style of Tupac Shakur," she gushes that Tupac's violent, obscene conspiracism offers "profound connections between the personal and the political, the psychic and the social, the individual and the larger relations of power. Such critical thinking is of course essential to the production of political consciousness."

Among the Antiracists

Those who authentically commit themselves to the people must re-examine themselves constantly . . . Conversion to the people requires a profound rebirth. Those who undergo it must take on a new form of existence; they can no longer remain as they were. Only through comradeship with the oppressed can the converts understand their characteristic ways of living and behaving, which in diverse moments reflect the structure of domination.

—*Paulo Freire,* Pedagogy of the Oppressed

Sandy, Jim, and Karen work at a downtown community center where they help low-income residents apply for rental housing. Sandy has a bad feeling about Jim: She notices that when black clients come in, he tends to drift to the back of the office. Sandy suspects racism. (She and Jim are both white.) On the other hand, she also notices that Jim seems to get along well with Karen, who is black. As the weeks go by, Sandy becomes more uncomfortable with the situation. But she feels uncertain about how to handle it. Test question: What should Sandy do?

If you answered that Sandy's first move should be to talk to Karen, and ask how Jim's behavior made her feel, you are apparently a better antiracist than I am: That, for what it's worth, was the preferred solution offered by my instructor at *Thinking About Whiteness and Doing Anti-Racism*, a four-part evening workshop for community activists, presented in early 2010 at the Toronto Women's Bookstore.

My own answer, announced aloud in class, was that Sandy should approach Jim discretely, explaining to him how others in the office might *perceive* his actions. Or perhaps the manager of the community center could be asked to give a generic presentation about the need to treat clients in a color-blind manner, on a no-names basis.

The problem with my approach, the instructor indicated, lay in the fact that I was primarily concerned with the feelings of my fellow Caucasian, Jim. I wasn't treating Karen like a "full human being" who might have thoughts and feelings at variance with her superficially friendly workplace attitude.

Moreover, I was guilty of "democratic racism"—by which we apply ostensibly race-neutral principles, such as "due process," constantly demanding clear "evidence" of wrongdoing, rather than confronting prima facie instances of racism head-on. "It seems we're always looking for more proof," said the instructor, an energetic thirtysomething left-wing activist named Sheila Wilmot who's been teaching this course for several years. "When it comes to racism, you have to trust your gut."

I felt the urge to pipe up at this. Racism is either a serious charge or it's not. And if it is, as everyone in this room clearly believed, then it cannot be flung around casually without giving the accused a chance to explain his actions. But I said nothing, and nodded my head along with everyone else. I'd come to this class not to impose my democratic racism on people, but to observe.

Most of the other thirteen students were grad student types in their twenties—too young to remember the late 1980s and early 1990s, when political correctness first took root on college campuses. The jargon I heard at the Women's Bookstore took me back to that age—albeit with a few odd variations. "Allyship" has replaced "solidarity" in the antiracist lexicon, for instance, when speaking about interracial activist partnerships. I also heard one student say she rejected the term "gender-neutral" as sexist, and instead preferred "gender-*fluid*." One did not "have" a gender or sexual orientation, moreover. The operative word is "perform"—as in, "Sally performs her queerness in a very femme way."

Wilmot's Cold War–era Marxist jargon added to the retro intellectual vibe. Like just about everyone in the class, she took it for granted that racism is an outgrowth of capitalism, and that fighting one necessarily means fighting the other. At one point, she asked us to critique a case study about "Cecilia," a community activist who spread a happy message of tolerance and mutual respect in her neighborhood. Cecilia's approach was incomplete, the instructor informed us, because she neglected to sound the message that "classism is a form of oppression." The real problem faced by visible minorities in our capitalist society isn't a lack of understanding; "it's the fundamentally inequitable nature of wage labor."

The central theme of the course was that this twinned combination of capitalism and racism has produced a cult of "white privilege," which permeates every aspect of our lives. "Canada is a white supremacist country, so I assume that I'm racist," one of the male students said matter-of-factly during our first session. "It's not about *not* being racist. Because I know I am. It's about becoming *less* racist." At this, a woman told the class: "I hate when people tell me they're color-blind. That is the most overt kind of racism. When people say, 'I don't see your race,' I know that's wrong. To ignore race is to be more racist than to acknowledge race. I call it neo-racism."

All of the students were white (to my eyes, anyway), and most said they'd come so they could integrate antiracism into their activism and community outreach efforts. A good deal of the course consisted of them unburdening themselves of their racist guilt. The instructor set the tone, describing an episode in which she lectured a junior black colleague about his job. "When I realized what I was doing, I approached him afterward and apologized," she told the class. "I said to him, 'I'm so sorry! I'm unloading so much *whiteness* on you right now.'"

Another woman, an activist with an expertise in media arts, took the floor to describe her torment when a friend asked her to give a presentation to a group of black students—an exercise that would have made a spectacle of her white privilege. "Should I say yes? Or is it my responsibility to say no?" she said, quite literally wringing her hands with apprehension. "But then he may say, 'I want *you* to do it—because you have a particular approach . . .'

"But wait! Could it be that the reason I *have* that particular approach is that I've been raised to think that I *could* have that particular approach, that I have the ability, that I am able to access education in a particular way? All these things are in my head, in my heart, not really knowing how to respond. On the other hand, I also recognize that the person asking me has the agency to decide that I'm the right person . . . so I say yes! . . . But them I'm still thinking, 'I don't know if I did the right thing.' I still struggle with this all the time . . ."

An especially telling moment came when someone raised the subject of Filipino nannies who immigrate to Canada under government-sponsored caregiver programs. The instructor told the class that the practice was inherently "superexploitative" (a Marxist term that, according to Wikipedia, means "exploitation that goes beyond the normal standards of exploitation prevalent in capitalist society"). She also pointed us to an article included in the week's reading, "Black Women and Work," in which Canadian author Dionne Brand argues that cynical employers use appeals such as, "You know that you're part of the family," to emotionally blackmail nannies, housekeepers, and elder-care workers into the continuation of abusive work relationships.

A community activist—I'll call her Kelly—interjected, apologetically. While she was all on board with the general thrust of the Brand article, she couldn't help but confess that her own family had employed a Filipino nanny who truly did seem "part of the family." Kelly had been a flower girl at the nanny's wedding, and became close friends with the nanny's own children, who'd spent much of their lives in Kelly's own house.

This little speech from the heart—one of the rare instances in which someone had actually stepped outside the dogmas of antiracism and told a story in real, human language—caused a ripple of discomfort in the class. One woman suggested that the nanny has adopted a "coping mechanism" to deal with her subordinate situation. This led to a discussion about how we must recognize the nanny's "agency"—a popular buzzword signifying that minority members must not be seen as passive victims. The instructor listened attentively—but couldn't offer much more except that the example demonstrated the "contradictoriness" of antiracism studies. We moved on while Kelly just sat there, looking somewhat confused. I felt sorry for her.

In fact, I felt sympathy for just about everyone in that class. Like communist die-hards confessing their counterrevolutionary thought-crimes at a Soviet workers' council, or devout Catholics on their knees in the confessional, they were consumed by their sin, seeming to regard their pallor as a sort of moral leprosy. Their guilt was never far from the surface: Even basic communication with friends and fellow activists, I observed, was a plodding agony of self-censorship, in which every syllable was scrutinized for subconscious racist connotations as it was leaving their mouths. While politically correct campus activists often come across as smug and single-minded, their intellectual life might more accurately be described as bipolar—combining an ecstatic self-conception as high priestesses who pronounce upon the racist sins of our fallen society, alongside extravagant self-mortification in regard to their own fallen state.

As cultural critics have been arguing for decades, the mindset I am describing betrays many of the hallmarks of totalitarianism: humorlessness, Orwellian neologisms, promiscuous accusations of thought-crimes, and the sanctification of doctrinal purity over candid emotional expression. But I also found it interesting to observe how closely this militant critique of society hewed to a traditional conspiracist narrative, which divides society between an elite, all-controlling oppressor class and everyone else. Or as Wilmot tells it: "In the blinding whiteness that controls our society—who gets what jobs, who is running the governments and business, who controls the media—the lives of people are generally erased."

Since Wilmot's dogmas are rooted in communist logic, this aspect should not be surprising: As noted elsewhere in this book, Marxism is, in its broad contours, itself a form of conspiracy theory that pits evil industrialists against the common workingman. But the rise of militant antiracism in the 1980s and 1990s injected a fresh element into conspiracist culture: the notion that the evildoers aren't Jews, or communists, or Bilderbergers, or aliens, or even capitalists—but rather *ourselves*. Under this politically correct, profoundly antipopulist form of conspiracism—which has found expression in not just radical antiracism, feminism, and anticapitalism, but a slew of more esoteric academic disciplines, such as postcolonial studies and queer theory—the very fabric of our society represents an invidious plot against anyone who doesn't happen to be rich, white, male, and straight.

The great irony is that all this was set in motion not by any of the epic crimes perpetrated by the white patriarchy (of which, let it be said, history records many), but by the civil rights movement and the legal and political victories that came in its wake. Once Western liberals launched themselves on the noble hunt for bald-faced bigotry, they expected to find their quarry everywhere—even once the hated creature had become virtually extinct.

Lessons from the *Yale Law Journal*

Yale University is a diverse place. When it comes to admissions, educational programs, and employment, the school claims in its official policy statements that it does not discriminate for or against any individual on the basis of race, color, or ethnic origin. But it's widely known that Yale officials take whatever informal measures are required to increase the representation of minorities on campus. During my time at the law school in the mid–1990s, just under 10 percent of each year's slots were assigned to African Americans—this, despite the fact that, as at other highly ranked U.S. law schools, few black applicants meet the school's general standard for undergraduate grade-point averages and scores on the Law School Admission Test (LSAT).

If the benefits of "diversity" are to be reaped anywhere, Yale Law School is the place. On some campuses, the ugliest aspect of affirmative action is that, by bringing in a population of less qualified students, it inevitably generates a racially stratified hierarchy of academic performance. At Yale Law School, on the other hand, classes are pass/fail affairs that, in practice, everybody passes. While it's possible for students to earn an "honors" grade in their course work, the school's culture actively discourages *Paperchase*-style competition. An aphorism frequently recited among the faculty in my day was that, once admitted to Yale, students were "off the treadmill."

But as my first year of law school wore on, it became clear that this was not quite true. Though grades count for less at Yale than at most schools, extracurricular activities count for more. The typical student has high ambitions. He does not merely dream of passing the local bar exam and joining a firm but rather aspires to become a judge, an academic, or a federal prosecutor—goals requiring, as a first step, the steady accumulation of accolades during one's term at law school itself. These include, most notably, membership on the editorial staff of the prestigious *Yale Law Journal*.

From the point of view of race relations, the *Journal* presents a problem. Under the rules in place during my time, applicants were required to complete a forty-eight-hour take-home exam testing their abilities in writing, editing, and the formatting of legal footnotes. The identities of the test-takers were unknown to the graders, and no accommodation was made for "underrepresented minorities." Out of eighty-four white applicants in my year, fifty-two made the cut, as did five out of twelve Asians. Out of the seven black applicants, none was successful.

This was not a one-time phenomenon. In the previous year's competition, eleven blacks had applied, of whom only one was accepted. The result was that, overall, the editorial membership of the *Journal* was overwhelmingly white and Asian. Out of 113 members, only two were black.

When these numbers were released, a scandal erupted. *Journal* officials convened a public meeting to discuss the problem, filling one of the law school's biggest classrooms with a standing-room-only crowd that stayed for three hours. It was an angry meeting—and also an awkward one. The problem was that no one dared mention the most obvious explanation for the racial imbalance that everybody decried. To refer, even obliquely, to the race-tagged stratification of talent at the school would have been humiliating for black students. So instead we censored ourselves and invoked esoteric theories of racial exclusion. The most popular of these was that black applicants approached the writing component of the *Journal* exam with a special "black" style that was routinely and unfairly marked down by the test's administrators. Some speakers argued that the test itself, like other such standardized exercises, amounted to a collection of culturally biased riddles. At the meeting, and in other campus discussions of the issue, many of my classmates folded their criticisms into a more general argument: the will of black applicants had been sapped by the "institutional racism" that allegedly pervaded Yale Law School.

It was around this time that I began noticing a broadening social estrangement at the school along racial lines. Since the only way to explain the racial gap at the *Law Journal* while simultaneously preserving the academic dignity of black students was to endorse various theories of alienation, black students were encouraged to see signs of such alienation in the neo-Gothic law school's every frieze and stained-glass medallion. A great deal was made of the absence of black "role models" on campus—especially black female role models. One of my fellow students argued in a public complaint that "in this environment, women students of color must fashion their professional personas out of thin air, because almost none of their professional mentors look anything like them." Another lamented: "How can I think that my ideas are respected here when people who are just like me—black women—aren't considered 'good enough' to teach here as full professors?"

Much grist was provided by small incidents. When a study group ejected one of its members, a black student whose contributions apparently were subpar, the spurned member posted a *J'accuse* manifesto charging racism. In another supposed manifestation of "micro-racism" (as such phenomena would later be described by antiracism advocates), one of my classmates complained in an essay that she'd been "excluded and alienated from the classroom environment" by her criminal-law professor, who had unconscionably confined discussion about race to a three-week segment of the semester.

In the classroom, certainly, the promised educational benefits of diversity rarely materialized. By promoting the idea that blacks thought and wrote in a special black style, the fallout from the *Law Journal* scandal reinforced the conceit that blacks and whites inhabit mutually impenetrable ideological worlds. Whites became increasingly reluctant to offer any comment that might be interpreted as threatening to blacks, while classroom comments by black students on any race-charged issue would almost always go unchallenged. Among my white peers, there was a feeling that sentiments expressed by black students had to be treated, in some abstract sense, as correct *for blacks*, and therefore immune from refutation. In general, most students were terrified of being accused of racism; when a subject connected to race came up, they either uttered platitudes or kept their mouths shut.

What helped me understand the benign origins of this surreal, emperor-has-no-clothes hunt for racist phantasms was the actual substance of my coursework—and, in particular, my classes on constitutional law—in which much of the material focused on the great victories against the very real racism embedded in America's legal framework until well into the 1960s, and arguably beyond that. (For instance, *Loving v. Virginia*, the U.S. Supreme Court case striking down Virginia's antimiscegenation statute, was not decided until 1967.) The 1954 case of *Brown v. Board of Education* in particular, was taken as the ultimate touchstone of America's moral redemption; just as its racist 1896 precedent, *Plessy v. Ferguson*—upholding the doctrine of "separate but equal"—was taken as a byword for racist hypocrisy. Like everyone else in my class, I remember being genuinely moved by *Brown* and similar cases, and by the back-stories of the litigants who'd fought them. While most of us knew we were destined to become anonymous corporate lawyers and litigators in large law firms, the civil rights crusade launched by our professional forebears filled us with lawyerly pride. Thanks to them, blacks were living Martin Luther King's dream of full racial equality, and overt racism had been pushed to the margins of American society. Armed with the same individual rights as the rest of us, we hoped and expected, blacks would quickly rise to the same level as their white neighbors.

Except, three decades after King's death, they hadn't—not where it counted, anyway: in jobs, education, housing, earning power, crime, or any other index of socioeconomic success. The complex reasons for this lie beyond the scope of this book (and, in any case, are so commonly catalogued by America's race-obsessed talking heads that I doubt anyone needs to hear them repeated, even in capsule form). But for the young and the idealistic, the fine points of gang culture, welfare-trap economics, and single parent-hood were beside the point: Racism, we'd all learned in school, was America's congenital disease. And the fact that blacks had not yet achieved full, practical equality meant it hadn't yet been fully treated. It was not a question of *whether* America was racist—that fact was answered by the data. It was a question of *how*. And if the answer couldn't be found in the plain language of laws and policy statements, it must somehow be lodged in hidden, even invisible, places, such as our own minds and words.

It was this benign but misguided instinct, not any inherently totalitarian urge to control others, that gave birth to political cor-rectness and the associated, increasingly conspiratorial witch hunt for racist phantasms within our souls. As illiberal as it seems, this conspiracist spirit is precious to those infused by it: Once one sur-renders to it, all of the inequities in our society—between men and women, blacks and whites—can be chalked up to the familiar, reassuringly simplistic bogeyman of bigotry.

Political correctness and radical identity politics have subsided slightly since their high-water mark in the early 1990s, in large part thanks to a backlash by right-wing culture warriors allied with principled leftist free-speechers. But like Marxism, it has left behind a toxic ideological residue on our intellectual coastline: a vague but powerful baseline belief among educated liberals that mainstream society is divided into victims and oppressors—and that the latter are largely white, male, straight middle-aged men who look a lot like George W. Bush and Donald Rumsfeld. After a few years spent wandering this coastline, the belief that these people might fly planes into the World Trade Center doesn't follow automatically, but it certainly becomes a lot easier to assimilate.

CHAPTER NINE

The *Protocols* Revisited: The New Face of Anti-Semitic Conspiracism

Showdown in the Bowery

There's an old joke about a lone Jewish sailor marooned on a tiny desert island in the middle of the South Pacific. After years of solitude, the castaway's signal fire is spotted by the captain of a passing freighter, who wades ashore to rescue the man. Thereupon, the captain is astonished to find that the Jew has built himself not one, but two small mud-and-straw synagogues side by side.

"Why *two*?" asks the captain.

"That one is where I pray," replies the Jew, gesturing solemnly to the synagogue on the left.

" . . . But as for *that* one," he adds, raising a rueful finger at the other building, "I wouldn't set foot in the place if you *paid* me."

That punch line neatly sums up the schismatic conspiracism on display over the weekend of September 11–13, 2009—the eighth anniversary of the 9/11 attacks—when lower Manhattan played host to not one, but two rival Truther conferences, just a few blocks from one another. Both events attracted hundreds of attendees, all convinced that the 9/11 attacks had been an inside job. Aside from that, the two groups had little in common.

The first group—call them the right-wing New World Order faction—was young, loud, and libertarian. Under the banner of

"We Are Change," they staged "street actions" outside Madison Square Garden, the Council on Foreign Relations (where they screamed "We won't be your New World Order slave puppets" to CFR president Richard Haass) and at Ground Zero itself. Their leader was Luke Rudkowski, a brooding twenty-three-year-old bullhorn activist (profiled in Chapter 5) who specializes in ambushing public figures on video with questions about 9/11. The most revered name on their lips was radio host Alex Jones; the most despised, the Bilderbergers ("scumbags trying to destroy humanity" was how one activist described them in a speech at Cooper Union). Everyone, it seemed, was carrying some form of digital camera, endlessly filming everyone else filming everyone else. Populism and patriotism were the binding ideological agents. Some of the speakers, in fact, were actual 9/11 first responders, former soldiers, and other uniformed types. Their speeches often were interrupted by chants of "U-S-A! U-S-A!"

Meanwhile, at St. Mark's Church in-the-Bowery, an entirely different conference was unfolding, this one under the banner of "We Demand Transparency: The Conference for Peace, Truth, and a New Economics." Here, the attendees were older, grayer, quieter—tweedy academics and activists in sportjackets and tennis shoes, with one foot still planted in Cold War–era pacifism. There were few cameras. Unlike at We Are Change's all-electronic right-wing jamboree, the people here were actually holding, reading, selling, and discussing old-fashioned *books*. These fathers and grandfathers did not go in for "street actions" or other noisy events. Instead, they sat in their pews and listened to a succession of wonky middle-aged men (they were all men) give Amerikan-themed history lessons about false flags, Vietnam, and the Bay of Pigs. The room was hot, and many of the attendees were clustered around the fans arrayed along the side walls. At a few points, I felt myself nodding off.

Then, Kevin Barrett took the podium, and everyone woke up.

Barrett is a balding, bespectacled man in his early fifties—the sort of fellow whose thumbnail photo might appear alongside the Yiddish-dictionary entry for *nebbish*. But from his base in Madison, Wisconsin, he's made a name for himself in Truther circles as one of the movement's say-anything bad boys. Born into a conventional midwestern Lutheran family (his father was Olympic gold-medal sailor Peter Barrett), Barrett converted to Islam in 1992, after marrying a Moroccan-born Muslim woman. Five years later, he earned a PhD in African languages and literature at the University of Wisconsin, where he remained employed as a lecturer until he created an uproar by publicly insisting that Muslims weren't involved in the World Trade Center attacks. ("Every single Muslim I know in Madison knew it was an inside job.") Since then, he's been arrested for alleged domestic abuse, run a fringe campaign for Congress, hosted conspiracist radio programs, launched a series of ugly feuds with competing conspiracists, and started up a creepy website that publishes the home addresses of police officers and other government officials "who are alleged to have seriously abused their power over others."

Barrett began his presentation at St. Mark's by arguing that the involvement of Muslims in the 9/11 operation would be an impossibility, since the tenets of Islam are incompatible with any sort of unprovoked violence. Instead, he said, the obvious villain is Israel—or, as he called it, the "genocidal settler colonial state in Palestine." But making this case to the American people is difficult, he said, because Jews are "wildly overrepresented in the American media," and all the major media companies are led by "Zionist Jewish CEOs." Nor can we trust the official 9/11 commission, Barrett says, since its executive director, Philip Zelikow, is an "ethnic Jew."

None of these claims would have been particularly surprising for anyone who'd studied Barrett's comments about Jews and Israel, in which he often recycles traditional anti-Semitic propaganda themes, as in this mass emailing addressing the Lebanese government's discrimination against Palestinians: "The hundreds of thousands of [Palestinian] refugees living in poverty in Lebanon, among other places, should be treated as honored guests; while the economic losses that ordinary Lebanese will suffer when the Palestinians compete with them in the work force, and all other losses suffered by the victims of Zionism, should be compensated ASAP by the seizure of Zionist money, starting with the Rothschild fortune along with those of the other 50% of American billionaires who are Zionist war criminals."

And it gets worse. Since leaving the University of Wisconsin, Barrett has become that rare breed: a *left-wing* Holocaust skeptic. Back in 2006, he described his views on the subject this way: "Whatever the facts about WWII, it seems tragic that systematic Zionist Big Lies [about the Middle East] have cast legitimate doubt upon ANYTHING Jews say about Jews and their recent history, including the Holocaust. As a rational person who is not a specialist in the subject of WWII, but who has studied the history of Zionist Big Lies vis-à-vis Palestine, I cannot possibly dismiss the arguments of people like [Mark] Green, [David] Irving, and even [Ernst] Zündel. And even if the 6-million-deliberately-murdered-for-purely-ethnic-reasons figure is correct—which it very well may be; I have grown agnostic on that after studying the Big Lies of Zionism—I would still have to characterize the Holocaust as it is taught in the U.S. as a hideously destructive myth."

As Barrett spoke, there was an uncomfortable stir in the crowd. One particular fellow—a middle-aged Truther with a boyish face and a shaggy 1970s-style mop of brown hair, seated about twenty feet to my right—could barely contain his exasperation. Later on, he identified himself to me as Steve Alten, a science-fiction author best known for his *Meg* action novels about a family of giant prehistoric sharks (the megalodon) that eat boats, helicopters, whales, and (in historical flashback) a Tyrannosaurus Rex.

When the Q&A began, Alten rose from his seat. "I consider you a friend, and I've been on your [Internet radio] show many times," he told Barrett. "But you start off with the idea that we shouldn't use racial profiling against Muslims, which I agree with, as a Jew. And then you completely become a hypocrite, and *blame* the Jews. You put up a list of Jewish people in the media, and immediately label them Zionist, and [suggest] that they have motivations for covering up 9/11, without any shred of evidence, without ever having met any of those people . . . You're actually hurting the 9/11 Truth movement by doing these things!" Then Alten sat down, to scattered applause.

A few minutes later, as the audience dispersed for lunch, Barrett came over to make peace with Alten. But their conversation degenerated into another argument. As I listened in, alongside a few others, I found myself in the odd position of cheering on one conspiracy theorist in what seemed to me a principled attack on a bigoted counterpart. (At one especially surreal point, Barrett—whom I'd interviewed previously—actually ushered me into the conversation to adjudicate some tangential point or other about Middle Eastern history.)

Later on, when I caught up with Alten, he told me that the whole episode symbolized what's wrong with the 9/11 Truth movement—an opinion shared by others I interviewed at St. Mark's. "I was shocked that they allowed Barrett to speak," he told me. "He's become so radical . . . I've basically cornered him into admitting his desire to see Israel wiped off the face of the map. Who would ever want to be associated with someone like that? He used to speak out about the facts of 9/11. But he now uses the 9/11 Truth podium to tie everything into the Jews."

Conspiracism's Hateful Sidekick

Not all conspiracy theorists are anti-Semitic. But all conspiracy movements—all of them—attract anti-Semites. Even UFO conspiracists manage, somehow, to project Jewish stereotypes on imagined visitors from other galaxies: A recurring theme in their literature is that outer-space visitors are divided into at least two categories—tall, virtuous, Aryan-seeming aliens (sometimes traced to the star Procyon, in the constellation Canis Minor); and malignant, gnomelike, big-nosed "Grays" (sometimes traced to the star Rigel, in the Orion constellation).

The roots of this ancient bigotry extend to the very moment when Jesus died on the Cross. "Most Christians did not want to be enemies of the Roman Empire and they soon sought to play down the role of the Romans in the [Biblical] story," Diarmaid MacCulloch explains in *Christianity: The First Three Thousand Years*. "So the Passion narratives shifted the blame on to the Jewish authorities"—a propaganda effort epitomized in the Gospel of Matthew, wherein the Jewish crowds are made to roar out "His blood be on us, and on our children!" (As MacCulloch archly notes, "It would have been better for the moral health of Christianity if the blame had stayed with Pilate.") In the superstitious medieval anti-Semitic tradition that eventually emerged—as described earlier in this book—the Jew was a sort of wandering demon, poisoning drinking water and murdering Christian babies to satisfy his inborn bloodlust.

Many centuries later—after the French Revolution and the wave of frenzied anti-Semitic conspiracism that accompanied it—the Jew became a symbol of the political, technological, and industrial forces threatening to overturn Europe's sleepy pastoral monarchies. Capitalism, in particular, along with the wrenching creative destruction that inevitably accompanied it, was imagined to be the creation of rootless Jewish financiers—*Luftmenschen*, or "people of the air," as German anti-Semites called them—who leeched their income off society's farmers, laborers, and artisans. In French society, this attitude came into full bloom during the Dreyfus affair; and, before it, the 1890s-era scandal surrounding the collapse of the Panama Canal Company, which the *Libre Parole* newspaper described as "a flagrant instance of the Jewish peril," and evidence that "all of Jewry, high and low" lay "congregated beneath the udder of this milch cow."

As discussed in Chapter 2, anti-Semitic conspiracists of this period played to the nostalgic, reactionary, backward-looking attitude that inevitably takes hold of insecure people in tumultuous times. Poisonous anti-Semitism penetrated all strata of European society in the decades leading up to World War II. But it found its most enthusiastic audience among romantic nationalists who fetishized their country's fading pastoral identity and aristocratic traditions, which the "rootless" urban Jew was seen to be undermining. This made the doctrine useful to Russia's czars, and Europe's other besieged monarchs, who pushed the idea that political liberalism was a Jewish plot to destroy Europe's Christian character.

As the influence of the *Protocols* swept west, Germany, afflicted with a particularly feverish strain of nationalism, showed itself to be especially vulnerable. "When [German anti-Semites of the *völkisch* variety] looked to the past, to the ideal state which they supposed to have preceded the modern age, they looked far beyond throne and altar, back to an infinitely remote and almost entirely mythical world," wrote Norman Cohn in *Warrant for Genocide*. "For them, 'the Jew' was not only, or mainly, the destroyer of kings and the enemy of the Church—he was above all the age-old antagonist of the Germanic peasant, he was the force which for two thousand years had been undermining the true, original German way of life."

Adolf Hitler put a pseudoscientific gloss on such dark superstitions by tethering them to the germ theory of medicine and associated notions of "racial hygiene." As early as 1919, when Hitler was still employed as an education officer with the German Army in Munich, he described Jewry as "the racial tuberculosis of the peoples." With the newly available tools of industrial slaughter, the Jew now could be scientifically eradicated in the same way that a hospital room could be sterilized. In pursuing this project, Hitler created a genocide so horribly systematic that it has become the standard of evil against which all other crimes against humanity have been measured ever since.

Hitler destroyed six million Jews. But he also destroyed anti-

Semitism as a semirespectable Western creed: In the shadow of the Holocaust, theories about Jews that had circulated for centuries suddenly seemed sinister and even lunatic. The presence of journalists among Europe's liberators (including Edward R. Murrow, whose April, 1945, report from Buchenwald concentration camp was one of the most memorable of his career) ensured that the effect on popular attitudes would be permanently etched in photographs and film—a reminder for future generations that could be summoned up whenever the language of murderous anti-Semitism fills the mouths of dictators (as, in fact, is now the case in Iran).

Soft anti-Semitism would stagger on for decades in Europe and North America—the sort that kept Jews out of certain country clubs and law firms till the 1970s and 1980s. But it would never again be permissible in the mainstream West to speak of Jews disparagingly as a race, or even to begin a dinner-party monologue with the words "The Jew." Overt anti-Semitism became dispersed to the fringes of intellectual life—the militant black ghetto and the Nation of Islam; neo-Nazi- and skinhead groups (which are largely extinct in North America, but still occasionally assert themselves in chants emanating from the cheap seats at European soccer games); and—as discussed at greater length in this chapter—militant, left-wing anti-Israeli obsessives, such as Kevin Barrett, who have made common cause with hatemongers in the Muslim Middle East.

Even most "mainstream" (if that word can be used) conspiracy theorists, I was surprised to discover, now go to extraordinary lengths to avoid the taint of Jew hatred. This is especially apparent among right-wing New World Order types, such as Alex Jones—despite the fact that their central narrative, the existence of a moneyed cabal of all-controlling globalists who oppress ordinary hard-working Americans, is precisely congruent with old-school anti-Semitism in just about every other aspect. Michael Ruppert, perhaps the most influential 9/11 Truther there was in the movement's early years, began his epic conspiracist tome *Crossing the Rubicon* with "special thanks" to "all of the American Jews who took to this book and my work in full recognition that we all worship the same God." Robert Bowman—the one-time head of the Star Wars missile defense program under Gerald Ford and Jimmy Carter, now a peace activist and 9/11 Truther—defends himself against allegations of consorting with Holocaust deniers by averring, "My father was an ethnic Jew." Even Barrett felt compelled to start up an odd organization called "Muslim-Jewish-Christian Alliance for 9/11 Truth" to give ecumenical cover for his conspiracy theories.

Perhaps my favorite example in the but-some-of-my-best-friends-are-Jewish conspiracist niche is Victor Fletcher, the editor and publisher of the *Toronto Street News*, a bizarre fortnightly newspaper sold for two dollars a copy by homeless people. While the publication was conceived as a way to provide dignity to beggars who otherwise would simply be asking passersby for a handout, its crackpot contents have instead reinforced the worst stereotype of homeless people as paranoid, hate-addled lunatics. One 2010 edition, for instance, contained an article titled "The Kaballah: The NWO's Satanic Bible," claiming that "the 'god' of the Kabbalah is not god at all. It is Lucifer. Freemasonry is based on the Kabbalah. Illuminati Jews and their Freemasonic allies are stealthily erecting a New World Order dedicated to Lucifer. That's why the ubiquitous logo of the City of Ottawa, where I am currently visiting, is an O with three tails. 666." Yet on the newspaper's masthead page, Fletcher—who once was forced to apologize for running an article calling for the murder of "Jew bankers"—proudly declares the *Street News* to be a "Jewish Newspaper, 60% written by Jews."

Of course, some conspiracy theorists do cross the line into out-and-out unapologetic anti-Semitism (and its inevitable cousin, Holocaust denial). But when that happens, they typically become radioactive to less radicalized conspiracists such as Jones, Alten, and most of the other leading conspiracy theorists whom I have profiled in this book. At this point, the typical pattern is for the anti-Semite to schism publicly from the movement—a melodramatic blog posting is now the usual medium for this maneuver—and set out down his own hateful, idiosyncratic path, adding his erstwhile conspiracists-in-arms to the long tally of Jewish and semitophilic conspirators he keeps tacked to the virtual bulletin board at the back of his mind.

The process can take years. By all appearances, Kevin Barrett is well on his way.

A New Home on the Left

Since the French Revolution, anti-Semitism typically had been a creature of the Right, in the European sense of the word—which is to say, the reactionary defenders of the established social, religious, and economic order: As already noted, the Jew was a stand-in for capitalism, mobility (physical and otherwise), new ideologies, and the marginalization of the sturdy gentile rural folk who plowed the fields, threshed the grain, and embodied the romantic pastoral core of the nation's collective identity.

This began to change in 1948, when the creation of the state of Israel, simultaneous with the extinction in the West of traditional anti-Semitism. Gradually, Jews would be spoken of less as social pollutants or passive victims within larger Western societies—and more as protagonists in the geopolitics of a once-obscure corner of the British Empire. After the Jews established their own state, it became impossible to typecast them as mere parasites contaminating foreign hosts. The Six-Day War of 1967, when Israel scored a crushing military victory against Egypt, Jordan, and Syria, furthered this transformation. Writing in that same year, one scholarly expert on the *Protocols* declared: "Today, the story is already almost forgotten—so much so that it is quite rare, at least in Europe, to meet anyone under the age of 40 who has even heard of these strange ideas."

Yet at the same time that an old breed of Jewish-focused conspiracism was dying, a new one was blooming on Israeli soil. As Columbia University professor Rashid Khalidi wrote in *The Iron Cage: The Story of the Palestinian Struggle for Statehood*, the Jews who arrived in Israel from Europe were mostly white, well educated, and politically sophisticated—alien beings amongst the largely rural, uneducated, and illiterate Arabs who populated the area. Far from the likes of David Ben Gurion, the Palestinian leaders of the British Mandate period were fez-wearing grandees held over from another age—feuding, risk-averse patriarchs who were far more concerned with preserving their traditional status than agitating for Arab rights, much less organizing a modern state. And so when civil war broke out between the two sides in 1947, the result was decisive.

Seen from North American shores, the Jews' transformation of Israel from an Ottoman backwater into a thriving, powerful Western nation continues to inspire: Here was an ancient people returning to their homeland following two millennia of statelessness and a European dictator's effort at extermination. But to the Arab peasants whose sleepy, agrarian society was being transformed into an alien landscape by immigrants speaking another language and embracing another religion, the Jews looked as much like colonialists as the British officials they replaced.

In the 1960s, Yasser Arafat would popularize this colonial narrative in the West by presenting himself as a sort of Arab Che Guevara. Equally influential was Palestinian American scholar Edward Said, whose books helped convince the Western intelligentsia that every corner of Western society—from the novels of Jane Austen to U.S. foreign policy—was soaked in bigotry and exploitation; and that the Western media, in particular, was poisonously disposed toward Eastern cultures. From the Palestinian point of view, the genius of this approach was that it cut through the complex history of Jews and Arabs, casting the Palestinian struggle as a simple microcosm of the Orient's larger battle against imperialism.

In the emerging propaganda against the Jewish state—which,

in the West, now takes its most common form on websites and campus posters announcing Israel Apartheid Week and other anti-Zionist events—the old anti-Semitic stereotypes have been revamped. In the centuries leading up to the Holocaust, the Jew often was seen as rich, but also physically flaccid, diseased, and somewhat wretched. Fagin, from Charles Dickens' *Oliver Twist*, for instance, was described as "disgusting." In *Ivanhoe*, the Jew Isaac is introduced as "a tall thin old man, who . . . had lost by the habit of stooping much of his actual height." By the 1970s, this stereotype was thrown into reverse: In the emerging propaganda, the Jew now was shown in the cockpit of a helicopter or fighter jet—an omnipotent, teched-up superman murdering defenseless Palestinian children from the sky. As in the Nazi era, the Jew isn't fully human—but now he's an all-powerful Nazgûl instead of a pitiful Gollum.

In the common usage of child victims to communicate the extent of the Jew's evil, the anti-Israeli propaganda of today is similar to the posters and textbooks of the Nazi era, which often showed shadowy Hebrews menacing German families. But the Nazis took care to personalize the Jew as a craggy, hook-nosed ghoul—an image meant to further the idea that Jews were so genetically inferior as to be literally inhuman. Aside from editorial cartoonists in the Arab world (many of whom continue to faithfully copy Nazi-era stereotypes to this day), anti-Semitic propagandists of our own age typically omit the Jew's features in favour of a faceless, Star-of-Zion-emblazoned machine of war. During the second Intifada, for instance, a photo genre much favored by newspapers was the image of a small boy throwing a rock at a monstrous chunk of moving steel—an Israeli tank or bulldozer.

In keeping with our society's obsession with victimhood, the propaganda strategy against Israel now is entirely passive-aggressive. While the Nazis dwelled on the virility and superhuman indomitability of Aryans, the Jews' enemies now are represented in propaganda by five-year-olds carrying teddy bears. In 2009, for instance, the worldwide organizers of Israel Apartheid Week circulated a slick sixty-second promotional movie on apartheidweek.org, in which they depicted a cartoon mock-up of Gaza's population containing no men of military age, just a group of sorrowful children, mothers, and grandparents. The complex moral dimension of the conflict has been replaced by a sentimental Marxist-inspired tale of the virtuous oppressed rising up against an evil oppressor. Slogans of racial purity have been replaced with the mantras of "social justice."

As a result, anti-Israel activism has drawn in the whole hodgepodge of leftist activists—and even world leaders—who know little about the Middle East, but who identify in a broad sense with the Marxist-inspired struggle of worker against capitalist, black against white, colonized against colonizer. During the 2008–2009 Gaza War, for instance, Hugo Chavez's "bolivarian" government in Venezuela declared its "unrestricted solidarity with the heroic Palestinian people" and denounced Israel's "criminal atrocities." A few months later, Chavez's deposed Honduran ally, Manuel Zelaya, told the world he was under siege from "Israeli mercenaries" armed with what a *Miami Herald* interviewer described as "high-frequency radiation" and "toxic gases" that "alter [Zelaya's] physical and mental state."

Back in North America, this merging of shrill anti-Zionism and traditional left-wing activism has produced bizarre juxtapositions—such as lesbian feminists who defend the *niqab* as a form of resistance against Western capitalism, and "peace activists" marching alongside *kafiyeh*-clad protesters who chant for Jewish blood in Arabic. Perhaps the most bizarre example I have witnessed is Toronto's annual Gay Pride parade, a popular tourist-friendly spectacle whose out-and-proud homoeroticism would constitute a death sentence for participants were the event held in the Arab world. Yet these parades have contained a contingent of "Queers Against Israeli Apartheid" who shout slogans against one of the most gay-friendly nations in the entire world. (Gays serve openly in the Israeli army, and there are gay pride parades in both Jerusalem and Tel Aviv.)

What makes such poisonous attacks on Israel especially notable is the fact that community activists in Toronto's gay community otherwise have shown themselves obsessively committed to the principles of nondiscrimination. The mission statement of the Pride committee, for instance, is a lengthy catalog of pledges to "value diversity" in regard to every imaginable sexual subniche. Yet, like many other left-wing activists, they often exhibit a single-minded hatred of Israel no less obsessive than the hateful campaigns once commonly launched by reactionary xenophobes. The same is true of the ultraliberal United Church of Canada, whose activists rarely raise a peep when Christians are slaughtered in Pakistan or Iraq, but militate for sanctions against one of the only nations in the Middle East where Christians can worship without fear. Then there is *Adbusters*, an ultra-*bien-pensant* Vancouver-based anticorporate magazine whose parent foundation earnestly describes itself as "a global network of artists, activists, writers, pranksters, students, educators, and entrepreneurs who want to advance the new social activist movement of the information age." In late 2010, *Adbusters* ran a photo spread (*Truthbombs on Israeli TV*) comparing the situation in Gaza to that of the Warsaw Ghetto during the Second World War—a feature so vile that Canada's largest drug-store chain pulled all copies of it off its shelves. Equally offensive was a 2004 *Adbusters* feature—"Why won't anyone say they are Jewish?"—ticking off all the powerful Jews who had pushed for the invasion of Iraq. After decades of political correctness, it has become clear that the hypertolerant mantras of modern leftism supply no defense against the mind-warping effects of conspiracism: They simply deflect the conspiracist impulse to more fashionable targets such as Israel and the Jews that support it.

Even Jews themselves sometime have been seduced by this phenomenon. Noam Chomsky is an example. So is leftist icon Naomi Klein, who, as noted earlier, believes that Israeli elites are somehow secretly complicit in the terrorist attacks against their country.

Another example is Toronto-based Jewish anti-Israel activist Diana Ralph, who co-founded a group called Independent Jewish Voices. Among the group's causes: a total economic boycott of Israel, defense of the UN's original anti-Semitic Durban conference, and promotion of the blood libel that Israel deliberately targets Palestinian "children playing on roofs." In a 2006 essay, Ralph argued that the Sept. 11 attacks were not perpetrated by al-Qaeda, but rather by American and Israeli conservatives seeking to implement "a secret, strategic plan to position the U.S. as a permanent unilateral super-power poised to seize control of Eurasia, and thereby the entire world"—a plan rooted in a 1979 Zionist conference organized by none other than future Israeli prime minister Benjamin Netanyahu.

Another member of Independent Jewish Voices is a twenty-nine-year-old University of Toronto sociology student named Jennifer Peto. In 2010, she submitted a master's degree thesis titled *The Victimhood of the Powerful: White Jews, Zionism and the Racism of Hegemonic Holocaust Education.* Peto's thesis—which can best be described as a confessional essay with footnotes—tells the story of her gradual transformation from religious Jewish Zionist to self-described "Palestine solidarity activist." In her thesis, she makes the astonishing argument that Holocaust education can have undesirable effects, because it reinforces Jews' sense of victimization, and thereby serves to indirectly strengthen their support for "the Israeli nation-state" (which she also refers to in the thesis as an "Apartheid State").

All of these figures represent minority opinions within the broader North American Jewish community. But they have attained outsized importance because their writings are promoted by anti-Zionist groups eager to escape the charge of anti-Semitism.

On this score, critics of Israel are perfectly correct that not all criticism of the Jewish state rises to the level of true anti-Semitism. But the boundary line is blurry and subjective. With *Protocols*-style anti-Semitism, things were simpler: The bell was rung whenever someone described Jews as a class of creatures, as fundamentally malignant or biologically deficient. But the left-wing variety nominally focuses on the actions of a state, not a people. And so the observer must instead rely on indirect (and therefore less conclusive) evidence of anti-Semitism, such as the anti-Zionists' obsessive focus on the victims of Israeli counterterrorist operations, while ignoring the terrorist provocations that led to them, not to mention the many other, far greater, human-rights abuses that occur regularly in other countries around the world.

The 9/11 Effect

If the Holocaust and the creation of the Jewish state jointly marked the first great turning point in the modern history of anti-Semitism, 9/11 marked the second. Following the attacks, supporters of Israel spoke of a silver lining: The war against militant Islam suddenly was a global one. Now, the whole world would see and understand the sort of nihilistic hatred that Israelis confronted every day.

But in Europe, this was not to be. Terrorism is effective because it causes people to choose sides—sending a tremor along the political fence, so that those sitting on it are cast on to one side or the other. Tens of millions of ordinary Europeans, the type who once might have thought themselves vaguely pro-Palestinian in their outlook, committed themselves to the belief that Israeli violence toward Palestinians—along with U.S. neoimperialism, globalization, and the like—was one of the "root causes" of not only 9/11, but also the Muslim militancy on display in the dilapidated immigrant ghettoes of Paris and other European cities.

Indeed, the period around 9/11—which also roughly coincided with the high point of the Second Intifada, and with the infamously anti-Semitic World Conference Against Racism in Durban, South Africa—featured a brief spasm of old-fashioned blood-libel anti-Semitism in Europe. During the April 2002 battle in the West Bank town of Jenin, in particular, European newspapers credulously reported false Palestinian claims that Israel was perpetrating a "massacre" of the town's civilians. In 2003, Dave Brown was named Britain's political cartoonist of the year for an image, published in the *Independent*, showing Ariel Sharon eating Palestinian babies in the style of Francisco Goya's *Saturn Devouring His Son*. Much of the hysteria died down in the middle of decade, as the Intifada gradually lost steam, and European attention turned toward George W. Bush and the Iraq War. But it was rekindled in 2006, during Israel's brief campaign against Hezbollah—and again in late 2008, during the Gaza conflict. Even as recently as 2009, a leading left-wing Swedish newspaper, *Aftonbladet*, published a lurid two-page spread alleging (falsely) that the Israeli army kills Palestinians to harvest their organs, a modern gloss on the age-old claim that Jews harvest the blood of gentile babies for their Passover matzo.

But in the United States (and Canada), where most observers previously had tilted to the other side of the fence, 9/11 had the opposite effect: America's fight became Israel's fight. Over the last decade, a period during which Republicans and Democrats have fought over every other subject imaginable, support for Israel has remained one of the few issues to attract virtually unanimous bipartisan support.

Among war-hawks on the Right, in particular, the sudden identification of militant Islam as America's greatest enemy capped a startling transformation in the perception of the American Jewish community. Whereas Jews might once have threatened the American Right in their roles as communists, anarchists, trade unionists, civil rights leaders, and Ivy League intellectuals, no Jew could ever be an Islamist. Just the opposite: The Jew was the perfect *anti-*Islamist, whose zeal and reliability in the war on terrorism was hard-wired into his political DNA thanks to six decades of Israeli warfare against Islamic terrorists in the Middle East. For the first time in the history of Western civilization, the Jew's "foreignness"

and mixed loyalties—to the United States, Israel, world Jewry—
became a source of respect and trust rather than suspicion.

A related phenomenon I have noticed through my interaction
with *National Post* letter-writers since 9/11—and this also must
rank as another unprecedented phenomenon—is that North American Jews now seem just as likely to *embrace* conspiracy theories as
to be targeted by them. Birther mythology, in particular (along
with its associated allegations that Barack Obama is Muslim, and
is secretly conspiring to destroy Israel) has become a bonding agent
between blue-state Jewish Zionists and red-state Evangelicals—a
conspiracist alliance that would have been unimaginable in the
days of the John Birch Society. Much has been made of the pre-
millennial beliefs of Christian Zionists, according to which Evangelicals stand by Israel because they believe an ingathering of Jews
in the Levant is required to fulfill the prophecy of Jesus' Second
Coming. But few have noticed that Jewish Zionists have returned
the favor—embracing Barack Obama conspiracy theories infused
with all manner of decidedly Christian eschatological influences.

As anti-Zionist conspiracy theorists have been only too happy
to remind us, many of the leading intellectuals and political figures who championed America's aggressive post–9/11 war against
terror were Jewish "neoconservatives" (to use the much-abused
shorthand)—a list that includes Richard Perle, Paul Wolfowitz,
Douglas Feith, Charles Krauthammer, Norman Podhoretz, Elliot
Abrams, Alan Dershowitz, Daniel Pipes, and Bill and Irving Kristol. Once reviled as counterfeit Americans by prewar conservative
nativists, Jews now found themselves at the very center of the intellectual firmament that surrounded the U.S. commander in chief
and his twenty-first-century war machine.

The post-9/11 alliance between Christian populists and Jews
has carried over into areas that have nothing to do with war or terrorism. On paper, for instance, the Tea Party movement—with its
suspicion of urban elites, social liberals, the Ivy League, the mainstream media, and much of America's corporate establishment—

would appear to provide the ideal ideological incubator for a revival of old-fashioned anti-Semitism. The same goes for the period in late 2009 and 2010 when the Tea Party movement took off, an era shot through with the sort of large-scale financial busts that, throughout history, typically have sparked the West's great anti-Semitic spasms. Yet even the disgrace of Bernie Madoff, a crooked Jewish financier plucked straight out of classic anti-Semitic stereotypes, failed to produce even the slightest hint of a mainstream revival in Jew hatred.

Or consider the case of George Soros, a billionaire Jewish Hungarian American financier who has earned the ire of conservatives by bankrolling a long list of liberal activist groups, including MoveOn.org. In November, 2010, FOX News host Glenn Beck profiled Soros on a segment he called *The Puppet Master*, which the network aired with ominous black-and-white newsreel-style graphics. Beck warned viewers of a shadowy "structure" being installed in America by saboteurs seeking to transform the country. "All the paths, time after time, really led to one man," Beck declared, pointing to a flowchart. "George Soros, one guy."

Soros' fingerprints, Beck declared, were on the "crisis collapsing our economy," as well as a plot to create a "One World Government." The FOX News hosts also claimed that "Not only does [Soros] want to bring America to her knees, financially, he wants to reap obscene profits off us as well."

As discussed in detail in this book, the idea that a secret cabal of all-powerful financiers and "puppet masters" is deliberately seeking to crash the world's economies and thereby create a "one-world government" has been kicking around right-wing conspiracist circles at least since the publication of *The Protocols of the Learned Elders of Zion*—in which the fictional Jewish "Elders" are shown as plotting to render "all the goy States to bankruptcy" and to create a "Super-Government Administration." This similitude helps explains why the Anti-Defamation League described Beck's rants against Soros as "offensive" and "horrific."

Yet, Beck's claim against Soros wasn't built around the financier's status as a Jew—but rather the claim that Soros isn't Jewish *enough*: At one point in his *Puppet Master* feature, Beck claimed that he is "probably more supportive of Israel and the Jews than George Soros is." He also declared that Soros is "an atheist who doesn't embrace his Jewish identity, and rarely supports Jewish causes."

These words bespeak an amazing transformation in right-wing American attitudes toward Jews. For centuries, Jewish bankers and financiers labored under the conspiracist accusation that they were fifth columnists—agents of a foreign Hebrew power that sought to control and oppress the gentiles. Now, decades later, Jews' fealty to their kind is presented as a saving grace (albeit one that, according to Beck, George Soros cannot claim).

Many American conservatives have internalized the idea that protection of Jews and Israel from the threat of a new, Iranian-sparked holocaust has become a sacred national duty on a par with protection of America's own homeland. At the February 2010 Tea Party National Convention in Nashville, for instance, I was shocked to hear a presiding minister bless Israel in the same breath as the United States during a prayer before Sarah Palin's speech. A few months later, when Barack Obama and Benjamin Netanyahu had a public spat over the construction of new Jewish homes in East Jerusalem, conservative pundits such as Charles Krauthammer (who denounced Obama's "kowtowing" to foreign leaders in just about every other context) openly took Israel's side. During this period, Joseph Farah's website, WorldNetDaily, even sent out an email asking readers for the "symbolic" amount of $19.48 to buy flowers for Israel's prime minister: "Obama treated our best friend in the Middle East, Israel, with disdain when Prime Minister Benjamin Netanyahu visited Washington. Now America is speaking up by sending the prime minister a tangible message of support that cannot be missed—yellow roses, the symbol of friendship! Stand against this terrible treatment!"

Farah and his followers, I have had to keep reminding myself, are part of a hyperpatriotic, even nativist, political movement animated by fears of Muslims and illegal Mexican immigrants taking over their Christian nation. Yet somehow, in the process, they have decided that a tiny Hebrew-speaking country six thousand miles from Washington is more apple-pie than their own president.

Jews Drift Right

The subject of this chapter has been anti-Semitism, and its evolving role within the larger framework of Western conspiracism. Before abandoning the subject, it is worth dwelling briefly on the way this evolution has affected the Jewish community itself.

For most of the twentieth century, North American Jews have identified with society's underdogs. On race issues in particular, many community leaders remain faithful to a political alliance struck between blacks and Jews a century ago. The affinity between the two groups had a cultural aspect: Both Jewish immigrants and religious blacks saw parallels between the story of Exodus and the end of modern slavery. Being disproportionately drawn to left-wing politics in the early part of the twentieth century, many Jews also tended to view blacks and other disadvantaged minorities through the prism of class struggle—an attitude comically epitomized by Alvy Singer's father in Woody Allen's *Annie Hall*, who defended his black cleaning lady against accusations of theft by famously insisting, "She's a colored woman, from Harlem! She has no money! She's got a right to steal from us! After all, who is she gonna steal from if not us?"

In the postwar years, all minorities—including not only Jews and blacks, but Muslims, gays, Hispanics, and Asians—were bound together by the fight for a meritocratic society in which people were judged not on the basis of their faith or skin color but by the content of their character. The fight against anti-Jewish quotas in universities and the fight to end Southern segregation were, in this respect, one and the same. As many other authors have noted, Jews were greatly overrepresented in the fight for civil rights in the United States. In Canada, Jewish community leaders led the charge for the network of human rights commissions set up in the 1970s.

Once the great battles of the civil-rights era had been won, however, things changed. Jews now truly were mingling at the best country clubs and checking into corner offices at white-shoe law firms, not to mention bestriding the inner circles of power in Washington and on Wall Street. The pretense that they were still bound up in the same struggles as other groups began to break down—even if many Jews, still playing the underdog role out of habit, refused to notice.

The 9/11 attacks forced them to notice. Virtually every major Jewish group in the United States lined up foursquare behind the war in Iraq—thereby estranging many Jews from the wider peace movement in which they'd once taken such an active part. The messy wars in Lebanon in 2006, and in Gaza in 2008–2009, during which many Jews were appalled to see Western leftists effectively take the side of terrorist groups as if they were legitimate "resistance movements," widened the fissure. As noted above, some Jews did follow the Chomskyite path, and continue to do so. But amid the carnage of 9/11 and the rise of suicide bombings as an everyday tool of Palestinian terrorists—tactics bespeaking existential hatred of Jews and Western society more generally—these dissenters no longer were met with the forbearance that formerly had greeted them by fellow Jews. That stock figure of left-wing synagogue life, the middle-aged peacenik holding bake sales for Gaza, was now regarded by some as a sinister dupe, not just a heterodox oddball.

In the years following 9/11, the group playing the civil-rights card was no longer blacks or Hispanics. Instead, it was America's Muslims and Arabs, whose community leaders typically have been strident critics of Israel, and—as author Daniel Pipes has documented in great detail—sometimes even apologists for terrorism. Among leftists, Jews once were understood to speak with moral authority on the subject of persecution. But no more. To quote Sheila Wilmot, my instructor in the *Thinking About Whiteness and Doing Anti-Racism* course I described in the last chapter, "Jewish people of European origin have a relationship to racism that is much closer to that of white non-Jews than to that of people of color."

The September 11 attacks changed America in a thousand different ways. Perhaps the most ironic, given the terrorists' intensely anti-Semitic ideology, was that it cemented the long process leading to Jews' full-fledged ascension into the American establishment.

CHAPTER TEN

Confronting Conspiracism

The conspiracy community regularly seizes on one slip of the tongue, mis-understanding, or slight discrepancy to defeat 20 pieces of solid evidence; accepts one witness of theirs, even if he or she is a provable nut, as being far more credible than 10 normal witnesses on the other side; treats rumors, even questions, as the equivalent of proof; leaps from the most minuscule of discoveries to the grandest of conclusions; and insists, as the late lawyer Louis Nizer once observed, that the failure to explain everything perfectly negates all that is explained.

—*Vincent Bugliosi,* Reclaiming History: The Assassination of
    President John F. Kennedy

A Pound of Cure

On July 17, 1983, a small Indian newspaper called the *Patriot* published a letter bearing the headline "AIDS may invade India: Mystery disease caused by U.S. experiments." The author—who requested anonymity, but described himself as "a well-known American scientist"—declared that AIDS had been created by the U.S. Army at its Fort Detrick, Maryland, testing facility, and warned that Washington was poised to transfer this potent new bioweapon to the government of neighboring Pakistan. While the letter went unnoticed in the West, it was picked up by the Soviet newspaper *Literaturnaya Gazeta*, and then by an energetic East German microbiologist named Jakob Segal. At the 1986 Confer-ence of Nonaligned Nations in Harare, Zimbabwe, Segal's forty-seven-page pamphlet, *AIDS—Its Nature And Origin*, became a sensation among African delegates. Western news outlets took notice. Even Britain's respectable *Daily Telegraph* printed an uncritical report on Segal's research.

Needless to say, the Fort Detrick–AIDS theory was baseless—a creation of the Soviet bloc's *aktivinyye meropriata* ("active measures") propaganda policy. As historian Thomas Boghardt argued in a 2009 *Studies in Intelligence* report, the original 1983 *Patriot* letter was almost certainly written by the KGB. As for Segal, he was a stooge of the East German Stasi, which fed the confused old man a steady stream of tantalizing documents to encourage his fantasy research.

The Soviet bloc's effort to pin AIDS on the Pentagon turned out to be brief—in part thanks to pressure imposed by the USSR's own medical establishment, which by the late 1980s was eager to access American data on HIV. In 1988, just three years after the *Patriot* letter appeared, official Soviet efforts to promote the conspiracy theory ceased. Speaking to the government newspaper *Izvestia*, the president of the Soviet Academy of Sciences declared: "Not a single Soviet scientist, not a single medical or scientific institution, shares [Segal's] position."

But the conspiracist cat already was out of the bag. Die-hard communists, black nationalists, and the full menagerie of Western conspiracy theorists all signed on.

To this day, the Fort Detrick–AIDS conspiracy theory and its variants remain popular in the African American community. In a 2010 study of 214 Los Angeles–area African American men undergoing treatment for HIV, 44 percent agreed that "HIV is a manmade virus." Thirty-five percent agreed that the disease was produced "in a government laboratory." And 31 percent said that AIDS "is a form of genocide, or planned destruction, against blacks." The study also found that a belief in AIDS conspiracy theories correlates negatively with adherence to prescribed antiretroviral drug regimens—suggesting that conspiracism itself, rather than any government plot, is killing black AIDS carriers.

In South Africa, meanwhile, former president Thabo Mbeki's obsession with AIDS denialism and crackpot theories of the disease's origins—and his consequent reluctance to distribute lifesaving medications—are estimated to have caused more than 330,000 otherwise preventable deaths. In 2000, as the world scientific community demanded that Mbeki's government act against the AIDS epidemic, he instead sent world leaders a paranoid letter, claiming that the pressure on Africans to adhere to "established scientific truths" comprised a "campaign of intellectual intimidation and terrorism." His like-minded health minister discouraged her citizens from taking antiretroviral drugs, which she called "poison," and instead promoted natural "remedies" like garlic and beetroot.

Education, many readers might assume, is the key to eradicating conspiracism. The Fort Detrick–AIDS conspiracy theory—and Mbeki's response to it—suggest the answer is more complicated.

The former South African president was one of the most intellectually sophisticated members of the African National Congress elite, having earned a BA in economics and a master's degree in African studies from the University of Sussex. Yet Mbeki's mind also was permanently scarred by his fight against apartheid. His father, Govan Mbeki, was a communist who'd been imprisoned for terrorism and treason. One of Thabo Mbeki's brothers died under mysterious circumstances in Lesotho. A son died trying to escape the country. Within the African National Congress, Mbkei became entangled in the group's vicious campaign to root out informants—and narrowly escaped being tortured by his fellow insurgents. Which is to say that Mbeki's whole early life had been one constant set of battles, tragedies, and dark plots. When a mysterious new epidemic suddenly broke out in his backyard, he saw it through this same conspiratorial lens. The notion that AIDS was spread through unprotected sex, in particular, seemed to strike Mbeki as a sort of blood libel against black people—not dissimilar to those spread by white bigots during the apartheid era. Medical schools, he complained, taught South Africans that they are "germ carriers, and human beings of a lower order that cannot subject its [sic] passions to reason . . . natural-born, promiscuous carriers of germs, unique in the world. [Scientists] proclaim that our continent is doomed to an inevitable mortal end because of our unconquerable devotion to the sin of lust."

Eventually, Mbeki relented, and permitted some distribution of AIDS medications in South African medical clinics. But he never fully backed off from his conspiracy theories, despite persistent appeals by the world's scientific community. Only when he was succeeded in the presidency by Jacob Zuma—a man with a fifth-grade education—did South Africa fully embrace the scientifically prescribed panoply of AIDS treatments and prevention programs.

As discussed later in this chapter, I believe a certain very specific kind of education can be helpful for inoculating young minds against conspiracy theories. But as Mbeki's example illustrates, conspiracism is only a nominally intellectual exercise. As argued in Chapter 5, it originates in an overlapping tangle of emotional and psychological factors that typically elude intellectual self-awareness, and which can't be refuted by logic and evidence: ethnic bigotry, fear of societal change and new technologies, economic uncertainty, midlife ennui, medical trauma, coming-of-age hubris, spiritual hunger, narcissism, the psychic scars left by past traumas, and outright psychosis.

This explains why arguing down a committed conspiracy theorist is impossible. Whenever I've tried to debate Truthers on the facts of 9/11, for instance, all of my accumulated knowledge about the subject has proven entirely useless—because in every exchange, the conspiracy theorist inevitably would ignore the most obvious evidence and instead focus the discussion on the handful of obscure, allegedly incriminating oddities that he had memorized. No matter how many of these oddities I manage to bat away (even assuming I have the facts immediately at hand to do so), my debating opponent always has more at hand.

In this game, the conspiracist claims victory merely by scoring a single uncontested point—since, as he imagines it, every card he plays is a trump. To quote 9/11 conspiracy theorist Richard Falk (better known as the UN official who suggested that Israel's actions in Gaza were akin to the Nazi Holocaust): "It is not necessary to go along with every suspicious inference in order to conclude that the official account of 9/11 is thoroughly unconvincing . . . Any part of this story is enough to vindicate [the] basic contention." The defender of rationalism, meanwhile, is stuck fighting for a stalemate.

Nor does it hold any water with conspiracists that their theories have been rejected and discredited by mainstream researchers, journalists, and government officials. As noted in the Introduction, the defining feature of a true conspiracy theory is that it has, embedded within its syllogistic circuitry, an explanation for why insiders refuse to go public with their information: Either they are coconspirators themselves, or they have been paid off, or threatened.

This is why so few experts are willing to take conspiracy theorists up on their frequent challenges to hold public debates. And those who do typically are sorry they did. In the 1990s, both Phil Donahue and Montel Williams made the disastrous decision to put Holocaust deniers on television. The Donahue episode, which aired on March 14, 1994, was a particularly bad train wreck, in which the host looked on helplessly as confused Auschwitz survivors bungled basic facts about the death camps (such as promoting the myth that prisoners were turned into soap) in the face of more authoritative-seeming deniers. One would think that someone who actually lived through the Holocaust would be able to out-debate a conspiracy theorist. But that assumption is wrong: As researchers Michael Shermer and Alex Grobman wrote in their 2000 book, *Denying History*: *Who Says the Holocaust Never Happened And Why Do They Say It*: "Most survivors know very little about the Holocaust outside of what happened to them half a century ago, and deniers are skilled at tripping them up when they get dates wrong."

I'll admit to feeling personally humbled by my failure to get the best of conspiracy theorists: What was the use in going through the official 9/11 report with a highlighter and Post-it notes, much less writing a whole book on the subject of Trutherdom, if I couldn't win an argument with a single college student? But on a more fundamental level, I also felt disillusioned by what this experience taught me about the limits of intellectual discourse itself. Even the reality of lived experience—the most direct path to truth there is—has been undermined by the conspiracist mindset, which overlooks eyewitness reports—of a plane flying into the Pentagon, or skyscrapers collapsing without any hint of internal demolition—in favour of tortured inferences from scattered esoterica.

Conspiracy theorists typically appear self-confident and even smug when they're discussing their area of obsession. But in many cases, it's an act: Since their entire identity is based on a nest of riddles that will unravel if they allow themselves to step outside their narrow conspiracist mindset, their emotional state is more fragile than they let on. When assembled in groups—either virtually, on the Internet, or in a real-life lecture hall—their group dynamics therefore tend to be brittle and cultish. "I simply asked logical questions that contradicted some of the conspiracy claims and demanded answers at the Loose Change Forum, [and] I got banned for that," reports one former quasi-Truther on a James Randi Educational Foundation discussion server. "[That] really annoyed me and I signed up again asking why they banned me for bringing up evidence against [a] fake Osama video, which got me banned again. All in all I got banned a hundred times or so."

During the course of writing this book, I became friendly with several conspiracy theorists—and in some cases, connected with them on Facebook. According to the earnest thinking I originally brought to this project, I imagined it would be possible for us to remain on friendly terms, even on the understanding that we disagreed on, say, the origins of 9/11 or the birthplace of Barack

Obama. This usually proved impossible: Every conversation with a conspiracy theorist tends to migrate, in one way or another, to their central obsession; and my refusal to accept their revealed "truths" always strained the relationship to the breaking point. (For this same reason, I've learned from interviewing a few "Truther widows," conspiracism often tends to create extraordinary rifts within marriages—unless both partners sign on to the same theory.)

Like all cults and cult-like movements, conspiracy theorists tend to become obsessed with dissidents, factions, internal schisms, and subplots. Many Truther purists, for instance, have seized on Noam Chomsky as a sort of Trotsky figure—primarily due to his refusal to expand his longstanding indictment of U.S. foreign policy to cover the crimes of 9/11. Some Truther books now have whole chapters dedicated to the "lies" of Chomsky and his fellow "left-wing gate-keepers." Anti-Chomskyite Truther websites and YouTube videos also have popped up, charging that the man is nothing less than "a deep cover agent for the New World Order, a master of black propaganda whose true motives become clear with a sober and honest examination." Truther Kevin Barrett, in particular, has made vilification of Chomsky a personal obsession, engaging the famous linguist in a 15,000-word email exchange, and then posting the whole thing to the Internet (against Chomsky's expressly stated wishes), complete with a final Barrett salvo declaring that the man has "done more to keep the 9/11 blood libel alive, and cause the murder of more than a million Muslims, than any other single person."

Though I would never presume to be loathed by Truthers at this epic level, my own investigations have earned me a modest taste of this treatment—sufficient to understand their radicalized us-versus-them mentality. (Google "Jonathan Kay" and "9/11" for a sampling.) The experience also has convinced me that any effort to engage committed conspiracy theorists in reasoned debate is a waste of time. Once someone has bitten down on the red pill, it's too late. As with any incurable disease, the best course isn't treatment, it's prevention.

The same is true of conspiracy *movements* themselves—which never entirely go away, even as the passage of years fails to vindicate their underlying theories. Even when conspiracists move on to fresh subjects, they tend to cite the truth of their old claims as validations for their new ones. Since the military-industrial complex killed JFK, why wouldn't it have destroyed the World Trade Center? Since the Bilderbergers had Bill Clinton and George W. Bush in their pocket, why not Barack Obama as well? In this way, conspiracy theories have built up like layers of rubble that smother what once were the intellectual foundations of rationalism.

An Ounce of Prevention

> "Nothing you will learn in the course of your studies will be of the slightest possible use to you in after life, save only this: That if you work hard and diligently you should be able to detect when a man is talking rot. And that, in my view, is the main, if not the sole purpose of education."
> —*Harold Macmillan, prime minister of Britain 1957–1963,*
> *quoting his classics tutor at Oxford*

Conspiracism is a stubborn creed because humans are pattern-seeking animals. Show us a sky full of stars, and we'll arrange them into animals and giant spoons. Show us a world full of random misery, and we'll use the same trick to connect the dots into secret conspiracies. For most of us, our desire to impose an artificial pattern on world events is held in check by our rational sense, which tells us that life often is cruel and unpredictable. Or we find compartmentalized, socially accepted outlets to give expression to our pattern-seeking—such as astrology or mainstream religion. Conspiracism takes root when, for the reasons discussed in this book, our pattern-seeking appetite overwhelms these containment mechanisms.

Yet this same pattern-seeking penchant is also the key to *fighting* conspiracism: By teaching ourselves to recognize conspiracism's unchanging basic structure—from its archetype in the *Protocols* to its modern incarnation in the 9/11 Truth movement—we can protect our brains from conspiracy theories before they have a chance to infect our thinking.

Conspiracism is deeply rooted in American thinking. Then again, the same once was true of racism. Exactly 150 years ago, the United States went to war with itself over the principle that a man could be chained up like an animal because of the color of his skin. It wasn't till 1954 that black and white schoolchildren were granted the constitutional right to attend the same schools. Even as recently as the 1970s, well within the living memory of middle-aged Americans, the idea that blacks and whites should be able to marry one another, or use the same swimming pools, was still controversial. And then, in the space of just a few decades, everything changed—capped by an extraordinary moment in early 2009 when it could be said that America's most powerful politician, beloved entertainment figure, and revered athlete all were black (Barack Obama, Oprah Winfrey, and Tiger Woods).

Women, meanwhile, went from ornamental second-class citizens in the typing pool and kitchen to full-fledged business-world equals. Perhaps most stunning of all was the transformation of our perception of gays. In 1973, homosexuality still was classified as a mental disorder by the American Psychiatric Association. Just 25 years later, NBC was airing a hit sitcom starring two gay men as part of its "must see" Thursday night lineup. Never in human history have social attitudes toward what we now (increasingly anachronistically) call "disadvantaged groups" been transformed so quickly. Never has human bigotry been winnowed at anywhere near this pace.

What developments in the Western intellectual condition permitted such a massive, wholesale shift in thinking? Whole libraries of books have been written about the struggle against racism, sexism, and homophobia, and I will not try to summarize them here. Instead, I will highlight just one essential factor, whose roots are in the Enlightenment, but which reached full bloom only in the twentieth century: civilizational self-awareness.

By this, I mean the habit of mind that permits us to stand back and objectively observe the flaws, hypocrisies, and double-standards embedded in our society. This ability is taken for granted in the modern Western world, so much so that we don't even recognize it as a special frame of mind. But it is: Throughout human history, and in most of the non-Western world today, the superiority of one's own tribe over others, of the faithful over the infidels, of the we over the they, has been entirely taken for granted—all corollaries of the reflexive tribalism that evolution has programmed into the hard-wiring of the human brain. Even the basic idea that a civilization should be "improved" can exist only in a society that is aware of its relationship to history and the outside world: It has little resonance in caste-ridden communities where the pace of technological change is slow, sons inherit their fathers' jobs, social mobility is nonexistent, and the established pecking order—with all its attendant forms of discrimination—is uncritically accepted as God-given and timeless.

Conspiracism cannot be eradicated any more than we can eradicate nationalism, midlife ennui, psychosis, or any of the other causes cataloged in Chapter 5. But among otherwise mentally healthy and open-minded individuals, it can be minimized by applying the same self-critical, self-aware mindset that has served to stigmatize racism, overt anti-Semitism, and related forms of bigotry in recent decades. As noted in Chapter 2 conspiracist mythologies tend to follow the same predictable pattern: There is no reason why people can't learn to recognize it.

This is an educational project that, to my knowledge, has never been attempted: For all the damage conspiracy theories have wrought, they traditionally have been regarded as mere intellectual curios, and so conspiracism never has been included in the canon of toxic *isms* targeted by educators. Instead, the approach has been to attack conspiracism's symptoms—often implementing a new brand of conspiracism as a cure for the old. Just as the fight against racism begat political correctness, the fight against communism begat McCarthyism, and the John Birch Society; and now, in our own era, the backlash against militant Islam and One World environmentalism has led to the Birthers.

What young minds need are the intellectual tools that not only permit them to identify established conspiracist creeds, but also allow them to identify the common features that bind all conspiratorial ideologies. The ideal time for students to receive these skills is when they are old enough to understand complex, abstract ideas, but before they have been exposed to conspiracism in a systematic way on campus or via the Internet: the freshman year of college. As the example of Luke Rudkowski shows, this also happens to be the time in life when many young people are looking to define their identity through the sort of radical, overarching secular faith conspiracism provides (which is one of the reasons so many college students fall hard for Karl Marx or Ayn Rand).

Of course, there already are numerous American intellectuals and organizations dedicated to the cause of fighting political radicalism, including the debunking of conspiracy theories. These include the James Randi Educational Foundation, an atheistic organization that specializes in refuting claims of paranormal and supernatural phenomena (and which recently has formed an education advisory panel); the Montgomery, Alabama–based Southern Poverty Law Center and Somerville, Massachusetts–based PublicEye.org, both of which take on right-wing conspiracists as part of their mandate to promote civil rights and fight bigotry; and the Skeptics Society, an Altadena, California–based group that describes itself as a "scientific and educational organization of scholars, scientists, historians, magicians, professors and teachers, and anyone curious about controversial ideas, extraordinary claims, revolutionary ideas, and the promotion of science."

(Thanks to his popular articles, books and speaking tours, Michael Shermer, the Skeptics Society's executive director, and the editor-in-chief of *Skeptic* magazine, likely ranks as the most effective debunker of junk science and conspiracy theories in America.) Also worthy of note is Snopes.com, an amateurish-looking but surprisingly authoritative resource for debunking urban legends; and, for vetting claims made by political candidates, Factcheck.org which is run by the Annenberg Public Policy Center.

But the limitation associated with all of these resources is that they preach mostly to the converted—i.e., mainstream educators, journalists, and activists who already take a deeply skeptical attitude toward conspiracist movements. As explained in Chapter 7, conspiracy theorists themselves tend to cut themselves off from all but the most radical information sources; and regard even independent, well-respected NGOs as complicit in the same power structure that envelops Washington and Wall Street. (This fact helps explain why there are so many more conspiracist books sold on the Internet than debunking books. "Debunking books don't sell," one New York City editor warned me when I told him that my original draft of *Among the Truthers* contained several long chapters explaining the logical fallacies within 9/11 Truth theories. "Conspiracy theorists won't believe you. And normal people don't need to be told what you're telling them. So you have no audience.")

Moreover, given the low level of trust that Americans have in their political leaders, it is out of the question that Washington, or even state governments, should be directly involved in the sort of educational project I am describing. Consider that in September 2009, when Barack Obama delivered a bland speech to the nation's students, urging them to work hard at their studies, many conservative Americans attacked the innocuous gesture as a form of statist propaganda—and some even kept their children home. One can only imagine the reaction if government officials instead were lecturing Americans about what sort of political ideas they should and shouldn't believe.

What would an anticonspiracist curriculum look like? The approach I've taken in this book, I like to believe, helps answer that question.

One of the reasons I chose to focus on *The Protocols of the Elders of Zion* in the second chapter is that its status as a hoax is now entirely uncontroversial among educated people in Western societies. While there exist tenured North American university professors who embrace conspiracy theories about 9/11—I have profiled a number of them—there is not a single faculty member on any first-tier university campus whose career would survive if he or she said they believed the *Protocols* was a legitimate historical document that described a real plot by Jews to enslave human civilization. The same is broadly true of any faculty member who denied the Holocaust (though I am aware of at least one tenured university professor who is on record with Holocaust-denial—Lincoln University's Kaukab Siddique, a Pakistan-born professor of English and Mass Communications who also believes that American Jews control "the entire economy," and who calls openly for Israel's destruction).

The Protocols and the Holocaust-denial movement thus would serve as generally uncontroversial objects of study in a university course that teaches students to recognize the patterns of conspiracist thought. More specifically, it would provide an opportunity to educate students about the basic themes contained in almost all systemic conspiracy theories—singularity, evil, incumbency, greed, and hypercompetence. These would be presented as warning signs in regard to the radical doctrines that students eventually will confront.

Teaching about Truthers, Birthers, anti-Bilderbergers, New World Order types, and all the rest also would be informative. But that would bring the curriculum I'm describing into the realm of current events—and thereby render it vulnerable to the charge of indoctrination or propaganda; which would in turn create friction between parents and school board trustees or university administrators, not to mention provide raw meat to the conspiracist blogosphere. Far better to have the next generation of students themselves connect the dots between the five conspiracist building blocks contained in the *Protocols* to more modern conspiracist movements.

Another advantage of a *Protocols*-centered curriculum is that it would reinforce traditional scholastic messaging promoting tolerance, especially if it also included modules on the KKK, anti-Mason agitation, Nazi propaganda, anti-Catholic hatred, and other historical examples that demonstrated the link between bigotry and conspiracism. This would help the project draw in the existing network of NGOs, education think tanks, and activists that are committed to the cause of antidiscrimination. Yet it would also be distinct from these existing campaigns: The fight against racism and its ilk typically is presented as a battle to eradicate hatred from people's hearts; but as I've described here, the fight against conspiracism is an intellectual project centered on pattern-recognition.

Finally, an anticonspiracist curriculum would aim to provide students with a grounding in Internet literacy. Students would be taught the difference between news and opinion; and between websites that are run by professional journalists, and those that are not. They would be taught the limitations associated with searching for information using Google and other search engines. And they would be instructed in the manner by which multimedia effects can be used to promote misinformation.

A study of conspiracism can have benefits that extend beyond merely inoculating young minds against conspiracy theories. On this score, I'll present myself as an example: The experience of writing this book has fundamentally altered my view of politics, faith, and the human capacity for rational thought.

That's not something I expected when I set out in early 2008. I then approached conspiracy theorists as if they were lab specimens to be poked and prodded from the other side of a tape recorder. On the Venn diagrams of human sociology, the "conspiracy theorist" was something I imagined to be a distinct and identifiable class of pathological thinker—a breed apart from humanity's "normal" rank and file that could be circled off in black ink.

Three years later, my view on that has changed: The tendency to imagine that world events are secretly controlled by some malign force that is seeking to corrupt the "true" course of human history manifests itself in many different personality types. Now that I have returned from book leave, and have resumed my regular work as comment-pages editor at a daily newspaper, I commonly spot this motif in the submissions that land in my inbox—from militant anti-Zionists who blame Israel for every imaginable geopolitical upheaval, to global warming skeptics who imagine that Greenpeace and Barack Obama are in league to create a one-world government.

This realization has taught me to be careful about my own ideological commitments, as well: I sometimes catch myself using forms of logic or turns of phrase that echo the conspiracy theorists whom I'd interviewed. For this reason, the act of writing this book has had a gradually moderating view on my attitude toward politics, and in my judgments of others. It has made me more self-aware when I bend the rules of logic in the service of ideology or partisanship.

Writing this book has also made me conscious of some of the biases that afflict my profession. As I've already noted at several points, one of the factors that has encouraged the growth of conspiracism in recent decades is the gradual erosion of popular trust in the media. To a certain extent, this trend is inevitable in a 500-channel universe: The more the mediascape fragments into disparate niches, the less prestige and influence will be retained by general-interest news outlets. But mainstream journalists often encourage this phenomenon by distorting the truth or pushing an ideological agenda. Many leftists—to cite one example from among many—grew disenchanted with their beloved *New York Times* when they learned that the case for war in Iraq had been buttressed by reporter Judith Miller, whose stories about Iraqi WMD were based on what we now know to be exaggerated intelligence reports. Many conservatives, meanwhile, became disgusted with the mainstream media during the 2008 election campaign, when fawning coverage of Barack Obama was broadcast and printed side-by-side with mockery of Sarah Palin and condescension toward her supporters. If tens of millions of middle-class Americans find Glenn Beck and Michael Moore more credible than the purportedly objective analysis offered by CBS, CNN, and NPR, journalists have to ask themselves: "Do we have anything to do with that?"

In no way do I believe that the mainstream media should give air time to the promotion of full-fledged conspiracy theories of the type I've described in this book. But nor should we muzzle or vilify those whose opinions are merely disquieting. When liberal journalists smear Tea Party types as racists merely because they ask why Barack Obama remained a congregant of Jeremiah Wright, for instance, it reinforces suspicions that the media is helping the president hide something. By denying the grain of truth in many conspiracy theories, the media betrays its own institutional biases and squanders the credibility it needs to exercise editorial judgment in regard to truly nefarious lies, genuine bigotry, and outright conspiracy theories.

We speak of the Enlightenment in the singular. But as historian Philipp Blom emphasizes in his recent book *Wicked Company*, there actually were several enlightenments; each led by a man of ideas trying to put his distinct stamp on the complex philosophical ferment of the seventeenth and eighteenth centuries. Yet all of them were bound up together by what we now describe as skepticism. Since the dawn of the scientific revolution, doctors, astronomers, and mathematicians had been challenging ancient dogmas through the exercise of reason and observation (the case of Galileo being only the most famous). Beginning with Descartes, this rigorous approach came to inform philosophy and even, as in the case of Voltaire's caustic response to the Great Lisbon Earthquake, theodicy.

In our own age, militant skepticism has become exalted as the truest mark of great intellect. Just about every conspiracy theorist I interviewed was very proud to tell me that they trust nothing they are told—and subject every claim to the most exacting scrutiny. This sounds intellectually noble—but in practice, it leads to a kind of nihilism, since there is no fact, historical event, or scientific phenomenon whose truth cannot, in some way, be brought into question by an inventive mind on the hunt for niggling "anomalies." In modest doses, skepticism provides a shield against superstition and false dogma. But when skepticism is enshrined as a faith unto itself, skeptics often will conjure fantasies more ridiculous than the ones they debunk.

The Church of Skepticism has tempted many of our era's most popular pundits. Christopher Hitchens, Richard Dawkins, and Sam Harris all have become best-selling authors by delivering scathing manifestos against organized religion, which they present as a sort of collectively experienced mental illness. Hitchens, the most influential of the trio, says he "value[s] the Enlightenment above any priesthood or any sacred fetish-object." Yet it is important to remember that the Enlightenment did not spell the end of serious Christian theology—and most of its giants likely would have been appalled by the exercise of their legacy to promote a Godless society.

Descartes, for instance, took care to divide the world into spiritual and material realms—making God lord of the former, and science lord of the latter. As for Voltaire—whose "moderate and deist form of Enlightenment thought" (in Blom's words) eventually would become synonymous with the Enlightenment itself—he believed that the existence of an "eternal, supreme, and intelligent being" could be established through the application of pure reason, and described religious belief as a necessary ingredient of a healthy society:

An atheist, provided he be sure of impunity so far as man is concerned, reasons and acts consistently in being dishonest, ungrateful, a slanderer, a robber, and a murderer. For if there is no God, this monster is his own god, and sacrifices to his purposes whatever he desires and whatever stands as an obstacle in his path. The most moving entreaties, the most cogent arguments have no more effect upon him than on a wolf thirsting for blood.

The philosopher was being perfectly sincere when he said *"Si Dieu n'existait pas, il faudrait l'inventer"*—if God did not exist, we would have to invent him.

Unlike Hitchens, Dawkins, Harris, and their followers, Voltaire understood that man cannot survive on skepticism alone—that society requires some creed or overarching national project that transcends mere intellect. When the appeal of traditional religion becomes weak, darker faiths assert themselves: including not only communism, fascism, tribalism, and strident nationalism, but also more faddish intellectual pathologies such as radical identity politics, anti-Americanism, and obsessive anti-Zionism. As I've argued, all of these provide rich soil for the seeds of conspiracism. As Europe is now learning, it is very difficult to maintain secular societies in a Godless limbo, fed by nothing but the materialist salves of wealth and the welfare state, without incubating malaise and ideological instability. As the Truthers show us, rootless thinkers eventually will find a devil to fear.

A healthy society is one in which faith and skepticism—both broadly defined—are in balance; where citizens feel a sense of trust and belonging in their society and its leading institutions, but also feel entitled to challenge prevailing biases, superstitions, and authority structures. The familiar historical phenomenon of faith overpowering skepticism is the problem of pre-Enlightenment societies. But since the murder of JFK, America has been dealing with the opposite, post-Enlightenment, problem: skepticism outdistancing faith. Like all the great traumas that America has suffered over the past half century, 9/11 has only made the yawning gap grow wider.

Diagnosing and fighting conspiracism is an important project, which is why I wrote this book. But ultimately, conspiracism is just one aspect of a larger crisis in American political culture; one that can be addressed only through a rehabilitation of the nation's public institutions. It is a large and difficult task—but also an urgent one. On 9/11, terrorists killed nearly 3,000 innocent people and destroyed the World Trade Center. Americans should not let their collective sense of truth be added to the list of casualties.

| INDEX |

Abdullah (king), 129
Abrams, Elliot, 302
Adbusters, 298
African National Congress (ANC), 311
Aftonbladet, 301
Ahmadinejad, Mahmoud, xxii, 157, 167
Ahmed, Nafeez Mosaddeq, 76
AIA. *See* American Institute of Architects
Akihito, Emperor, 129
Akol & Yoshii, 154
Allen, Arthur, 172, 173
Allen, Woody, 305
al-Qaeda, 6, 9, 15, 21, 76, 259, 299
Alten, Steve, 288–89
American Institute of Architects (AIA), 154–55
American Psychiatric Association, 317
ANC. *See* African National Congress
Anderson, Brian, 234–35
Andreas, Dwayne, 58
Annenberg Public Policy Center, 320
Anti-Cancer Club, 55
Anti-Defamation League, 169, 219, 303
Arafat, Yasser, 48, 295
Arizona State University, 271
Arouet, François-Marie. *See* Voltaire
Aryan Pride, 61
Aspen Institute, 58
Assange, Julian, xvii
ATF. *See* Bureau of Alcohol, Tobacco, and Firearms

Atta, Mohammed, 12, 50
Auschwitz, 313
Avery, Dylan, 86, 104
Azande tribe, 205–7

Baader-Meinhof, 116
Bacon, Delia, 183–84
Bacon, Francis, xvi, 162, 183–84, 189, 195
Badillo, Manny, 174
Baigent, Michael, 73, 213
Baker, Russ, 51
Balsamo, Robert, 49, 110–11, 120
Bannon, Stephen K., 132
Baraka, Amiri, 168–69
Bard College, 261
Barkun, Michael, 21, 62
Barrett, Kevin, 167, 237–38, 286–94, 315
Barrett, Peter, 287
Barruel, Augustin, 29–30, 87
Basiago, Andrew D., 92
BBC (British Broadcasting Corporation), 114, 179
Beck, Glenn, 13, 110, 138–46, 240, 242, 303, 324
Benedict XVI, Pope, 242
Bennett, James, 192
Berlet, Chip, 215
Bernhard (prince), 57
Bernstein, Carl, 94, 248
Betts, Charles, 55, 56
Bilderberg Group, 15, 47–60, 96, 114, 201, 217, 221, 244, 278, 286, 316
Bill Gates Foundation, 58

Bin Laden, Osama, 4, 9, 17, 103, 167, 314
Black, Conrad, 57–58, 113
Blakeney, Joshua, 271
Blanchard, Brent, 20
Blom, Philipp, 324
Bloom, Allan, xvi
Bloomberg, Michael, 3
Blumenthal, Sid, 43
Boggs, Hale, 44
Boghardt, Thomas, 310
Bolsheviks, 53
Bonaparte, Napoleon, 87
Bottum, Joseph, 149
Bouvier family, 51
Bowman, Robert, 211, 293
BP (British Petroleum), 128, 243
Branch Davidians, 199
Brand, Dionne, 276
Brandes, Georg, 160, 161
Bratich, Jack, 272
Breitbart, Andrew, 126
Bridle, Susan, 269, 270
Brigham Young University, 192
British Broadcasting Corporation. See BBC
British Columbia Ministry of Health Library, 6
British Green Party, 179
British Petroleum. See BP
Brookings Institution, 58
Brown, Bridget, 56
Brown, Dan, xxi, 29, 48, 60, 181, 213, 215
Brown, Dave, 301
Brown and Root, 185, 186
Bryan, William Jennings, 83–84, 127
Brzezinski, Zbigniew, 117–18, 200–202
Buckley, William F. Jr., 191, 236
Bugliosi, Vincent, 42–44, 47, 309

Bureau of Alcohol, Tobacco, and Firearms (ATF), 16
Burke, Edmund, 29
Burrows, Terry, 78, 111
Bush, George H. W., 8, 61, 87–88, 115
Bush, George W., xix, 5, 9, 14, 22, 83, 102, 138, 144, 242, 256, 283, 301
Bush, Jeb, 118
Bush, Marvin, 256
Bush, Prescott, 14

Cabet, Étienne, 212
Cable News Network. See CNN
Cable-Satellite Public Affairs Network. See C-SPAN
Cameron, James, 126
Campbell, Colin, 181
Canadian Broadcasting Corporation. See CBC
Canis Minor, 290
Cantril, Hadley, 144–45
Cantwell, Robert, 231
Carlyle Group, 13
Carter, Jimmy, 117, 293
Castro, Fidel, 42, 55, 106–9
CBC (Canadian Broadcasting Corporation), 248
CBS (Columbia Broadcasting System), 324
CENTCOM (United States Central Command), 244
Central Intelligence Agency (CIA), xvii, 4, 6, 13, 15, 43, 44, 47–48, 49, 50, 51, 54–55, 88, 91, 106–9, 184
CFR. See Council on Foreign Relations
Chang, Iris, 166
Charles V (king), 75
Chavez, Hugo, 92, 157, 186, 297

Cheney, Dick, 6, 13, 66, 73, 102–3, 116, 118, 186, 229, 242
Chiang Kai Shek, 165
Chomsky, Noam, 18, 102, 156, 167, 261, 298, 315
Chossudovsky, Michel, 11
Christian Identity, 61
CIA. See Central Intelligence Agency
Citizen Investigation Team, 194
Claremont School of Theology, 104, 154, 193
Clarke, Steve, 21
Clinton, Bill, 43, 86, 118, 119, 235, 316
Clinton, Hillary, 73
Cloward, Richard, 169
Club of Rome, 58
CNN (Cable News Network), 11, 125, 170, 238, 242, 324
Cobain, Kurt, 47
Cohn, Norman, 65, 70, 78, 134, 210, 291
Colbert, Stephen, 138, 202
Colorado Public Television, 152
Columbia Broadcasting System. See CBS
Columbia University, 169, 170, 243, 295
Committee for State Security. See KGB
Committee to Investigate Communist Influences at Vassar College, 40
Committee to Re-elect the President, 20–21
Connally, John, 45
Connell, Michael, 11
Cooper, John Sherman, 44
Cooper, Milton William, 72–73
Corbett, James, 257
Corsi, Jerome, 242

Coughlin, Charles, 37–38, 85–86
Council on Foreign Relations (CFR), 2, 58, 60, 200, 201, 242, 286
Counter Intelligence Program, 219–20
CounterPunch, 240
Coventry City, 179
Cronkite, Walter, xviii
C-SPAN (Cable-Satellite Public Affairs Network), 123

Daily Kos, 240
Daly, Mary, 268–70
Dawkins, Richard, 325, 326
deHaven-Smith, Lance, 271
DeMint, Jim, 122
Democrats, 4, 18, 83, 128, 301
Democratic National Committee Headquarters, 20–21
Democratic Underground, 240
Denison University, 272
Derrida, Jacques, 261–64
Dershowitz, Alan, 302
Descartes, René, xvi, 10, 324–25
Dewdney, Alexander Keewatin, 89, 184
Diana (princess), 47, 48
Dickens, Charles, 296
Directorate of Propaganda and Agitation of the Central Committee, 253–54
Dobbs, Lou, 242
Domitian, Emperor, 135
Donahue, Phil, 313
Donnelly, Ignatius, 36–37, 182, 187–90, 220
Dreyfus, Alfred, 20–21
Dulles, Allen, 44

Eastern Illinois University, 228
Eisenhower, Dwight, 32, 41, 232

Elizabeth II (queen), 180
Elliott, Brenda, 247–48
Estulin, Daniel, 15, 57–60, 96, 114, 186, 217, 248
European Union (EU), 58, 63
Evans, Margaret, 25–26
Evans-Pritchard, Edward Evan, 205–7
Ewing, Patrick, 234

Facebook, 237, 254
Factcheck.org, 320
Falk, Richard, 313
Fanon, Franz, 265–66
Farah, Joseph, 31, 121–24, 134, 170, 304, 305
Farrakhan, Louis, 163, 169
Fayed, Dodi, 47, 48
FBI. *See* Federal Bureau of Investigation
FCC. *See* Federal Communications Commission
FDA. *See* Food and Drug Administration
Federal Bureau of Investigation (FBI), 46, 82, 116, 169, 219–20, 227, 228
Federal Communications Commission (FCC), 235
Federal Emergency Management Agency. *See* FEMA
Federalists, 35
FederalJack.com, 245–46
Federal Reserve, 2, 13, 82, 244, 249
Feith, Douglas, 302
FEMA (Federal Emergency Management Agency), xix, 62, 102, 197, 243, 257
Fetzer, James, 50
Figes, Orlando, 166
Fisk, Robert, xxiii

Fitzgerald, Craig, 2–3
Fletcher, Victor, 293
Food and Drug Administration (FDA), 172, 176
Ford, Gerald, 44, 293
Ford, Henry, 72
Foucault, Michel, 263
FOX News, 235, 236, 240, 242, 303
Fox Piven, Frances, 169
Free, Lloyd, 144–45
Freemasons, xxi, 29, 35, 41, 72, 83, 87–88, 229, 293
Freemason Secret Society, 58–59
Free Republic, 240
Freire, Paulo, 266, 273
Freud, Sigmund, 160
Friedman, Milton, 75
FrontPage Magazine, 158
Fukuyama, Francis, xv
Fulford, Robert, 166

Gaddafi, Moammar, 50
Gage, Richard, xxi–xxii, 100, 104, 105, 151–55, 159, 211
Galati, Rocco, 114
Galileo, 324
Gallup Poll, 144–45
Galton, Francis, 247, 257
Gandhi, Mohandas Karamchand, 192
Ganser, Daniele, 113
Garofalo, Janeane, 128
Garrison, Jim, 43
Gasset, Jose Ortega y, 149
Gates, Bill, 58
Gaylord Opryland Hotel, 124–25
Gearhart, Sally Miller, 269
George III (king), 34
Georgia Institute of Technology, 273
Gibbs, Robert, 157

Gidion, Gabriele, 41–42
Giffords, Gabrielle, xxii
Giuliani, Rudy, 202
Godwin, Mike, 240
Gold, Jon, 174
Goldberg, Bernard, xviii
Goldberger, Paul, 48–49
Goldman Sachs, 128
Goldwater, Barry, 251
Google, xviii, 243–44, 249
GOP (Grand Old Party), 126, 202
Gorbachev Foundation, 58
Goya, Francisco, 301
Grand Old Party. *See* GOP
Green, Mark, 288
Greenberg, Hank, 58
Green Party, British, 179
Greenpeace, 323
Griffin, David Ray, 6, 49–50, 91, 104, 119, 154, 190, 193, 230
Grobman, Alex, 166, 313
The Guardian, 14, 240
Guelph University, 10–11
Guevara, Che, 295
Gurion, David Ben, 295

HAARP. *See* High Frequency Active Auroral Research Program
Haass, Richard, 2, 286
Halcyon Company, 60
Hall, Anthony J., 168, 271
Halliburton, 13, 185
Hamlet, 160–61
Hampton, Fred, 43
Hansen, Dallas, 13–14
Hanson, Jay, 80
Harris, Sam, 325, 326
Harvard Law School, 238–39
Harvard University, 145, 261
Hasan, Nidal Malik, 244
Hearst, William Randolph, 231
Heaven's Gate, 199

Heinz, Jack, 58
Helms, Richard, 271
Henry J. Kaiser Family Foundation, 145
Hereford United, 179
Herman, Arthur, 55
Hersh, Seymour, 54
Herzl, Theodor, 67–69, 81, 96
High Frequency Active Auroral Research Program (HAARP), 92
Hiss, Alger, 232
Hitchens, Christopher, 325, 326
Hitler, Adolf, xx, 14, 30, 41, 48, 58–59, 69, 85, 101, 167, 240, 251–52, 291–92
Hofstadter, Richard, 34–35, 41, 231, 232–33
Hoggatt, Greg, 99
Homer, 207, 208
Hoover, J. Edgar, 54, 101
Horowitz, David, 122
Huffington Post, 240
Hufschmid, Eric, 219
Hughes, Lesley, 4, 5
Hunt, E. Howard, 13
Hurricane Katrina, 75
Hussein, Saddam, 112
Huxley, Aldous, 53
Hydrick, Rick, 142

ICC. *See* International Criminal Court
Icke, David, 72, 73, 91, 179–81, 182
Ignotus, Miles, 117
Illuminati, 3, 29–30, 35, 41, 57, 60–61, 72, 73–74, 83, 87, 180, 221, 293
IMAIM. *See* Industrial Military Academic Intelligence Media complex
IMF. *See* International Monetary Fund

Industrial Military Academic Intelligence Media complex (IMAIM), 97

Infowars, 17

Instapundit, 240

Institute for Policy Studies, 58

International Criminal Court (ICC), 63

International Monetary Fund (IMF), 13

Inter-Services Intelligence (ISI), 13

Irving, David, 288

ISI. *See* Inter-Services Intelligence

Ivy League, xviii, 265, 302

Izvestia, 310

Jackson, La Toya, 48

Jackson, Michael, 48

James I (king), 111

James Randi Educational Foundation, 220, 314, 319

James VI (king), 111

Jarrah, Ziad, 50–51

Jenkins, Ken, 40, 99–106, 112, 180, 213, 215

Jersey Girls, 21–22

Jesuit General, 220

Jesus Christ, 192, 213, 214

Jews, 78, 81, 83, 85–88, 93, 96, 124, 149, 162, 167, 169, 180, 210, 212, 214, 218–20, 252, 262–63, 269, 278, 285–307, 321

John Birch Society (JBS), 30, 40, 41, 73, 130, 319

Johnson, Lyndon B., 112, 250–51

Joint Chiefs of Staff, 106

Joly, Maurice, 69

Jones, Alex, 2, 16–19, 60, 63, 76–77, 79, 101, 113, 197, 221, 286, 292

Jones, Ernest, 162

Jones, LeRoi. *See* Baraka, Amiri

Jones, Steven, xxii, 192, 211

Jones, Van, xxii

Kagan, Robert, 118

Kaiser, Henry J., 145

Karadzic, Radovan, 166

Kazin, Michael, 141

Keefer, Michael, 10–13

Keeley, Brian, 21

Keen, Andrew, 249

Kelly, Michael, 93

Kennedy, Jacqueline, 41, 51

Kennedy, John Fitzgerald, xiii, 2, 17, 41–51, 55, 72, 106, 113, 230, 254, 309, 326–27

Kennedy, Robert, 42, 43, 47–48, 50, 72

KGB (Committee for State Security), 114, 310

Khalidi, Rashid, 295

Khalizad, Zalmay, 118

Khashoggi, Adnan, 13

King, Larry, 170–71

King, Martin Luther, Jr., 42, 43, 72, 139–40

Kirov, Sergey, 111

Kissinger, Henry, 13, 79, 117

KKK. *See* Ku Klux Klan

Klein, Aaron, 247–48

Klein, Naomi, 75, 298

Kleist, David von, 110

Knight, Peter, 272

Knights Templar, 28

Kolar, Jay, 50–51

Koresh, David, 16

Krauthammer, Charles, 5, 21, 302, 304

Kravis, Henry, 58

Kristol, Irving, 302

Kristol, William, 118, 302

Krugman, Paul, 242

Ku Klux Klan (KKK), 22, 33, 35, 322

LAPD. *See* Los Angeles Police Department
Lapham, Lewis H., xix
LaRouche, Lyndon Hermyle, 74, 115
Leigh, Richard, 73, 213
Leman, Patrick, 47
LeMay, Curtis, 271
Lenin, Vladimir, 53, 77
Lepacek, Matt, 258
Lepore, Jill, 144
Leverett, Hillary Mann, xxii
Libby, I. Lewis, 118
Liberal Party (Canada), 4
Libre Parole, 290
Life, 254
Limbaugh, Rush, 121, 234–36, 243
Lincoln, Henry, 73, 213
Lincoln University, 321
Lindbergh, Charles, 38
Lindbergh, Charles August, 81–83
Litvinenko, Alexander, 112
Lloyd, Henry Demarest, 231–32
London School of Economics, 180
Looney, J. T., 219
Loose Change Forum, 314
Los Angeles Police Department (LAPD), 125, 185
Loughner, Jared, xxii
Love, Courtney, 47
Lowenstein, Allard, 43
Luchet, Jean Pierre Louis, 29
Luther, Martin, 135
Luttwak, Edward, 117

MacCulloch, Diarmaid, 205, 290
Machiavelli, Niccolò (prince), 99
Machon, Annie, 112
Macmillan, Harold, 316

Madoff, Bernie, 303
Mainstream Media. *See* MSM
Malcolm X, 49
Malloy, Steve, 130–31
de Man, Paul, 261–64
Mandela, Nelson, 242
Mao Tse Tung, 77
Marcello, Carlos, 185–86
Marchand, Philip, 191–92
Marlowe, Christopher, 10, 195
Marsden, Victor E., 216–17
Marx, Karl, xx, 31, 42, 142, 212, 319
Mary Magdalene, 213
Mavell, Roger, 251
Mazza, Jerry, 3, 168
Mbeki, Govan, 311
Mbeki, Thabo, 311–13
McCarthy, Jenny, 170–73, 174, 177, 178
McCarthy, Joseph, 34–35, 38–39
McCarthy, Mary, 261
McCloy, John J., 44
McGlowan, Angela, 129
McIlvane, Bob, 174
McKertich, Mark, xvii
McLuhan, Marshall, 191–92
McMurtry, John, 88
McNamara, Robert, 106
McVeigh, Timothy, 16, 228
Meigs, James, 91, 92
Melley, Timothy, 54
Metz, Mikey, 256
Meyssan, Thierry, 79
MI5, 184
MI6, 47, 58
Miami Herald, 297
Mikics, David, 262–64
Military Intelligence, Section 5. *See* MI5
Miller, Edith Starr, 35
Miller, Judith, 324

Miller, Shane, 228
Milligan, Linda, 61–62
Mobley, Gregory, 209–10
Mohamad, Mahathir, 89
Moher, Frank, 168
Molé, Phil, 192–93
Monroe, Marilyn, 47
Moore, Michael, 33, 324
Moore, Roy, 130
Morgenthau, Henry, Jr., 85–86
Moro, Aldo, 115–16
Mossad, 58, 180
MoveOn.org, 303
MSM (Mainstream Media), 238
Murdoch, Rupert, 58
Murrah, Alfred P., 16, 113
Murrow, Edward R., 292
Mustaine, Dave, 196–99

Napolitano, Andrew, xxii
NASCO. *See* North America's
  SuperCorridor Coalition, Inc.
The Nation, 169
National Broadcasting Company.
  See NBC
National Cancer Institute, 80
National Institute of Standards and
  Technology, 20
National Post, 55–56, 57, 113, 238,
  302
National Public Radio. *See* NPR
National Review Online, 240
National Rifle Association. *See* NRA
National Transportation Safety
  Board (NTSB), 227
Nation of Islam, 292
NATO (North Atlantic Treaty
  Organization), 9, 17, 54, 113,
  114–15
Nazi Party, 13, 14, 166, 251–52, 296
NBC (National Broadcasting Com-
  pany), 317

Netanyahu, Benjamin, 304
Newsweek, 262, 263
New Yorker, 48–49
New York Giants, 8
New York Times, xiii–xiv, 238, 242,
  324
Nilus, Sergei, 75
Nirvana, 47
Nixon, Richard, 71–72, 271–72
Nizer, Louis, 309
NORAD (North American Aero-
  space Defense Command), 6–7,
  9, 12, 15, 101, 102–3, 229
Norris, Frank, 231–32
North American Aerospace Defense
  Command. *See* NORAD
North America's SuperCorridor
  Coalition, Inc. (NASCO), 242
North Atlantic Treaty Organiza-
  tion. *See* NATO
Novick, Peter, 266, 267–68
NPR (National Public Radio), 235,
  324
NRA (National Rifle Association),
  235
NTSB. *See* National Transportation
  Safety Board

Obama, Barack, xviii, xxi, 16,
  18, 31, 39, 76, 121–24, 126,
  130–32, 134–39, 169–70, 241,
  242, 304, 314–15, 316, 320, 323
Occidental College, 157
Olmsted, Kathryn, 82
OPEC (Organization of the Petroleum Exporting Countries),
  117
Orwell, George, 52, 53, 164,
  252–53, 255, 261, 278
Oswald, Lee Harvey, 42–46,
  49–50, 51, 115, 116, 184
Oswald, Marina, 46

Owen, Orville Ward, 195
Oxford University, 21

Paine, Thomas, 34
Pajamas Media, 158
Palin, Sarah, 33, 126, 127, 129,
    132–33, 304
Palmer, A. Mitchell, 82
Panama Canal Company, 290
Patrick, Dennis, 235
Paul, Rand, 128
Paul, Ron, 2
Pelosi, Nancy, 130
Perle, Richard, 302
Perot, Ross, 33, 127
Peto, Jennifer, 299
Philip IV (king), 28
Pierce, Charles, 31–32
Piereson, James, 42
Pipes, Daniel, 28–29, 302, 307
Pitzer College, 21
PNAC. *See* Project for the New
    American Century
Podhoretz, Norman, 302
Politico, 125
Pope, Alexander, xiii
Popper, Karl, 205
Populist Party, 33, 35–40, 128,
    141–45
Powers, Thomas, 41
Presley, Elvis, 48
Procyon, 290
Project for the New American Cen-
    tury (PNAC), 17, 118–19
PublicEye.org, 319
Pynchon, Thomas, 270

Quinn, Eithne, 273

Radar, 17
Raiskila, Vesa, 111–12
Ralph, Diana, 299

Rand, Ayn, 114, 319
RAND Corporation, 58, 60, 117
Randi, James, 220, 314, 319
Ranke, Craig, 194–95
Rankin, J. Lee, 44
Reagan, Ronald, 61, 87–88, 115,
    122, 123, 144, 235
Red Brigades, 115
Reed, Jebediah, 17
Reeves, Keanu, 216
Reid, Harry, 130
Reno, Janet, 16
Republican Party, xxi, 18, 35,
    121–22, 126, 128–29, 154, 162,
    187, 234, 235, 301
Republicans in Name Only. *See*
    RINOs
Rich, Frank, 242
Ridge, Martin, 189
Riefenstahl, Leni, 251, 253, 255
RINOs (Republicans in Name
    Only), 126
Rivero, Mike, 105
Roberts, Gregg, 95–96
Roberts, Mark, 20
Robertson, Pat, 60–61, 73–74
Robison, John, 29
Rockefeller, David, 1–2, 13, 57, 201
Rockefeller, Nelson, 2
Roosevelt, Franklin Delano, xv, 33,
    38, 41, 112–13
Roosevelt, Theodore, 230–31
Rothschild, Evelyn de, 58
Rothschild (family), 41, 58
Rove, Karl, 11, 244
Royal Hospital, Lisbon, xi
Royal Institute of International
    Affairs, 58
Royal Military College, 10
Ruby, Jack, 50
Rudkowski, Luke, 1, 114, 200–203,
    255, 286, 319

Rumsfeld, Donald, 6, 118, 187, 283
Ruppert, Michael, 50, 76, 79–80, 86, 91, 102–3, 104, 185–87, 217–18, 292
Russell, Bertrand, 45–46, 50, 66
Russell, Richard B., 44
Rutgers University, 272

Said, Edward, 295
St. Mark's Church in-the-Bowery, 286
Sandanistas, 13
Sartre, Jean-Paul, 265
Saul, John Ralston, 267
Savio, Mario, 156
Scarborough, Rick, 131, 133–34
Schlessinger, Laura, 234
Schumpeter, Joseph A., 160
Scientology, 236–37
Scripps Howard poll, xxi
SEC (Securities Exchange Commission), 103, 128
Segal, Jakob, 309–10
Shakespeare, William, 10, 161, 183, 189, 195, 219
Shapiro, James, 160, 243
Sharon, Ariel, 301
Shayler, David, 184
Sheen, Charlie, xxii
Shermer, Michael, 26–27, 166, 313, 320
Shulevitz, Judith, 264
Siddique, Kaukab, 321
Sikh Golden Temple, 241
Silverstein, Larry, 7, 229
Sinclair, Upton, 231–32
Singer, Alvy, 305
Skeptic, 320
Skeptics Society, 26–27, 319–20
Skoda, Mark, 131, 133
Snopes.com, 320

Sobran, Joseph, 191
Social Democrats of West Germany, 40
Society of Fellows, Harvard, 261
Soldier Readiness Center at Ford Hood, 244
Solway, David, 156–59
Somers, Suzanne, 174–78
Soros, George, 303–4
Southern Poverty Law Center, 319
Soviet Academy of Sciences, 310
Special Olympics, 8
Stack, Joseph, 25
Stalin, Joseph, 2, 77, 111, 166, 233, 252
Starr Miller, Edith, 35
State University of New York. *See* SUNY Albany
Steffens, Lincoln, 231–32
Stewart, Jon, 138–39
Stinnett, Robert, 112
Stone, I. F., 93
Stone, Oliver, 71–72
Strauss, Leo, 117
Street News, 293
Summerlin Center Mall, 155
Sunjata, Daniel, xxii, 256
Sunstein, Cass, 238–39
SUNY Albany (State University of New York), 256
Surowiecki, James, 247
Synarchist Movement of Empire, 58–59

Tanenhaus, Sam, 39
Tarpley, Webster, 74, 87–88, 111, 114–16
Tavistock Institute for Behavioural Analysis, 58
Taylor, Philip, 251
Tea Party, 124–35, 138, 143, 145, 235, 269, 302–3

Temple, William, 131
Thatcher, Margaret, 122
Thompson, Damian, 220
Thorn, Victor, 137
Thorns, Paul, 49
Thucydides, 53
Tippitt, J. D., 46
Tonkin Gulf, xvii
Trans-Texas Corridor (TTC), 241–42
Trilateral Commission, 58, 60, 200–201
Trochmann, David, 93
Truman, Harry S., 113, 232
Tsioniaon, Brenda, 267
TTC. *See* Trans-Texas Corridor
Twin Towers, xiii, 48–49, 66, 92, 95, 104, 105, 168, 219
Tyler, Dan, 215
Tyree, J.M., 189

UN. *See* United Nations
UNESCO (United Nations Educational, Scientific and Cultural Organization), 58
United Church of Canada, 298
United Nations (UN), xiv, 31–32, 50, 54, 62, 106, 154, 257
United Nations Educational, Scientific and Cultural Organization. *See* UNESCO
United States Army, 309
United States Central Command. *See* CENTCOM
Unity movement, 211
University of Lethbridge, 168, 271
University of Michigan, 25
University of York, 181
Unocal, 13
U.S. Navy, 227
U.S. Army, 309

Venetian Black Nobility, 58
Ventura, Jesse, xxii
de Vere, Edward, 219
Virgil, 207
Virginia Commonwealth University, 272
Voltaire (François-Marie Arouet), xi–xiii, xv, 39, 325–26
Vreeland, Delmart, 186

Wade, Henry, 46
Wagner, Richard, 252
Walesa, Lech, 131
Wallace, George, 43
War Department, U.S., 253
Warren, Earl, 44, 46
Warren Commission, xvii, 43, 44–45, 230, 271–72
Washburne, Elihu, 187, 189
Washington Post, 21, 145
Waters, Anita, 272
Webster, Nesta, 35
Weisberg, Harold, 230
Welch, Robert, 39–41, 253–54
Wellstone, Paul, 47–48
WFAN (sports radio station), 233
WHO. *See* World Health Organization
Wikipedia, 17, 241, 246, 247
Will, George, 236
Williams, Montel, 313
Willman, Skip, 273
Wilmot, Sheila, 274–75, 278, 307
Wilson, Woodrow, 65
Winfrey, Oprah, 171, 178–79, 317
Wohlstetter, Albert, 117
Wolfowitz, Paul, 6, 118, 229, 302
Women Against Labor Union Hoodlumism, 40
Woods, Ian, 78, 111
Woods, Tiger, 317

Woodward, Bob, 94, 248
Woodworth, Elizabeth, 6
World Bank, 44
World Health Organization
  (WHO), 80
WorldNetDaily, 121–23, 128, 170,
  240–41, 247–48, 304
World Trade Center, xxi, 2–14, 17,
  20–22, 48–49, 66, 88, 96, 103,
  108, 152, 154–56, 168, 211,
  228, 248–50, 255–56, 283, 287,
  316, 327
World Wide Web, xvi–xvii, 228
Wray, T.J., 209–10
Wright, Jeremiah, 157, 324
Wright, Lawrence, 20

Yale Law Journal, 279–83
Yale Law School, 40, 279–80

Yale University, 279
Yousef, Ramzi, 228
YouTube, 254, 258–59

Zamyatin, Yevgeny, 36, 51–53
Zapruder, Abraham, 254
Zarathustra, 209
Zarembka, Paul, 50, 51, 190, 194
Zelikow, Philip, 258–59, 287
Zinn, Howard, 102, 167
Zizakovic, Lubo, 8–9, 12–13, 15,
  114, 163
Zuma, Jacob, 312
Zündel, Ernst, 182, 219, 288
Zwicker, Barrie, 94, 97, 190, 191